Grade **3**

Teacher's Guide and Lesson Plans

Great Source Education Group

a Houghton Mifflin Company

Wilmington, Massachusetts

www.greatsource.com

AUTHORS

Laura Robb
Author

Powhatan School, Boyce, Virginia

Laura Robb, author of *Teaching Reading in Middle School, Teaching Reading in Social Studies, Science, and Math, Redefining Staff Development,* and *Literacy Links,* has taught language arts at Powhatan School in Boyce, Virginia, for more than 35 years. She is a co-author of the *Reader's Handbooks* for grades 4–5 and 6–8, as well as the *Reading and Writing Sourcebooks* for grades 3–5 and the *Summer Success: Reading Program.* Robb also mentors and coaches teachers in Virginia public schools and speaks at conferences throughout the country.

April Nauman
Contributing Author

Northeastern Illinois University, Chicago, Illinois

April D. Nauman, Ph.D., is a teacher educator at Northeastern Illinois University in Chicago. For more than 10 years she has worked with Chicago area elementary and high school teachers to improve literacy instruction for their students, mostly in high-needs city schools. Dr. Nauman has authored many papers on literacy learning.

Donna Ogle
Contributing Author

National-Louis University, Evanston, Illinois

Donna M. Ogle, Professor of Reading and Language at National-Louis University in Evanston, Illinois, served as President of the International Reading Association 2001–2002. Her extensive staff development experiences include working in Russia and other eastern European countries as part of the Reading and Writing for Critical Thinking Project from 1999–2003. Her latest books are *Coming Together as Readers* (2001, Skylight Professional Books) and *Reading Comprehension: Strategies for Independent Learners,* co-authored with Camille Blachowicz (Guilford, 2000). She is also a senior consultant for McDougal Littell's history text, *Creating America* (2000).

Editorial: Developed by Nieman Inc. with Phil LaLeike

Design: Ronan Design: Sean O'Neill

Illustrations: Mike McConnell

Printed in the United States of America
International Standard Book Number: 0-669-51427-6
1 2 3 4 5 6 7 8 9—CK—10 09 08 07 06 05 04

Consultants

Marilyn Crow
Wilmette Public Schools
Wilmette, IL

Ellen Fogelberg
Evanston Public Schools
Evanston, IL

Reviewers

Julie Anderson
Hawken Lower School
Lyndhurst, OH

Jay Brandon
JB Murphy Elementary School
Chicago, IL

Harriet Carr
Holladay Elementary School
Richmond, VA

Lisa Clark
Lebanon Elementary School
Lebanon, WI

Erin Hansen
Concord Elementary School
Edina, MN

Carol Hauswald
Karel Havlicek School
Berwyn, IL

Eleanor Johnson
Weaver Lake Elementary School
Maple Grove, MN

Elma Jones
Swarthmore-Rutledge School
Swarthmore, PA

Paula Kaiser
Irving Elementary School
West Allis, WI

Amber Langerman
Jane Vernon Elementary School
Kenosha, WI

Brenda Nixon
Las Lomitas Elementary School
Atherton, CA

Pat Pagone
St. Emily School
Mt. Prospect, IL

Kelli Phillips
Maryvale Elementary School
Rockville, MD

Krista Sackett
Lawson Elementary School
Johnston, IA

Carole Skalinder
Orrington Elementary School
Evanston, IL

Dr. Karen Smith
Manoa Elementary School
Havertown, PA

Sandra Sparacino
Longfellow Elementary School
West Allis, WI

Linda Vlasic
Ormondale Elementary School
Portola Valley, CA

Dawna Work
Normandy Village Elementary
Jacksonville, FL

Student Contributors

Nicole Barbian
Longfellow Elementary School
West Allis, WI

Cara Camardella
Holladay Elementary School
Richmond, VA

Sarah Cunningham
Meadow Ridge Elementary
Orland Park, IL

Jessica Ellis
Normandy Village Elementary
Jacksonville, FL

Elizabeth Garrett
Botsford Elementary School
Livonia, MI

Charlotte Jones
Las Lomitas Elementary School
Atherton, CA

Emma Kerrigan
St. Joseph School
Wilmette, IL

Sarah Langston
Holladay Elementary School
Richmond, VA

John Lee
McKenzie Elementary School
Wilmette, IL

Sophie Lee
McKenzie Elementary School
Wilmette, IL

Nicole Naudi
Jane Vernon Elementary School
Kenosha, WI

Kate O'Donnell
Creek Valley Elementary School
Edina, MN

Tyler Peay
Pearsons Corner Elementary
   School
Mechanicsville, VA

Bekka Rood
Prairieland Elementary School
Normal, IL

Caroline Ruwe
Weaver Lake Elementary School
Maple Grove, MN

Savannah Shields
Vandergriff Elementary School
Fayetteville, AR

James Thornberg
W.A. Porter Elementary School
Hurst, TX

Maria Tuite
St. Cecilia School
San Francisco, CA

Thomas R. Vanderloo
St. Jude School
Chattanooga, TN

Christian Vetter
Sacred Heart School
Lombard, IL

Jessica Walters
Karel Havlicek School
Berwyn, IL

Kiernan Ziletti
St. Bridget's Catholic School
Richmond, VA

Teacher's Guide and Lesson Plans

Lessons

What Happens When You Read

The Reading Process

Skills for Active Reading

Words and Their Meaning

Understanding Paragraphs

4

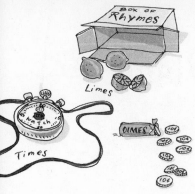

Reading for Information

Reading for School

Reading Stories and Poems

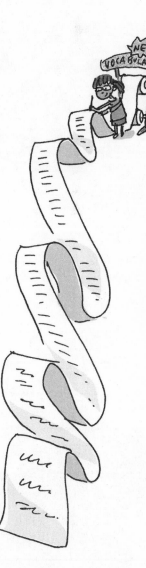

Reading for Tests

Reading Tools Blackline Masters.....458

Program Components

The *Reader's Handbook* program includes the materials on the following pages in addition to the handbook.

Teacher's Guide

The *Teacher's Guide and Lesson Plans* book follows the lessons in the *Reader's Handbook*, highlights what to teach, and suggests ways to extend the lessons.

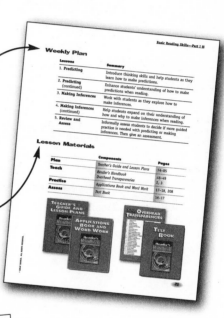

The **Weekly Plan** outlines what material will be taught on a day-to-day basis.

The **Lesson Materials** chart lists where to find additional materials that supplement the lesson.

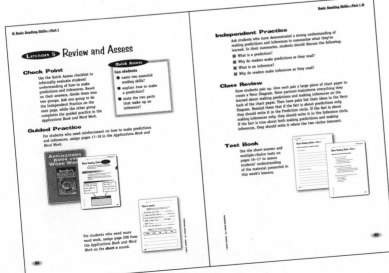

At the end of each lesson, you informally assess the students and then have them apply the skills either a) independently or b) in guided practice in the *Applications Book and Word Work*.

Applications Book and Word Work

The *Applications Book and Word Work* extends the lessons with opportunities to practice skills and strategies introduced in *Reader's Handbook*. It also includes practice sheets for students to work with phonics and word structures.

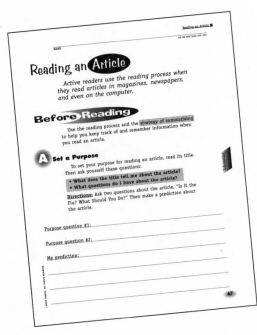

The lessons allow students to practice their reading skills, apply tools to a new selection, and use reading strategies.

The *Applications Book and Word Work Teacher's Edition* includes the answers.

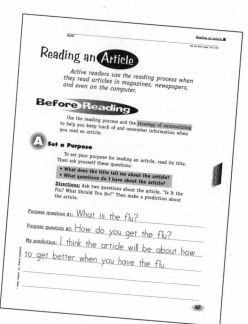

Overhead Transparencies

The *Overhead Transparencies* display key parts of the handbook to help in-class teaching of important concepts, such as the reading process and previewing different kinds of reading.

Test Book

The *Test Book* contains two kinds of tests for each lesson in the *Reader's Handbook*.

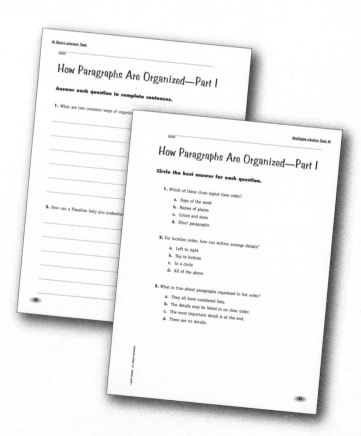

Assess students' understanding of the handbook lessons through short-answer and multiple-choice tests.

How to Use a

Teacher's Guide Lesson

Begin by reading the **Goals**. You may want to read them aloud to the class and inform them that they will be assessed on these goals.

A **Background** section helps you connect the lesson with students' prior knowledge and previous lessons.

Introduce the unit or week's lessons with an **Opening Activity**.

WEEK 29

Reading a Novel

Goals

Here students read an excerpt from the novel *Flat Stanley*. This week's lessons will help them learn to:

☑ understand the characters, setting, and plot of a novel
☑ use the reading strategy of using graphic organizers

Background

Help students connect this week's lessons to their prior knowledge by asking them to:

■ discuss what they know about novels
■ think about how to apply the reading process when reading a novel
■ compare reading novels with reading other types of fiction
■ explore the more challenging aspects of reading novels

Opening Activity

Write the following headings on the board: *Title, Interesting Characters, Exciting Plot,* and *Other Reasons.* Hold a class discussion about favorite novels. Begin by sharing your own favorite novels from childhood. Provide a brief summary, and explain why these are your favorites. List your titles on the board, and then place a tally mark under one of the three headings (provide specifics under *Other Reasons*). Invite volunteers to share their favorite novels. Add their reasons under the correct heading(s). After completing the activity, tally the marks to see which story element was mentioned most as a reason for considering a novel a favorite. Were students surprised by the results? What does this informal poll tell students about what they look for most when choosing novels?

362

Reading a Novel ▓

Weekly Plan

Lessons	Summary
1. Before Reading: Novel	Review with students the steps of the Before Reading stage of the reading process and discuss how to apply each step to a novel.
2. During Reading: Novel	Explore how to apply the During Reading stage of the reading process to a novel, particularly the story elements of plot and characters.
3. During Reading: Novel (continued)	Apply the During Reading stage of the reading process to a novel. Reinforce their understanding of setting and making connections as they read.
4. After Reading: Novel	Apply the After Reading stage of the reading process to a novel.
5. Review and Assess	Informally assess students to decide if more guided practice is needed. Then give an assessment.

Lesson Materials

	Components	Pages
Plan	Teacher's Guide and Lesson Plans	362–373
Teach	Reader's Handbook	282–293
	Overhead Transparencies	29, 30
Practice	Applications Book and Word Work	147–155, 232
Assess	Test Book	64–65

TEACHER'S GUIDE AND LESSON PLANS

APPLICATIONS BOOK AND WORD WORK

OVERHEAD TRANSPARENCIES

TEST BOOK

363

The **Weekly Plan** lists the week's lessons and gives a brief summary of what will be covered on a day-to-day basis.

The **Lesson Materials** chart lists all supplementary materials that support the lesson.

Daily Instruction

The **Focus** section summarizes what will be taught in the day's lesson.

Use the **Getting Started** activity to grab students' attention as you begin the lesson.

The **Teaching Approach** section guides you through the lessons in the *Reader's Handbook.*

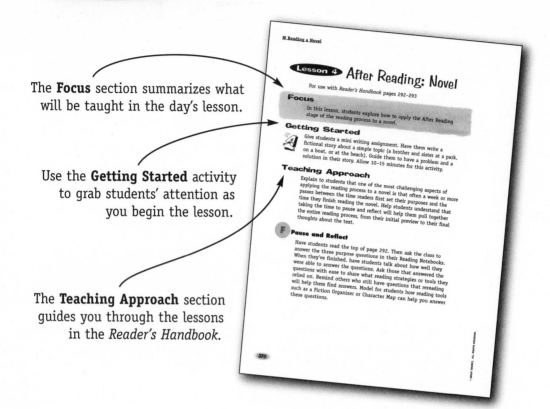

Reading a Novel

Lesson 4 After Reading: Novel

For use with *Reader's Handbook* pages 292–293

Focus

In this lesson, students explore how to apply the After Reading stage of the reading process to a novel.

Getting Started

Give students a mini writing assignment. Have them write a fictional story about a simple topic (a brother and sister at a park, on a boat, or at the beach). Guide them to have a problem and a solution in their story. Allow 10–15 minutes for this activity.

Teaching Approach

Explain to students that one of the most challenging aspects of applying the reading process to a novel is that often a week or more passes between the time readers first set their purposes and the time they finish reading the novel. Help students understand that taking the time to pause and reflect will help them pull together the entire reading process, from their initial preview to their final thoughts about the text.

F Pause and Reflect

Have students read the top of page 292. Then ask the class to answer the three purpose questions in their Reading Notebooks. When they've finished, have students talk about how well they were able to answer the questions. Ask those that answered the questions with ease to share what reading strategies or tools they relied on. Remind others who still have questions that rereading will help them find answers. Model for students how reading tools such as a Fiction Organizer or Character Map can help you answer these questions.

376

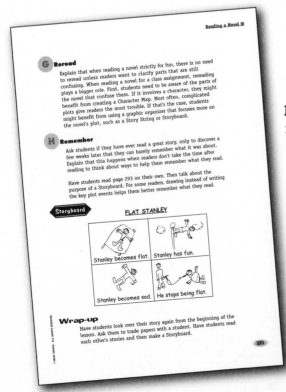

Reading a Novel

G Reread

Explain that when reading a novel strictly for fun, there is no need to reread unless readers want to clarify parts that are still confusing. When reading a novel for a class assignment, rereading plays a bigger role. First, students need to be aware of the parts of the novel that confuse them. If it involves a character, they might benefit from creating a Character Map. Most often, complicated plots give readers the most trouble. If that's the case, students might benefit from using a graphic organizer that focuses more on the novel's plot, such as a Story String or Storyboard.

H Remember

Ask students if they have ever read a great story, only to discover a few weeks later that they can barely remember what it was about. Explain that this happens when readers don't take the time after reading to think about ways to help them remember what they read.

Have students read page 293 on their own. Then talk about the purpose of a Storyboard. For some readers, drawing instead of writing the key plot events helps them better remember what they read.

Storyboard

FLAT STANLEY

Stanley becomes flat.	Stanley has fun.
Stanley becomes sad.	He stops being flat.

Wrap-up

Have students look over their story again from the beginning of the lesson. Ask them to trade papers with a student. Have students read each other's stories and then make a Storyboard.

371

Reading Tools are highlighted in each lesson. They point out how the reading purpose and the type of reading affect which strategy or tool to use.

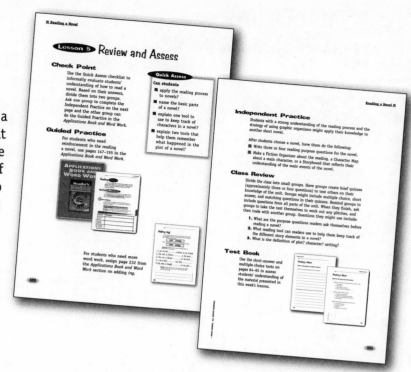

Review and Assess includes a **Quick Assess** checklist that teachers can use to evaluate students' understanding of the lesson. This section also proposes three ways to extend the lesson.

1. Students who need more guided practice can use a new selection in the *Applications Book and Word Work*.

2. Students who need more word work can use the page from the Word Work section of the *Applications Book and Word Work*.

3. Students able to work on their own are directed to apply the strategies to a suggested activity for independent practice.

 Throughout this book there are **Activity Icons** placed in the margins. This icon highlights activities that teachers can use to extend the lesson beyond the *Reader's Handbook* pages. These activities are designed to create more meaning and make the material more memorable to the student.

A **Class Review** is included to bring all students together for a final review before a test is taken.

Use the *Test Book* pages to assess students on the material in the lesson.

Reading Strategies Overview

Reading Lesson	Selection	Reading Strategy
Reading an Article	"Bubble, Bubble, Spittlebug"	Summarizing
Reading a Biography	from *Benjamin Franklin* by David A. Adler	Note-taking
Reading Social Studies	"A Capital for the U.S.A."	Using Graphic Organizers
Reading Science	"How Plants Make Food"	Note-taking
Reading Math	"Multiply with 2"	Visualizing and Thinking Aloud
Reading a Folktale	"The Lion and the Mouse"	Summarizing
Reading a Novel	from *Flat Stanley* by Jeff Brown	Using Graphic Organizers
Reading a Poem	"Michael Is Afraid of the Storm" by Gwendolyn Brooks	Using Your Own Words
Reading a Test and Test Questions	"The Boatman"	Skimming

Focus Lesson	Selection	Reading Tools
Focus on Information Books	from *Giant Pandas* by Patricia A. Fink Martin from *Giant Pandas: Gifts from China* by Allan Fowler	Summary Notes
Focus on a Website	San Diego Zoo website	Summary Notes Website Card
Focus on Graphics	"Top 5 Heaviest Land Mammals" "The 5 Largest States"	Think Aloud
Focus on Word Problems	Sample Word Problem	Think Aloud
Focus on Questions	from "Earth Moves Around the Sun"	Think Aloud
Focus on Plot	from *The Skirt* by Gary Soto	Story Organizer Plot Diagram
Focus on Characters	from *Jake Drake Know-It-All* by Andrew Clements	Character Map Character Change Chart
Focus on Setting	from *Stone Fox* by John Reynolds Gardiner	Setting Chart Summary Notes
Focus on Reading Tests	Sample Reading Test	Think Aloud
Focus on Language Tests	Sample Language Test	Think Aloud
Focus on Writing Tests	Sample Writing Test	Process Notes
Focus on Math Tests	Sample Math Test	Think Aloud

Correlations

Overview

The *Reader's Handbook* is a multifaceted guide to reading, and it easily supplements several other Great Source reading and writing products. Use the correlation charts that follow to complement lessons with different materials.

1. *Daybook of Critical Reading and Writing,* Grade 3

Like the *Reader's Handbook,* the *Daybooks* show students how to become active readers. The *Daybooks* complement the *Reader's Handbook* by offering further opportunities to practice using reading strategies and tools, the reading process, and reading skills. The *Daybooks* have been correlated to the *Reader's Handbook* through the genre of the selections. In other words, nonfiction selections from the *Daybooks* are suggested for the Reading for Information chapter in the handbook, poetry selections with the Reading Stories and Poems chapter, and so on.

Reader's Handbook Chapter	*Daybook,* Grade 3	Pages
The Reading Process		
Skills for Active Reading	from *A Mouse Called Wolf*	10–13
	"A Fire-Breathing Dragon"	14
	from *Solomon the Rusty Nail*	16–18
	from *Real Live Monsters!*	88–89
Words and Their Meaning	"Cricket Jackets"	49
	"I'm an Amiable Dragon"	52
	"The Multilingual Mynah Bird"	53
Understanding Paragraphs	from *How to Think Like a Scientist*	21–22
	from *Fireflies in the Night*	82–83

2. Reading and Writing Sourcebook, Grade 3

One way the *Reader's Handbook* can be used is to help struggling readers. The *Sourcebooks* focus on struggling readers, teach a reading process and reading tools, and encourage students to become active readers. In these three ways, the *Sourcebooks* complement the *Reader's Handbook*. To facilitate using both programs, each *Sourcebook* selection has been correlated to an appropriate chapter in the *Reader's Handbook*.

3. *Write on Track* (©2002)

The main goal of the *Reader's Handbook* is to teach all students how to become better readers. *Write on Track* directly complements the handbook through its teaching of the writing process and the organization of different types of writing. The correlation below shows which parts of *Write on Track* best complement individual chapters in the *Reader's Handbook*.

Reader's Handbook Chapter	*Write on Track*	Pages
Introduction	writing process	12–53
The Reading Process		
Skills for Active Reading		
Words and Their Meaning	using strategies to read new words	198–199
	building vocabulary skills	207–213
	dictionary of prefixes, suffixes, and roots	214–223
Understanding Paragraphs	writing paragraphs	55–63
Reading for Information	reading graphics	193–197
Reading for School	writing classroom reports	144–151
	writing to learn math	274–275
	improving math skills	366–375
Reading Stories and Poems	writing realistic stories	159–163
	writing free-verse poetry	177–183
	writing other forms of poetry	184–190
	performing poems	240–245
	telling stories	256–261
Reading for Tests	taking tests	284–294
Almanac	becoming a better speller	224–227

Frequently Asked Questions

How did you define what a reading strategy is, and how did you choose which ones to use in the handbook?

In the *Reader's Handbook,* a **strategy** is defined as having a broad application across different genres. A strategy can serve a number of purposes. For example, you can *summarize* or *take notes* with fiction or nonfiction, a textbook, or a test. But some skills, such as *drawing conclusions* or *comparing and contrasting,* are so fundamental that they underlie almost all kinds of reading. That's why these skills are called **basic reading skills.** The handbook also refers to **reading tools,** which are more specialized and have a specific use or purpose. The Almanac lists 30 key reading tools used throughout the handbook. A K-W-L Chart, for example, is used with nonfiction texts; Story Strings work specifically with fiction; a Double-entry Journal is most appropriate for poetry. These distinctions between strategies, basic skills, and tools are an attempt to use terms consistently in the absence of any consensus and an attempt to create a set of terms teachers can use within a school to create a shared, common language.

How did you decide on these specific steps of the reading process?

Reading is infinitely complex. It—like writing—hardly follows any single process or, for that matter, works in any single direction. But students need specifics on what to do. They need a good model, and they need to develop good habits. So, rather than presenting reading in all its complex splendor, the handbook organizes reading around an easy-to-remember process, explaining what students need to do Before, During, and After Reading. It breaks down the process into brief, easy steps. As with the writing process, students may sometimes skip a step, go backward occasionally, or spend a long time on one of the steps. That's OK. The reading process will help students make the decisions they need in order to be effective readers.

What kinds of students is the handbook for?

The *Reader's Handbook* is for all students. Different students will take away different things from the handbook. Good readers will refine the strategies they use and learn some new reading tools, and perhaps they will learn even more about how different kinds of texts are organized. Average readers will add to the reading strategies and tools they use, and they'll develop a stronger understanding of the reading process. In addition, students who struggle will acquire some good strategies, tools, and understanding of the reading process.

Where should I begin as a teacher?

For help in teaching the handbook, start with the *Teacher's Guide and Lesson Plans* and *Overhead Transparencies.* To see if students can apply the strategies, utilize basic skills, and implement tools, use the *Applications Book and Word Work.* If students need extra help with phonics, use the Word Work section of the *Applications Book and Word Work.*

How does the *Teacher's Guide and Lesson Plans* book work?

It offers weekly plans and daily lessons. There are 36 units of five lessons that correlate with the pupil's edition. The first four lessons are geared toward direct instruction of the material. Each daily lesson includes a Getting Started activity, Teaching Approach, and a Wrap-up activity. The fifth lesson in the unit is for review and assessment. An informal review helps the teacher decide who can move to independent practice and which students need more guided practice.

How can I adapt the *Reader's Handbook* program to meet the individual needs of my students?

To succeed as readers, students need to work with appropriate-level materials. Materials that are too hard, albeit on grade level, will only frustrate struggling readers and deepen their aversion to trying and failing again. To avoid this problem, the *Reader's Handbook* program has been organized so that teachers can accommodate students' varying reading levels.

The basic idea is simple. If the unit is too hard, you can reinforce your teaching with the *Applications Book and Word Work,* which is designed to help the struggling readers in each lesson. It is easy to adjust for the individual differences of readers with the *Reader's Handbook*. This will help them work within their "comfort zone" where they can learn.

Likewise, for advanced students, you can step up to higher levels of the handbook and the *Applications Book and Word Work.*

On pages 20–21 of this book, you will find a chart that explains how to individualize the *Reader's Handbook, Applications Book and Word Work,* and Great Source products to meet your students' needs.

Why is the tone of the handbook so casual and informal?

The *Reader's Handbook* is written for students. The voice behind the book is an informal, friendly, guiding one, as if the narrator was poised behind the student, arm around the shoulder, speaking in the student's ear as he or she reads. The attempt is to guide students as they read. To create that tone and voice in the writing, the wording of each sentence becomes important.

The handbook "talks" to the student. To give the feel of speaking to students, style rules were set for the handbook that were deliberately a little informal.

Meeting Students' Individual Needs

The Reader's Handbook *program is organized so that teachers can accommodate students' varying reading levels. The handbook itself is written to the third-grade level, but that readability does not limit the usefulness of the handbook for students who are very highly developed in reading or for students who are struggling.*

For Highly Developed Readers

Even strong readers will benefit from the *Reader's Handbook*. The reading strategies and tools explained in the handbook are rarely in common usage, even with the very best readers. The desire to use "harder" or "more sophisticated" materials should extend more to the reading materials to which students are applying the handbook's strategies and tools. The world of students' reading is what is more sophisticated, not necessarily their command of reading strategies and tools.

Here are some ideas to try with your most highly developed readers:

1. Independent Application
Ask students to apply the strategy and tools in a specific lesson to their own materials. For example, after teaching Reading Social Studies, ask students to apply the strategy of note-taking and the note-taking tools to a chapter in their own social studies text.

2. Buddy Learning
Ask students to "teach" the lesson to other students in small groups. Use the highly developed readers to "tutor" students who need more help. The experience of explaining the strategy and reading tools to other readers will reinforce the ideas, as well as help the students who are being tutored.

3. Reading Exercises
To stretch students to the topmost level of their learning zone and challenge them, create reading exercises using materials that are specifically two, three, or even four years above grade level. By experiencing a difficult text and having to rely on the strategies and tools, students will be challenged to use more than just one or two reading strategies. As a teacher, you need to monitor students' frustration levels so that they do not become discouraged. The point of the exercises is to give students' command of reading strategies and tools a test, not to break their spirit.

For Struggling Readers

Struggling readers can also benefit greatly from the *Reader's Handbook*. Most struggling readers use few reading strategies and tools, and their grasp of the reading process is probably vague, if they see it as a process at all.

As a teacher, try not to focus on having students "cover" the material. Instead, help students develop a stronger reading process and become adept with **one reading strategy** and **two or three reading tools**. Focus, too, on the reading materials to which students are applying the handbook's strategies and tools.

Here are some ideas to try with your struggling readers:

1. Easier Texts

Ask students to apply the strategy and tools in a specific lesson to texts that are very easy for them. Help students find a text that is appropriate to their reading level. Then help them apply the reading process, a reading strategy, and a reading tool to it. Success with an easy text will show students how to apply these strategies to more challenging materials.

Limit your objectives for these students to a few main things:

■ Focus on one (or perhaps two) reading strategies at most.

■ Try out three to five reading tools and help struggling readers master one or two so that they are comfortable using them.

■ Help students apply the single strategy and reading tool to their own textbooks.

2. Guided Reading of the Handbook

Before beginning a lesson, work with students to preview the material in the handbook. Have students predict what they think the chapter or lesson will be about. Then explain that you will use a reading process. Reading starts *before* the eyes begin moving. Preferably, you will work with a small group of students, leading them through the lesson. Focus on the basic parts of the reading process, building background for students at each step. Help students understand the importance of rereading. After they finish reading the first time, help them see that they don't have to "know it all." This is the time to go back and "fix up" the holes in their understanding, using another strategy or tool.

3. Paired Reading and Questioning

By pairing students, you can help struggling readers by giving them a "buddy" to help guide them through a lesson. Then, ask students to ask each other questions on each page.

Reading First Connections

Section in *Reader's Handbook*	Connection to Reading First

WORDS AND THEIR MEANING (continued)

Learning New Words	*Vocabulary*
Using a Dictionary	*Vocabulary, Phonics*
Using Context Clues	*Vocabulary, Comprehension*
Synonyms and Antonyms	Vocabulary, Comprehension
Surrounding Sentences	Vocabulary, Comprehension
Definitions	Vocabulary, Comprehension
Examples	Vocabulary, Comprehension
Repeated Words	Vocabulary, Comprehension
Answering Vocabulary Questions	*Phonics, Vocabulary, Comprehension*
Definition Questions	Phonics, Vocabulary, Comprehension
Synonyms and Antonym Questions	Vocabulary, Comprehension
Paragraph Questions	Vocabulary, Comprehension

UNDERSTANDING PARAGRAPHS

What Is A Paragraph?	*Comprehension*
Paragraph Signals	*Comprehension*
Finding the Subject	*Comprehension*
Finding the Main Idea	*Comprehension*
Main Idea in First Sentence	Comprehension
Main Idea in Last Sentence	Comprehension
Implied Main Idea	Comprehension
Kinds of Paragraphs	*Comprehension*
Narrative Paragraphs	Comprehension
Descriptive Paragraphs	Comprehension
Persuasive Paragraphs	Comprehension
Expository Paragraphs	Comprehension
How Paragraphs Are Organized	*Comprehension*
Time Order	Comprehension
Location Order	Comprehension
List Order	Comprehension
Cause-Effect Order	Comprehension
Comparison-Contrast Order	Comprehension

READING FOR INFORMATION

Reading Nonfiction	*Fluency, Comprehension*
Reading an Article	Fluency, Comprehension
Reading a Biography	Fluency, Comprehension
Focus on Nonfiction	*Comprehension*
Focus on Information Books	Comprehension
Focus on a Website	Comprehension
Focus on Graphics	Comprehension
Elements of Nonfiction	*Vocabulary, Comprehension*
Bar Graph	Vocabulary, Comprehension
Circle Graph	Vocabulary, Comprehension
Details	Vocabulary, Comprehension
Diagram	Vocabulary, Comprehension
Email	Vocabulary, Comprehension
Encyclopedia	Vocabulary, Comprehension
Fact and Opinion	Vocabulary, Comprehension
Line Graph	Vocabulary, Comprehension
Main Idea	Vocabulary, Comprehension
Map	Vocabulary, Comprehension
Table	Vocabulary, Comprehension
Timeline	Vocabulary, Comprehension
Topic Sentence and Supporting Details	Vocabulary, Comprehension
Website	Vocabulary, Comprehension
World Wide Web	Vocabulary, Comprehension

Section in *Reader's Handbook*	Connection to Reading First
READING FOR SCHOOL	
Reading Textbooks	***Comprehension***
Reading Social Studies	Comprehension
Reading Science	Comprehension
Reading Math	Comprehension
Focus on Textbooks	***Comprehension***
Focus on Word Problems	Comprehension
Focus on Questions	Comprehension
Elements of Textbooks	***Vocabulary, Comprehension***
Glossary	Vocabulary, Comprehension
Headings and Titles	Vocabulary, Comprehension
Illustrations and Photos	Vocabulary, Comprehension
Index	Vocabulary, Comprehension
Maps	Vocabulary, Comprehension
Previews	Vocabulary, Comprehension
Table of Contents	Vocabulary, Comprehension
READING STORIES AND POEMS	
Reading Kinds of Literature	***Fluency, Comprehension***
Reading a Folktale	Fluency, Comprehension
Reading a Novel	Fluency, Comprehension
Reading a Poem	Fluency, Comprehension
Focus on Stories	***Fluency, Comprehension***
Focus on Plot	Fluency, Comprehension
Focus on Characters	Fluency, Comprehension
Focus on Setting	Fluency, Comprehension
Elements of Literature	***Vocabulary, Comprehension, Fluency, Phonemic Awareness***
Alliteration	Vocabulary, Fluency, Comprehension
Characters	Vocabulary, Comprehension
Dialogue	Vocabulary, Fluency, Comprehension
Fiction	Vocabulary, Comprehension
Imagery	Vocabulary, Comprehension
Metaphor	Vocabulary, Comprehension
Mood	Vocabulary, Fluency, Comprehension
Narrator	Vocabulary, Comprehension
Onomatopoeia	Vocabulary, Comprehension
Personification	Vocabulary, Comprehension
Plot	Vocabulary, Comprehension
Poetry	Vocabulary, Comprehension
Rhyme	Vocabulary, Fluency, Comprehension, Phonemic Awareness
Rhythm	Vocabulary, Fluency, Comprehension
Setting	Vocabulary, Comprehension
Simile	Vocabulary, Comprehension
Stanza	Vocabulary, Comprehension
Style	Vocabulary, Comprehension
Theme	Vocabulary, Comprehension

Section in *Reader's Handbook*	Connection to Reading First
READING FOR TESTS	
Reading a Test and Test Questions	*Comprehension*
Focus on Tests	*Comprehension, Phonics*
Focus on Reading Tests	Comprehension
Focus on Language Tests	Comprehension, Phonics
Focus on Writing Tests	Comprehension
Focus on Math Tests	Comprehension
READER'S ALMANAC	
Strategy Handbook	*Comprehension*
Note-taking	Comprehension
Skimming	Comprehension
Summarizing	Comprehension
Using Graphic Organizers	Comprehension
Using Your Own Words	Comprehension
Visualizing and Thinking Aloud	Comprehension
Reading Tools	*Comprehension*
Cause-Effect Organizer	Comprehension
Character Change Chart	Comprehension
Character Map	Comprehension
Double-entry Journal	Comprehension
Fiction Organizer	Comprehension
5 W's and H Organizer	Comprehension
Key Word Notes	Comprehension
K-W-L Chart	Comprehension
Main Idea Organizer	Comprehension
Plot Diagram	Comprehension
Process Notes	Comprehension
Setting Chart	Comprehension
Storyboard	Comprehension
Story Organizer	Comprehension
Story String	Comprehension
Summary Notes	Comprehension
Timeline	Comprehension
Venn Diagram	Comprehension
Web	Comprehension
Website Card	Comprehension
Word Workshop	*Phonics, Phonemic Awareness, Vocabulary*
Letters and Sounds	Phonics, Phonemic Awareness
Spelling	Phonics
Word Parts	Vocabulary

WEEK 1

Introduction

Goals

Here students will learn about the content and organization of the *Reader's Handbook*. These lessons will help them to

- ☑ learn how to use the *Reader's Handbook*
- ☑ recognize how the book is organized
- ☑ define what reading is
- ☑ explore why they read
- ☑ understand what happens when they read

Background

Help students connect this week's lessons to their prior knowledge by asking them to

- ◼ explain the term *handbook*
- ◼ compare the *Reader's Handbook* with their other textbooks
- ◼ think about the reasons they read
- ◼ talk about reading for pleasure vs. reading for school

Opening Activity

 Divide students into small groups and explain that you would like them to work together to complete a *Reader's Handbook* "scavenger hunt." Give each group a list items in the handbook. Ask them to search for each item and record the page number on which they find it. You might ask them to "scavenge" for the following items or make your own list.

- ◼ the first page of the Table of Contents
- ◼ the section called "How to Use This Book"
- ◼ the final page of "Reading Social Studies"
- ◼ the folktale "The Lion and the Mouse"
- ◼ the poem "Noodles"
- ◼ the section called "Elements of Textbooks"
- ◼ the last page of "Reading a Test and Test Questions"
- ◼ the Reader's Almanac

When students have finished, discuss their initial impressions of the book.

Weekly Plan

Lessons	Summary
1. **Using the Handbook**	Introduce the *Reader's Handbook*.
2. **Organization**	Work with students as they learn the handbook's organization.
3. **What Is Reading? Why Do You Read?**	Explore what reading is and why it is important.
4. **What Happens When You Read**	Help students understand what happens when they read.
5. **Review and Assess**	Informally assess students to decide if they have an understanding of the material. Then give an assessment.

Lesson Materials

	Components	Pages
Plan	*Teacher's Guide and Lesson Plans*	26–37
Teach	*Reader's Handbook*	13–29
Practice	*Applications Book and Word Work*	6–10, 204
Assess	*Test Book*	8–9

Lesson 1 · Using the Handbook

For use with *Reader's Handbook* pages 13–16

Focus

In this lesson, students learn how to use the *Reader's Handbook*.

Getting Started

Work with students to set up a Reading Notebook. Have them divide their notebooks into three sections: *Notes, Terms and Strategies,* and *Writing about Reading*.

Teaching Approach

Open the lesson by asking students to reflect on their reading habits. Ask them to describe their favorite place to read and what makes it conducive to reading. On the cover of their Reading Notebooks, have them draw a picture of themselves reading in their favorite spot.

How to Use This Book

Ask students to turn to page 13 in the handbook and follow along as you read aloud the text under the head "How to Use This Book." Explain that knowing how to use the book and how it will help them will be beneficial throughout the year.

Goals

Next, explore the three goals of the handbook (page 14). Use them as a springboard into a discussion of students' own goals for this year's reading class. Have students write a letter to themselves about the goals they discussed or thought about. Encourage them to come up with at least three reading goals for the year. Goals could range from grades on tests, number of books they want to read, or a specific book they would like to read. Ask each student to put the letter in a sealed envelope. Collect them and tell students they will get their letters back at the end of the year.

Uses for the Handbook

Ask students to turn to page 15. Read aloud the introductory text at the top of the page. Then introduce the various uses for the handbook. Explain that they should check the handbook whenever they need help with:

■ completing a homework assignment

■ reading a textbook chapter

■ writing a book report

■ reading aloud

■ preparing for a test or quiz

Briefly explain how the handbook can help with each of these activities. Then ask students to read pages 15–16 on their own. Have students keep a list of ways in which the handbook will help for each use. Then come together as a class and discuss notes they made from the reading. Model for students how to think aloud by demonstrating it yourself.

Wrap-up

To help students further explore the information presented in the lesson, ask them to create a "My Reading Habits" page in the *Writing about Reading* section of their notebooks. Here they can answer the following questions.

■ What is your favorite book?

■ What do you like to read about?

■ What do you do well when you read?

■ What can you work on to be a better reader?

When they finish, read students' work and use it when conferencing with students individually. Be sure students understand a number of ways that the *Reader's Handbook* can help them.

 Lesson 2 Organization

For use with *Reader's Handbook* pages 17–21

Focus

Here students will explore the organization of the *Reader's Handbook*.

Getting Started

 Tell students they are going to plan a book. Explain that they need to pick a topic they've learned about in school and map out the parts of the book and how many pages each part is. Emphasize that they are not writing the book; they are only figuring out what the different parts will be. Encourage them to think about what they already know about books. Allow students to look at a variety of books in your class library. Have students share their "plans" when finished. Keep a list on the board of different book parts.

Teaching Approach

Ask volunteers to demonstrate what they do before reading a new book. Do they read the table of contents and then thumb through the entire text? Or do they spot-check chapters of particular importance? Explain that these activities are all examples of previewing and that readers preview a text in order to get a sense of how the book is organized and what they can expect in terms of subject matter.

Next, guide students through a preview of the *Reader's Handbook*. Point out key features of the book, including the Table of Contents, the Author and Title Index, and the Skills and Terms Index. Tell the class that you'll discuss these elements and model how to use them in a future lesson.

Then begin your discussion of the four main parts of the handbook.
■ Reading Lessons
■ Focus Lessons
■ Elements Mini-lessons
■ Reader's Almanac

Reading Lessons

Have students turn to page 17. Explain that the handbook has lessons of different sizes, with the Reading Lessons being the longest. These lessons explore major school subjects as well as novels, articles, poems, and tests. Explain that the purpose of these lessons is to show students step-by-step how to use the reading process with a particular text. Then ask students to read page 17.

Focus Lessons

Next, discuss the purpose of the Focus Lessons. Explain that the Focus Lessons explore small aspects of the Reading Lessons. For example, the reading lesson "Reading a Novel" is followed by the smaller lessons "Focus on Plot," "Focus on Characters," and "Focus on Setting." Ask a volunteer to read aloud the information on page 18.

Elements Mini-lessons

Move on to an explanation of the Elements Mini-lessons, which appear at the end of the major chapters of the handbook. Ask students to learn about the purpose of these lessons by reading page 19 to themselves.

Reader's Almanac

Have students read pages 20 and 21. Then direct them to the Reader's Almanac (pages 392–439). Point out the three parts of the Almanac: Strategy Handbook, Reading Tools, and Word Workshop. Explain the purpose of each section.

Wrap-up

Ask a volunteer to review the four parts of the handbook. Have students make a poster that advertises the book and shows the parts. Then explain the different ways students will be using the handbook over the course of the year.

Lesson 3 # What Is Reading?
Why Do You Read?

For use with *Reader's Handbook* pages 24–27

Focus

Here students will explore what it means to read and the various opportunities they have to read, both in school and outside of school.

Getting Started

Ask students to choose five key terms that relate to the handbook. Have them to hide the terms in a word search they create on their own. Allow them to trade word searches with a partner and check to see how many reading words they can find. Extend it by having students write the definitions or a description of the words in the *Terms* section of their Reading Notebooks.

Teaching Approach

Have students think of all the things they have read since waking up this morning. Have some volunteers share their lists with the class. Ask students if they were surprised to learn that they have read almost constantly through the day.

What Is Reading?

Begin the lesson by telling the class that there is more to reading than they might think. Explain that reading is a skill all students have, although it's a skill that requires time, effort, and practice. Compare being a good reader to being a good athlete. Like athletes, readers need to practice in order to stay in tip-top condition, and the more they practice, the better they get at it.

Next, direct students to follow along as you read aloud page 24. Then have students preview silently the information on page 25. Ask the class, "What is reading?" Reading is also a tool—one that students will need to use for the rest of their lives. Then explain that reading is also a process, or a series of steps, to follow. Tell students that in lessons to come, they'll learn the steps of the reading process and then apply what they learned to a variety of different texts.

Why Do You Read?

Write the question "Why do you read?" on the board. Have students spend the first few minutes quickwriting an answer. Remind them that there might be more than one answer to the question. Direct students to handbook pages 26–27. Tell the class that there are several reasons to read.

▮ It is fun.

▮ It gives you information.

▮ Reading changes you.

Read aloud the text under "Reading Is Fun." Ask, "What is fun about meeting interesting characters? Which book or story characters are your favorites? Why?" Point out that it can also be fun to learn about real people, places, and events.

Next, read the text under "Reading Gives You Information." Ask the class what kinds of information they can get from reading. Point out that there are all types of informational texts, including maps, graphics, websites, and so on.

Last, have students read silently the text under "Reading Changes You." When they finish, ask, "How can a book or article change a person? How can a reading change someone's goals?"

Wrap-up

Draw the following table on the board.

Reading Is . . .	Reading Is Not . . .

Have students work in small groups to complete the table on chart paper. Encourage them to think carefully about their responses before adding them to the list. Discuss the charts the students created.

⬭ Lesson 4 ⬭ What Happens When You Read

For use with *Reader's Handbook* pages 28–29

Focus

In this lesson, students will explore what happens when they read. They'll do this in preparation for learning the reading process.

Getting Started

Post on the board the three questions shown at the top of page 28.

■ How would I describe reading to someone?

■ What goes on in my head while I'm reading?

■ What does reading look like?

Teaching Approach

Have each child choose one of the questions. Ask them to illustrate their answers. When students are finished have them explain their picture and then post it on the board or wall. Keep the pictures in the three groups.

Ask students, "What other questions do you have about reading?" Students might wonder why we read left to right, for example, or why reading is particularly easy/difficult for them. Add these questions to the list and explain that the purpose of the day's lesson is to think about what happens when you read.

Visualizing Reading

Ask students to turn to page 28 in the *Reader's Handbook*. Point out the questions at the top of the page, and then ask the class to read the text under "Visualizing Reading." Ask, "What does it mean to visualize something?" Help students understand that visualizing is like creating a picture in their minds. Give students an opportunity to practice visualizing. Describe a fictional scene and have them draw what they hear. Allow students to compare their pictures with those of other students when they are done. Next, ask students to complete the activity described on page 29. Explain the individual steps and then have them draw in their Reading Notebooks a picture of themselves reading.

Visualizing

Pick up a book.
Hop in bed.

Read my book.

Put my book at
the end of my bed.

Go to sleep.

Thinking of Ourselves as Readers

The purpose of the activity is to help students learn to think consciously of reading as a process. Talk together about how they move from start to finish, just as they do when they use the writing process, conduct a science experiment, or perform another type of activity. If students think of themselves as readers, they will become better at reading and have more confidence in themselves as readers.

Wrap-up

Finish the lesson by reiterating to students that reading takes time and effort, but that the rewards can be too numerous to count. It's important for students to know that even the best readers will find some texts challenging and that they're not alone if they feel like they struggle with reading. Share your own experiences as a reader with the class. Reassure the class that the *Reader's Handbook* offers tips and strategies that can make almost any type of text more accessible and interesting to read.

Lesson 5 Review and Assess

Check Point

Use the Quick Assess checklist to informally evaluate students' understanding of the *Reader's Handbook*. Based on their answers, divide students into two groups. One group can do the Independent Practice on the next page while the other group completes the guided practice in the *Applications Book and Word Work*.

Quick Assess

Can students

- ☑ list several ways the *Reader's Handbook* can help them?
- ☑ come up with their own definition for reading?
- ☑ tell two things that they can learn from reading?

Guided Practice

For students who need reinforcement in understanding the *Reader's Handbook,* use pages 6–10 in the *Applications Book and Word Work.*

For students who need more word work, assign page 204 from *Applications Book and Word Work* on rhyming words.

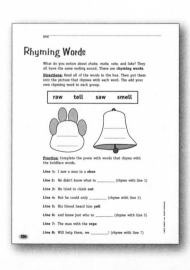

Independent Practice

Encourage students who have demonstrated a strong understanding of the content and organization of the *Reader's Handbook* to quickwrite their thoughts about how the handbook can help them. Use these prompts and have students illustrate their writing.

■ When I first saw the *Reader's Handbook*, I . . .

■ I think the *Reader's Handbook* is . . .

■ Something I wonder about the *Reader's Handbook* is . . .

Class Review

Divide the class into small groups. Have groups create a multiple-choice or short-answer quiz that tests their classmates' knowledge of the *Reader's Handbook*. Make sure they write an answer key. Then ask students to trade tests with another group. Questions students could use on their tests include:

■ What is the *Reader's Handbook*?

■ What are the four parts of the book?

■ Why should you use reading tools?

Test Book

Use the short-answer and multiple-choice tests on pages 8–9 to assess students' understanding of the material presented in this week's lessons.

The Reading Process— Before Reading

Goals

Here students will explore the Before Reading stage of the reading process. In addition, they'll consider the ways the reading process is similar to the writing process. These lessons will help them to

- ☑ think of reading as a process similar to the writing process
- ☑ understand the three stages of the reading process
- ☑ set a purpose for reading
- ☑ preview a reading passage
- ☑ develop a plan for reading

Background

Help students connect this week's lessons to their prior knowledge by asking them to

- ◼ think about the term *process* and what it means
- ◼ retell the steps in a simple activity such as tying their shoes
- ◼ recall what they know about the writing process
- ◼ discuss what they do now to get ready to read

Opening Activity

Invite students to reflect upon the steps involved in an everyday activity such as preparing a sandwich for lunch. Then divide the board into three large columns and label them *Before, During,* and *After.* Ask students to list the steps they go through before, during, and after preparing lunch. For example, in the Before column, students might suggest activities such as gathering the bread, turkey, and lettuce and getting a plate, napkin, and knife.

Weekly Plan

Lessons	Summary
1. **The Writing Process and Reading Process**	Introduce the three stages of the reading process: Before, During, and After. Compare the reading process to the writing process.
2. **Set a Purpose**	Help students explore in detail how to set a purpose for reading.
3. **Preview**	Support students as they learn how to preview a text.
4. **Plan**	Help students to make a plan that can help them meet their reading purpose.
5. **Review and Assess**	Informally assess students to decide if they have an understanding of the Before Reading stage of the reading process. Then give an assessment.

Lesson Materials

	Components	Pages
Plan	*Teacher's Guide and Lesson Plans*	38–49
Teach	*Reader's Handbook*	30–36
Practice	*Applications Book and Word Work*	11–12, 205
Assess	*Test Book*	10–11

Lesson 1 The Writing Process and Reading Process

For use with *Reader's Handbook* pages 30–31, 34

Focus

In this lesson, students will learn the steps of the writing process and begin their exploration of the reading process.

Getting Started

Have students turn to the *Notes* section of their Reading Notebooks. Ask them to divide a notebook page in half. Have them label the left column *My Writing Process* and leave the right-hand column blank. Ask them to list the steps they take when they write on the left and then illustrate each step on the right side of the page.

Teaching Approach

Review the meaning of the term *process*. Encourage the class to brainstorm other activities that are a process. List these on the board. Then ask the class to turn to page 30. Read aloud the explanatory text at the top of the page. Discuss the staircase analogy. Next, have students turn to page 31 and look at the individual steps of the writing process.

The Writing Process

1. **Prewriting**

2. **Drafting**

3. **Revising**

4. **Editing and Proofreading**

5. **Publishing**

Explain the purpose of each step. Model the writing process with a simple topic, such as "Riding the School Bus." Walk students through each step to show how a topic can go from the prewriting phase to a paragraph ready to "publish." Then forge a link between the writing process and the reading process.

The Reading Process

1. **Before Reading**
2. **During Reading**
3. **After Reading**

Read aloud the three stages of the reading process and explain that each stage contains two or three separate steps to follow. Then direct students to turn to page 34.

Read aloud the top of the page. Have students skim the middle of the page. Ask, "What stands out on this page? What do you think it means?" Discuss with students how they think the illustration and the Before Reading steps may go together.

Before Reading

A. Set a Purpose

B. Preview

C. Plan

Ask students to illustrate the boxes in a Story String (page 421 in the *Reader's Handbook*) on what they think happens during each of the above steps. They can use the topic of the "broken bike" to be their reason for reading.

Wrap-up

Give students an opportunity to use the writing process to write about the Before Reading stage of the reading process. At this point they do not know the details about the steps, so have students write a short paragraph about what they currently do before they begin reading.

Lesson 2 Set a Purpose

For use with *Reader's Handbook* page 34

Focus

Here students will learn the first step of the reading process, Set a Purpose.

Getting Started

List on the board chores your students might do at home or in school.

■ take out trash   ■ finish homework

■ feed pet dog   ■ go to soccer practice

■ wash the dishes   ■ set the dinner table

Ask students what the purpose is for each chore. Point out that there may be different purposes. Tell students they will learn to set a purpose for reading too.

Teaching Approach

All too often, students dive right into reading without taking the time to consider what they're about to read or why they're reading it. The reading process helps students to spend a few moments thinking before they begin reading. As a first step, they'll think about their purpose for reading. Setting a purpose can make it easier for students to find information they need and create meaning from a text. In this lesson, you'll help students learn to develop purpose questions that are text-specific.

Setting a Purpose for Reading Nonfiction

Write *Set your purpose for reading* on the board. Ask what they think that means. Next, model how to set a purpose for various texts. Point out that an easy way to set a purpose for a nonfiction text is to turn the title of the material into a question using *who, what, where, when, why,* or *how*. For practice, have students write reading purpose questions for a variety of nonfiction books you show the class. Allow students to share their purpose questions. Another way to set a purpose for reading nonfiction is to create a K-W-L Chart and then use the questions listed in the W column as the purpose for reading.

K-W-L Chart

WHAT I KNOW	WHAT I WANT TO KNOW	WHAT I LEARNED

Setting a Purpose for Reading Fiction

Explain to students that setting a purpose for reading fiction is as important as setting a purpose for reading nonfiction. The process, however, is slightly different. Very often, students' purpose for reading fiction will involve learning about the characters and finding out what happens in the plot. Here is a student's purpose for reading the novel *Charlotte's Web*.

■ What happens in *Charlotte's Web*?

■ Who is Charlotte?

■ Where and when does the action take place?

With some selections—poetry, in particular—students' purpose for reading will be to create meaning. Here are purpose questions for this type of text.

■ What is "Good Luck Gold" about?

■ What does the poem mean?

Wrap-up

Display a variety of reading materials, such as novels, poetry books, textbooks, magazines, newspapers, advertisements, schedules, menus, and so on. Ask students to choose one text and then set a purpose for reading. Have them write at least two purpose questions that they will share with the class. Make the point that a reader's purpose changes when the text changes and that no two readers will have the exact same purpose for reading.

Lesson 3 Preview

For use with *Reader's Handbook* pages 31–35

Focus

In this lesson, students will learn the second step of the reading process, Preview.

Getting Started

 Put students into small groups and distribute five or six different restaurant menus to each group. Tell them they must decide where they would like to order from in the next few minutes. When the time is up, have each group tell their choice and their reasons. Explain that they just previewed the menus and they will learn how to do that with books in this lesson.

Teaching Approach

Explain to the class that in this lesson, they'll learn the importance of previewing a text before they begin reading.

Preview Techniques

Ask students to reflect upon the previewing techniques they currently use. (Reiterate that reading through the table of contents, reading a book's back cover, and thumbing through the pages of a text are all previewing techniques.) Make a list on the board of the previewing activities students use. Then ask the following questions.

■ What is your favorite previewing technique? Why?

■ How do your previewing techniques change as the text changes?

■ How do you think previewing can help you become a better reader?

Next, have students turn to page 35 in the *Reader's Handbook*. Work with students to understand that their first step when previewing will often be to look at the title (or book cover) and consider what they think the book might be about.

Previewing a Book

Model the process by holding up a book for students to see and then commenting on the elements on the cover that grab your attention. Then, with your students' help, post two Preview Checklists on the board: one for nonfiction and the other for fiction. You may want to have a fiction and nonfiction book to show students as you make the lists. Explain to students that these checklists are general enough to work with most texts. As they read the handbook, they'll learn about checklists that are text-specific.

◆ Preview Checklist for Nonfiction ▷

√ the title and any headings
√ any names, dates, or words that are repeated or set in boldface
√ any pictures, maps, charts, or diagrams and captions
√ any questions or study guides

◆ Preview Checklist for Fiction ▷

√ the title and author
√ any repeated words or phrases
√ any background information or other type of introduction
√ the first paragraph or two
√ any pictures

Finish the lesson by doing a preview of a book or magazine. Create a Preview Chart similar to the one below.

◆ Preview Chart ▷

Book Title:	My Thoughts
What I noticed about the front and back covers	
I noticed these repeated words and phrases	
Here's what I learned from the background information	
Here's what I learned from the first and last paragraphs	

Wrap-up

Ask students to draw a Preview Chart in their notebooks and use it to help them preview a book of their choice.

Lesson 4 Plan

For use with *Reader's Handbook* page 36

Focus

In this lesson, students will learn the third step of the reading process, Plan.

Getting Started

Divide the class into small groups. Give each group a different vacation spot. Be sure to vary the types of destinations. Ask groups to list what they would pack for this trip. Have each group present their suitcase contents. Lead students to realize that they just planned their trip. Also, emphasize that all plans were different.

Teaching Approach

Once students understand how to set a purpose and preview, they are ready to move on to the third step of the Before Reading stage: Plan. Begin by explaining the purpose of this step. Help students understand that they can read in different ways. Students should know, however, that the same plan won't work for every text. For example, the plan they make for reading a poem will be different from the plan they make for reading a math chapter.

A large part of the Plan step involves choosing a reading strategy and the tools that can support that strategy. Explain the difference between a strategy and a tool (see page 18). Refer students to pages 393 and 406 of the Reader's Almanac in the handbook. You'll notice that the *Reader's Handbook* makes suggestions about which strategies to use with which types of texts. Take these as suggestions only. If, for example, your students have great success with the strategy of using graphic organizers, you may want to help them apply it to several types of texts. The chart that follows contains information about the types of texts discussed in the *Reader's Handbook,* as well as a list of suggested strategies and tools to use with each text.

Suggested Reading Strategies and Tools

Text Type	Reading Strategy	Reading Tools
Article	Summarizing	5 W's and H Organizer, Main Idea Organizer, Summary Notes
Biography	Note-taking	Key Word Notes, Cause-Effect Organizer, Timeline
Social Studies	Using graphic organizers	K-W-L Chart, Timeline, Web
Science	Note-taking	Process Notes, Cause-Effect Organizer
Math	Visualizing and thinking aloud	Summary Notes
Folktale	Summarizing	Story String, Fiction Organizer
Novel	Using graphic organizers	Fiction Organizer, Storyboard, Character Map
Poem	Using your own words	Double-entry Journal, Think Aloud
Tests and Test Questions	Skimming	Think Aloud

Explain that the Strategy Handbook (pages 393–405) describes six different strategies (summarizing, note-taking, using graphic organizers, visualizing and thinking aloud, using your own words, and skimming) and how they work. Then have students preview the Reading Tools section. Tell the class that these will be very useful throughout the year.

Wrap-up

Divide the class into three groups. Assign each group one step of the Before Reading stage of the reading process to discuss. Then have each group make a poster that explains the step. Keep the posters on display so that students can consult them as needed.

Lesson 5 Review and Assess

Check Point

Use the Quick Assess checklist to informally evaluate students' understanding of how to use the Before Reading stage of the reading process. Based on their answers, divide students into two groups. One group can do the Independent Practice on the next page while the other group does the guided practice in the *Applications Book and Word Work*.

Guided Practice

For students who need reinforcement with the Before Reading stage of the reading process, assign pages 11–12 in the *Applications Book and Word Work*.

Quick Assess

Can students

☑ name the three steps of the Before reading stage?

☑ say why it's important to set a purpose for reading?

☑ explain what to do in a preview?

☑ describe how to make a plan for reading?

☑ discuss similarities between the reading process and the writing process?

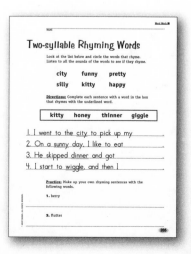

For students who need more word work, assign page 205 from the *Applications Book and Word Work* on two-syllable rhyming words.

Independent Practice

Students who have demonstrated a strong understanding of the Before Reading stage of the reading process should practice applying what they've learned to a library book. After they've completed the three steps, ask students to report on the following:

■ the title of the book or article they chose

■ their purpose for reading

■ what they found on their preview

■ their plan for reading the selection

Class Review

Continue encouraging students to think of themselves as active readers. Ask them to visualize what they do for each step of the Before Reading stage of the reading process. Then have them draw a three-panel poster that shows them setting a purpose, previewing, and planning to read a selection.

Test Book

Use the short-answer and multiple-choice tests on pages 10–11 to assess students' understanding of the strategies presented in this week's lessons.

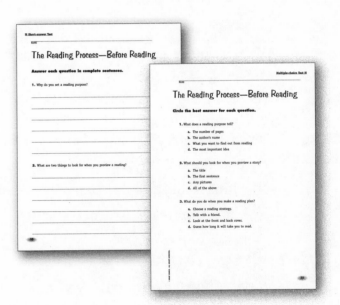

The Reading Process— During Reading

Goals

Here students explore the During Reading stage of the reading process. In these lessons, students will learn to

- ☑ read with a purpose
- ☑ use a reading strategy to help them create meaning
- ☑ make connections while reading

Background

Help students connect these lessons to their prior knowledge by asking them to

- ■ recall the steps of the Before Reading stage of the reading process
- ■ discuss their current techniques for reading fiction and nonfiction
- ■ think about graphic organizers they've used in the past
- ■ reflect on reading "trouble spots"

Opening Activity

Have students work with you to create a reading corner in your classroom. Separate the reading area from the rest of the classroom with bookshelves or a trifold screen that you cover with posterboard. Ask students to suggest their favorite fiction and nonfiction library books to keep in the area. Have them design their own library cards using crayons and index cards. On the back of the card, they can keep track of the books they browsed and the books they read.

Weekly Plan

Lessons	Summary
1. **During Reading**	Introduce the During Reading stage of the reading process and what it means to be an "active reader."
2. **Read with a Purpose**	Continue helping students explore how to read with a purpose.
3. **Connect**	Support students as they learn how to connect to a text and see how reading connects to their lives.
4. **Connect (continued)**	Work with students as they develop questions and make their own connections to a classroom text.
5. **Review and Assess**	Informally assess students to decide if they understand the During Reading stage of the reading process. Then give an assessment.

Lesson Materials

	Components	Pages
Plan	*Teacher's Guide and Lesson Plans*	50–61
Teach	*Reader's Handbook* *Overhead Transparencies*	37–38 1, 40, 41
Practice	*Applications Book and Word Work*	13–14, 206
Assess	*Test Book*	12–13

Lesson 1 During Reading

For use with *Reader's Handbook* page 37

Focus

Here students will learn about the During Reading stage of the reading process and what it means to be an "active reader."

Getting Started

Ask students to form small groups and discuss the "hardest" books they've ever read. Have each group member name at least one book. Then ask a group secretary to record students' comments about what made the books challenging. For example, some may say they found the vocabulary difficult. Others may say the story was too hard to follow. Later, make a class list of reading challenges. As you work through the *Reader's Handbook,* see how many of these problems can be solved by skills and strategies introduced in the handbook.

Teaching Approach

Display Overhead Transparency 1 and discuss the steps of the During Reading stage of the reading process.

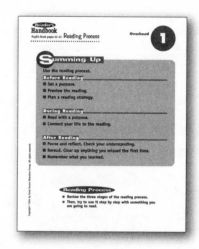

During Reading Steps

Ask students to turn to page 37. Point out the importance of creating pictures in your mind of what the author is saying (visualizing), asking questions, and making comments as you read.

During Reading

D. Read with a Purpose

E. Connect

Becoming an Active Reader

You can help students better understand the notion of reading with a purpose if you explain what it means to be an active reader. Active readers find ways to *engage* with the text. Rather than allowing their eyes to merely float past the words on the page, one sentence after another, they "talk back" to the author by asking questions, making comments, and activating personal connections to the text.

Brainstorm with students a list of the kinds of questions and comments active readers make while reading a text. These include:

- What do you mean by that word?
- Why is that detail important?
- What are you talking about here?
- This part is important.
- I don't understand what's going on here.
- I remember something like this happening to me once.

Model this kind of active reading for students. Read a few paragraphs out loud from a story and ask yourself questions that come to you so that the class can see what making meaning from the text and reading with a purpose means.

Explain to students that asking questions as well as making comments while reading is like holding a private conversation with the author. Point out that this can make a text easier to understand and more enjoyable to read.

Wrap-up

Finish the lesson by asking students to write a definition for the term *active reader* in the Terms and Strategies section of their Reading Notebooks. Ask them to include with their definitions some of the questions and comments an active reader might have when reading fiction and nonfiction.

Lesson 2 Read with a Purpose

For use with *Reader's Handbook* page 37

Focus

In this lesson, explain to students what it means to read with a purpose.

Getting Started

Present the class with the following problem: A cat is stuck in a tree outside your classroom window. Ask students to come up with a plan to save the cat. Allow students to share their ideas. Keep a tally on the different strategies. Explain that these solutions use different strategies and tools but they all had the same purpose, to save the cat. Tell them that choosing strategies and tools is important in reading as well.

Teaching Approach

Begin by reviewing the various reading strategies students can use to help them read with a purpose. Direct students' attention to the Strategy Handbook (pages 393–405) and have students read silently the definition for each strategy.

Reading Tools

Have students thumb through the Reading Tools section of the handbook (pages 406–426). Tell the class that many of the tools shown here work well as during-reading organizers. Students can use them to record their thoughts and ideas as well as key details from a text. Explain that some tools work best with fiction, while others are better for nonfiction. Show Overhead Transparency 40 as an example of an organizer to use with fiction. Then show Overhead Transparency 41 and explain that this tool works well with nonfiction.

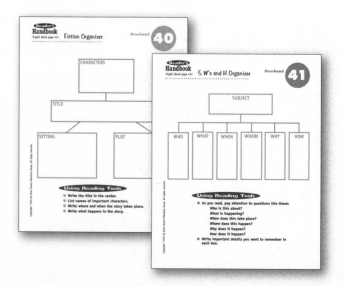

Purpose Questions

After your general discussion of strategies and tools, remind students of the importance of starting out with a clear purpose in mind. Explain that, over the course of the year, students will learn how to phrase purpose questions for a variety of texts. Then point out that you'd like them to get into the habit of writing their purpose questions on note cards and keeping the note cards tucked between the pages of the reading. This way they can remind themselves of their purpose as needed and even make adjustments to their purpose questions if the text warrants it.

Note Cards

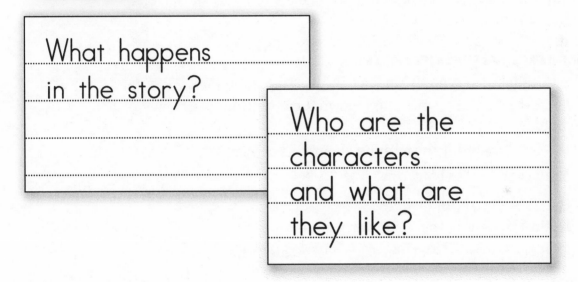

What happens in the story?

Who are the characters and what are they like?

Wrap-up

Ask students to quickwrite for a minute or so about how to set a purpose and why this step is important. When they finish, ask them to read what they wrote and highlight what they think is their most important thought. Invite volunteers to share their ideas with the class.

Lesson 3 Connect

For use with *Reader's Handbook* page 38

Focus

In this lesson, students will learn about another part of the During Reading stage, Connect.

Getting Started

Tell the class about your favorite story and explain your personal connection to it. Have students tell a favorite story and explain why they like it. Chances are they made some sort of personal connection to it.

Teaching Approach

Ask students to turn to page 38 in the *Reader's Handbook*. Read aloud the text and write the following connection questions on the board:

■ Do I already know anything about this subject?

■ How do I feel about this?

■ What do I think about this?

■ How or why is this important to me?

■ Have I seen or read something like this before?

Explain to students that when they make a connection between the text and themselves, they forge a valuable link between what the author is saying and their own thoughts and feelings. Point out that connecting to a text will make reading more interesting to them, and it will help them get more from what they read.

Help students understand that completing the Connect step of the reading process can serve to activate prior knowledge and bring relevance to the material.

Use a Double-entry Journal to model how a reader can connect a word, phrase, or sentence to his or her own life.

Double-entry Journal

Quotes	My Thoughts and Feelings
Write quotations from the text here.	Ask students to write their responses to the quotations here.

Next, have students choose a study partner. Ask them to discuss the Connect step and how it is used. Then discuss what it means to make a personal connection to a text. Explain that connection comments can take different forms. Share with the class the following chart.

Making Connections Chart

Type of Connection	Examples
Connection to the writing	This ending was a complete surprise! I never thought the story would turn out that way.
Connection to self	I remember when something like this happened to me.
Connection to others	Our school had a parade like this once.

Wrap-up

Ask students to reread page 38 and take notes on the information in the Notes section of their Reading Notebooks. Spot-check for confusion about the purpose of the Connect step and how to apply the step to different types of reading.

Lesson 4 Connect (continued)

For use with *Reader's Handbook* pages 37–38

Focus

Students further their understanding of the Connect step.

Getting Started

Gather a selection of eight to ten picture books. Give a summary of each book and have students raise a hand if they think they can connect to it. Ask them to write a sentence on how it may connect them. Then have the students think of their favorite picture book or fairy tale and write how they connect to it.

Teaching Approach

Proficient readers read with a purpose, and they know how to change or adjust their purpose during reading, if necessary. Often, the connections readers make to a text—and their ongoing "conversation" with the author—will bring about a change in purpose.

Questioning to Connect

Finding texts to which students can make connections is particularly important in order to get struggling or reluctant readers involved with reading. The questions on page 38 of the handbook are just a few to get them started. Work with students to create a list of questions they can ask themselves. Have students work in groups of four or five. Ask each student to come up with a question that will help him or her connect to a reading. Have them write their questions on a piece of chart paper. Display it and use it as they practice making connections.

Encourage students to connect by writing these prompts on the board.

■ What I wonder about is . . .

■ This reminds me of . . .

■ What I think about this is . . .

Making Connections

After you discuss the types of connection questions readers make to a text, encourage students to reflect on what *they* think about when reading. Do they slow down to make sense of important information? Do they compare the characters and situations in books to their own lives?

Next, model for students how to make the connection to a text. Show them a novel or short story you've read in class. Then offer a few comments that show you are connecting text to yourself. You can set up an organizer like the one below on the board to show students one way of keeping track of their thoughts and ideas about a reading.

Making Connections Chart

Story Element	Connection Comments
the wolf	This wolf reminds me of the wolf from "Little Red Riding Hood." He's mean, but he's not very smart.
the little pigs	These little guys are funny. They fight a lot, but you can tell they care about each other. They are much smarter than the wolf.

Wrap-up

Have students try out the Connect step with a partner. Ask students to work in pairs. One student will read aloud from a classroom novel. The other student will come up with a question for the reader that connects him or her to the reading. The reader will then answer the question. Tell students to switch places at the end of each page. Giving students time to practice making connections with a partner will help them internalize what to do and give them a "safe" way to try out their understanding of this idea.

Lesson 5 Review and Assess

Check Point

Use the Quick Assess checklist to informally evaluate students' understanding of how to use the During Reading stage of the reading process. Based on their answers, divide them into two groups. One group can do the Independent Practice on the next page while the other group does the guided practice in the *Applications Book and Word Work*.

Guided Practice

For students who need reinforcement with the During Reading stage of the reading process, assign pages 13–14 in the *Applications Book and Word Work*.

Quick Assess

Can students

- ☑ name the two steps of the During Reading stage?

- ☑ tell how to read with a purpose?

- ☑ discuss the importance of using a reading strategy, such as note-taking and using graphic organizers?

- ☑ write three questions that can help them make a connection while reading?

For students who need more word work, assign page 206 from the *Applications Book and Word Work* on consonant sounds.

Independent Practice

Students who have demonstrated a strong understanding of the During Reading stage of the reading process should practice applying what they've learned to a short story or article from your classroom library. Before they begin reading, ask:

- ▮ What is your purpose for reading?
- ▮ What strategy will you use to help you meet your purpose?
- ▮ What reading tools will you use to support the strategy?
- ▮ What is your plan for reading the selection?

Then have students read the short story or article they chose. Ask them to show the Read with a Purpose and Connect step.

Class Review

Ask students to create a booklet about the reading process that is geared toward emergent readers. Explain that young readers rely on pictures to help them understand what the text on the page means. Have students draw pictures of a child following the steps of the reading process and then write simple text as accompaniment for each picture. When they finish, have students put aside their booklets so that they can add to them during the lessons on the After Reading stage of the reading process.

Test Book

Use the short-answer and multiple-choice tests on pages 12–13 to assess students' understanding of the material presented in this week's lessons.

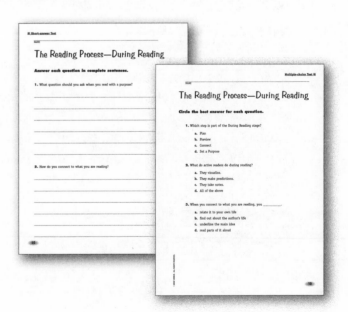

WEEK 4

The Reading Process—After Reading

Goals

Here students explore the After Reading stage of the reading process. In this week's lessons, students will learn to

☑ pause and reflect after finishing a selection

☑ reread to find more information

☑ remember what they've read

Background

Help students connect this week's lessons to their prior knowledge by asking them to

■ recall the steps of the Before and During Reading stages of the reading process

■ discuss what they currently do after reading ideas

Opening Activity

Read the above list of unit goals to the class. Then show students the chart that follows. Ask them to list in the left-hand column something they read last week. In the right-hand column, have them note what they did when they finished it. For example, did they talk about an article with a family member? Did they draw a picture of the story? Did they take notes on a textbook? Discuss the various after reading activities as a class.

After Reading Chart

Type of Text Read	What I Did After I Finished Reading

Weekly Plan

Lessons	Summary
1. **After Reading**	Introduce the three steps of the After Reading stage of the reading process.
2. **Pause and Reflect**	Explore what it means to pause, reflect, and monitor their understanding.
3. **Reread**	Support students as they reread for more information.
4. **Remember**	Work with students as they find ways to remember what they've read.
5. **Review and Assess**	Informally assess students to decide if more guided practice is needed with the After Reading stage of the reading process. Then give an assessment.

Lesson Materials

	Components	Pages
Plan	*Teacher's Guide and Lesson Plans*	62–73
Teach	*Reader's Handbook*	39–43
	Overhead Transparencies	1, 3, 4
Practice	*Applications Book and Word Work*	15–16, 207
Assess	*Test Book*	14–15

Lesson 1 After Reading

For use with *Reader's Handbook* pages 39–43

Focus

In this lesson, you'll introduce the three steps of the After Reading stage of the reading process.

Getting Started

Without any direction, give each student an easy picture book to read and a time limit of ten minutes (considerably longer than what they will actually need). Observe what students do when they are done with their reading. Then have students tell what they did with their time and record this information on the board. Explain that in this week's lessons they will learn what to do when they finish reading something.

When readers make the effort to reflect upon what they've read, they recall more of what they've learned and gain a deeper appreciation of the text's meaning. Unfortunately, most students don't take the time to pause and reflect. Instead, they close the book or turn to the next article the minute they've finished. Encourage students to allocate plenty of time for reflecting, rereading, and remembering.

Teaching Approach

Remind students that the reading process does not end the minute they finish the last page of a selection. Rather, there are three fairly quick steps for them to follow before they're ready to put the book or article away.

Introducing the Ideas

Display Overhead Transparency 1 and discuss the steps of the After Reading stage of the reading process.

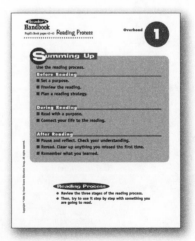

Being Active Readers

Help students understand that they are active, rather than passive, readers and that their dialogue with the author should continue even after they finish reading. Brainstorm with students a list of the questions and comments active readers might ask the author and themselves after they finish reading a piece of fiction or nonfiction. These can include the following:

- Why did you end the story that way?
- What is your message for readers?
- What's the most important thing I learned?
- What do I need to remember?
- How would I describe this to a friend?
- This article reminds me of . . .

Explain to students that asking questions and making comments after reading can help them think their way through important ideas in a text. This, in turn, can make the text easier to understand and more enjoyable to read.

Wrap-up

 Finish the lesson by asking students to write what it means to be an active reader at the After Reading stage of the reading process. (You'll recall that they did this same exercise after Lesson 1 of "The Reading Process—During Reading," pages 52–53.) Ask them to include some of the questions and comments an active reader might have when reading fiction and nonfiction.

Lesson 2 Pause and Reflect

For use with *Reader's Handbook* page 39

Focus

In this lesson, students will discuss the importance of the Pause and Reflect step of the reading process.

Getting Started

Ask students to think about the Before and During Reading stages of the reading process. Then have them use what they know to make predictions about the Pause and Reflect step. Read aloud one to two pages of a book you are reading to the class. Give students five minutes to respond freely to the text. They can draw or write their reflections.

Teaching Approach

Explain to students that they need to work at understanding what the author is trying to say. It will probably not happen on its own.

Introducing This Step

Point out that this step in the Reading Process will involve asking questions, making inferences, and drawing conclusions. Remind students of the thinking skills by displaying and then discussing Overhead Transparencies 3 and 4.

Explain, too, that this step in the reading process gives them a chance to ask questions and "fix up" their understanding of what they read.

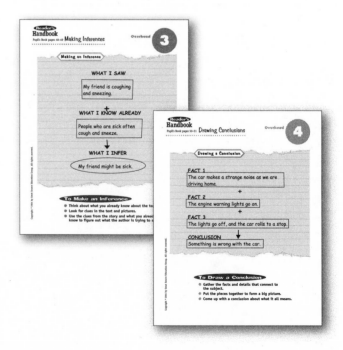

Modeling the Step

Next, ask students to turn to page 39. Ask, "What does it mean to 'collect your thoughts'? How do you do that?"

Then read aloud the information under "Pause and Reflect." Tell the class that, after they read a text, they need to stop and reflect upon what they've learned. Lead students to understand that *reflect* means "to think seriously and carefully." Explain to the class that the best way to reflect is to return to the original purpose for reading and ask yourself the following questions:

■ Are all of my questions answered?

■ Do I have any new questions?

■ What part of the reading confused me?

■ Was I unclear about anything?

Explain to students that the way to answer these additional questions is to reflect on what they read. They may decide to reread parts of the selection to gather more information or clarify key points. But readers first have to reflect.

Try reading a short selection. Model for students some of the questions you have when you reflect. Let them hear you reflecting out loud. Check how well they understand. Then help students to try out this step with a selection.

Wrap-up

Ask students to talk with a partner for a minute or so about how to pause and reflect and why this step is important. When they finish, ask them to share what they discussed and to tell what they think is their most important idea.

Lesson 3 Reread

For use with *Reader's Handbook* page 40

Focus

In this lesson, students will learn about the Reread step of the reading process.

Getting Started

Begin the lesson by explaining that most readers—even the most skillful ones—need to do a little rereading to be sure they understand what the author is saying. This is especially true when they're reading textbook chapters, some fiction and poetry, nonfiction, and even real-world writing, such as directions and schedules. Tell the class that the key to rereading successfully is doing so *with a purpose in mind*.

Teaching Approach

Ask students to turn to page 40 in the *Reader's Handbook*. Talk about reasons to reread and write students' responses on the board.

Reasons to Reread

■ To learn more details about a plot, character, or idea

■ To clear up misunderstandings about an event or detail

■ To retrace a sequence of events or steps in a process

■ To look again at the author's main idea or message

■ To enjoy again a part you really liked

How to Reread

Explain to students that sometimes rereading means returning to the text and reading word for word. More often, however, rereading means skimming for the information you need and then rereading only small parts word for word. Make the analogy between patching up your understanding as a reader and patching a hole in some clothing.

Choosing a Strategy and Tool

Ask students to recall the Plan step of the Before Reading stage. There they chose the strategy and reading tool that they thought would work best with the selection they were about to read. At the Reread step, students may want to choose a *different* strategy or tool. Help students understand that this will encourage them to look at the text with a "fresh eye" and perhaps notice words, phrases, and ideas that they missed the first time around.

Direct students to thumb through the Reader's Almanac. Explain that once they become accustomed to using the strategies and tools shown here, they'll have no problem swapping one for another at the Reread stage.

If you have time, discuss the Double-entry Journal and Main Idea Organizer. Explain that these are two all-purpose tools that will work for many selections.

Double-entry Journal

QUOTES	MY WORDS

Main Idea Organizer

SUBJECT

MAIN IDEA

DETAIL	DETAIL	DETAIL

Wrap-up

Ask students to reread page 40 and choose one of the tools above to fill in. Clear up any confusion about the purpose of the Reread step and how to use it with different types of texts.

Lesson 4 Remember

For use with *Reader's Handbook* pages 41–43

Focus

In this lesson, students will discuss the importance of the Remember step and learn techniques they can use to help them remember what they've read in nonfiction and fiction texts.

Getting Started

Do students find it easy to remember a funny story but hard to remember facts about history? Explain that the more involved they can be in a reading, the easier it will be for them to remember what they've learned. The strategies they'll read about and practice this year—such as visualizing and thinking aloud, using your own words, and note-taking—are effective because they help readers get involved. Demonstrate this by taking a new science concept and making it into a song or rap. Discuss with students how they think this will help them remember it.

Teaching Approach

Brainstorm with students a list of activities they could do to remember the material they read. Several are listed in the middle of page 41. Students might also suggest that they

■ make an organizer

■ describe the ending

■ draw a sketch or picture

■ talk with a friend about the reading

In Your Own Words

Next, ask students to work with a partner to read and take notes on page 41. Then discuss, and point out the final sentence on the page: "By writing or explaining something in your own words, you will make it easier to remember." Ask students to explain what this means and tell whether they've used an "in your own words" technique before.

Have a few students attempt to "tell in their own words" what happened in the last story that was read in class.

Review the Reading Process

Use the final part of this lesson to review all three stages of the reading process. Direct students to reread key parts of the handbook and then display Overhead Transparency 1 once more. Have a volunteer summarize the individual steps of the process. Finish by reading aloud "Summing Up" on pages 42–43 of the handbook.

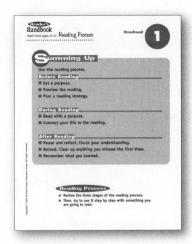

The Reading Process

The reading process has three main stages.

Before Reading

- Set a purpose.
- Preview the reading.
- Plan a reading strategy.

During Reading

- Read with a purpose. Look for information that fits your purpose.
- Connect your life to the reading.

After Reading

- Pause and reflect. Look back to see if you learned what you wanted to learn.
- Read some or all of it again. Clear up anything you missed the first time.
- Remember what you learned. Write something about it, or share it with a friend.

Wrap-up

Divide the class into three groups. Assign one group the Pause and Reflect step, the next group the Reread step, and the third group the Remember step. Have group members make a poster that tells about their step. Keep the posters on display during the year.

Lesson 5 Review and Assess

Check Point

Use the Quick Assess checklist to informally evaluate students' understanding of how to use the After Reading stage of the reading process. Based on their answers, divide them into two groups. One group can do the Independent Practice on the next page while the other group completes the guided practice in the *Applications Book and Word Work*.

Quick Assess

Can students

- ☑ name the three steps of the After Reading stage of the reading process?

- ☑ explain the importance of reflecting on a selection?

- ☑ tell why they might need to reread?

- ☑ give examples of ways to remember what they've read?

Guided Practice

For students who need reinforcement in the reading process, assign pages 15–16 in the *Applications Book and Word Work*.

For students who need more word work, assign page 207 from the *Applications Book and Word Work* on the **short a** sound.

Independent Practice

Students who have demonstrated a strong understanding of the After Reading stage of the reading process should practice applying what they've learned to a story or article you've read in class. Ask students to make After Reading notes in their Reading Notebooks. Then, come together as a class and ask:

■ What are the three steps of the After Reading stage of the reading process?

■ How does each step work?

■ What techniques do you know for remembering what you've read?

Class Review

Ask students to add to the Reading Process booklet they started in Week 3 (see page 61 of this *Teacher's Guide*). Remind the class that young readers rely on pictures to help them understand what the text on the page means. Have students draw pictures of a child following the After Reading steps of the reading process and then write simple text to accompany each picture.

Test Book

Use the short-answer and multiple-choice tests on pages 14–15 to assess students' understanding of the material presented in this week's lessons.

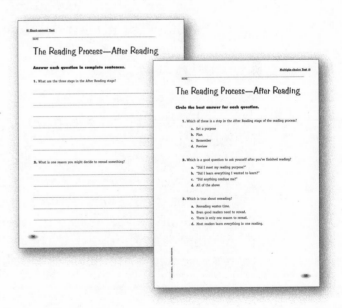

Basic Reading Skills—Part I

Goals

Here students explore specific skills to help them become more active readers. In this week's lessons, students will learn the importance of

- ☑ making predictions as they read
- ☑ understanding why predictions change
- ☑ making inferences as they read

Background

Help students connect this week's lessons to their prior knowledge by asking them to

- ▮ share times when they have made predictions
- ▮ tell what they think *making inferences* means
- ▮ talk about what reading strategies they use now as they read

Opening Activity

Describe the following to students: *Your birthday is tomorrow. None of your friends can play with you and your family doesn't mention it. Your dad takes you out for the day. When you come home, all the lights are off. As you open the front door, you hear giggling in the family room. Your mom calls out, "Hi, honey. Come in the family room. I have something to show you." What happens next?* Write students' ideas on the board. Explain that they just made predictions. They took what they heard plus their prior knowledge of surprise parties to guess what will happen next.

Next, retell the scenario. Ask students to "read between the lines" to figure out what is going on. For example, "Why does no one mention your birthday? Why does your dad take you out for the day?" Write students' ideas on the board. By taking what they heard plus what they know about surprise parties, students made inferences. Explain that both predictions and inferences are essential reading skills that students will learn more about in this unit. Stress to students that the skills used to make predictions and inferences do overlap.

74

Weekly Plan

Lessons	Summary
1. **Predicting**	Introduce thinking skills and help students as they learn how to make predictions.
2. **Predicting** (continued)	Enhance students' understanding of how to make predictions when reading.
3. **Making Inferences**	Work with students as they explore how to make inferences.
4. **Making Inferences** (continued)	Help students expand on their understanding of how and why to make inferences when reading.
5. **Review and Assess**	Informally assess students to decide if more guided practice is needed with predicting or making inferences. Then give an assessment.

Lesson Materials

	Components	Pages
Plan	*Teacher's Guide and Lesson Plans*	74–85
Teach	*Reader's Handbook*	46–49
	Overhead Transparencies	2, 3
Practice	*Applications Book and Word Work*	17–18, 208
Assess	*Test Book*	16–17

 **Lesson 1** Predicting

For use with *Reader's Handbook* page 46

Focus

Here students learn about thinking skills and how to make predictions.

Getting Started

 Write the following on the board: *I make predictions whenever I read.* Do students agree or disagree with this statement? Have students discuss this statement and share their responses. Take a vote to see how many students think they make predictions when they read and how many don't. Tell students that, even if they are not aware of it, readers are constantly making predictions about what will happen next in a story. Have students write down a story about something that happened to them in the past few days. It can be in the form of a list. Ask a few students to tell the story, but they need to stop their story before the ending. Have another student predict how it ends.

Teaching Approach

Explain to students that they will explore five basic reading skills:

- Predicting
- Making Inferences
- Drawing Conclusions
- Comparing and Contrasting
- Evaluating

Reassure students that they already use those skills every day. The goal is that they learn to use them as they're reading. Explain that, because these five skills are so important for active reading, the class will spend quite a bit of time on each of these skills, beginning with predicting. To reinforce students' prior knowledge of predicting, create a Web, such as the one on the next page.

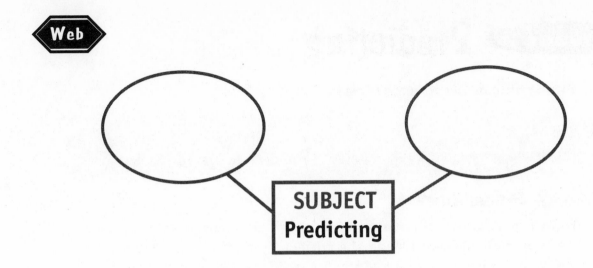

Web

SUBJECT
Predicting

Write *Predicting* in the center circle. Have the class brainstorm ideas about predicting, such as what they think it means, times when people make predictions, and any other thoughts they have related to the topic. Keep the Web on the board as you work through the lesson and add to it as students continue learning about the skill.

Talk about the definition of *predicting*. Make clear that predictions are not just wild guesses. Good predictions are always based on what students know about the subject. Reinforce this key point by looking over the sample predictions on page 46. Ask students what information would make someone predict that it will rain. Compare the definition of *predicting* with the definitions students brainstormed in the Web. Add to or modify the Web as necessary.

Wrap-up

Have one student give a brief summary of predicting. Then tell the class they are all going to make predictions. Pull out the sports section of the newspaper and choose five sporting events that will take place tonight. Show the most current league standings so they have some prior knowlege about the teams. Have students write their predictions of who will win each game in their Reading Notebooks. Tell students they will check the scores in the following days to see if their predictions came true.

Lesson 2 Predicting (continued)

For use with *Reader's Handbook* page 47

Focus

In this lesson, students expand on their understanding of predicting.

Getting Started

Begin the lesson by checking the scores of the chosen games. See how many students made the correct predictions. Look over the Web and have students add any new ideas they have about making predictions. Make sure students are clear on the following three points.

■ Making predictions is a basic reading skill.

■ People make predictions all the time.

■ Good predictions come from using what you know about a subject to make a guess about what will happen next.

Teaching Approach

Explain that because predicting is one of the five essential reading skills, it is time to narrow the discussion to how predicting can help students become more active readers.

Have students turn to page 47 of the *Reader's Handbook*. Work with them as they examine how one reader made a prediction about a book called *Becoming a Butterfly*. Help them see that the reader used what he or she knew— the book's title, its cover, and information from the teacher to make a prediction about what the book will be about. Then have students read the rest of page 47 on their own. Use Overhead Transparency 2 to demonstrate how to predict.

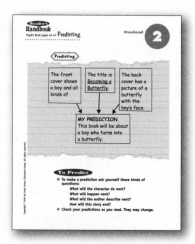

Predicting Chart

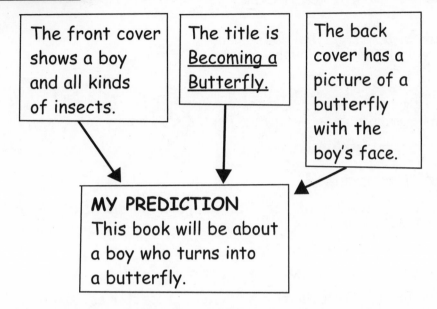

The front cover shows a boy and all kinds of insects.

The title is <u>Becoming a Butterfly.</u>

The back cover has a picture of a butterfly with the boy's face.

MY PREDICTION
This book will be about a boy who turns into a butterfly.

After students complete their reading, help them see that the act of predicting automatically pulls readers into the reading material. Readers want to read on to find out if their predictions are correct. Make clear as well that students' predictions will change as they keep reading and gather more clues about a character or a subject. Explain that returning to an original prediction to change it or correct it is an important part of the predicting process.

Using the first page or two of a story or picture book, model how active readers make predictions as you read aloud. After you have made one or two predictions, stop and illustrate how you made them by creating an organizer such as the one above.

Wrap-up

Use the sports section from a newspaper. Pick a few games or matches. Have students write down which team they think will win. Then tell them each team's win/loss record. Ask students if they want to change their prediction. Then tell them who won the last time these two teams played each other if this information is available.

Have students draw a Predicting Chart in their Reading Notebooks. Tell them to list what they know about the two teams in the top boxes. Remind them to use these facts as a basis for making their prediction in the bottom box. Invite students to share with the class their prediction on who will win.

Lesson 3 Making Inferences

For use with *Reader's Handbook* page 48

Focus

In this lesson students will begin exploring the basic reading skill of making inferences.

Getting Started

Start the lesson with this scenario: *Imagine you are at the grocery store. You see a woman buying a birthday cake, balloons, and plates decorated with toy fire trucks.*

Now ask students to answer the following questions:

■ Why do you think the woman bought these items?

■ Is the party most likely for a boy or girl? How old do you think the child is?

Invite volunteers to share their answers and explain how they came up with them. Once students understand that the party was probably for a little boy, describe the scene again. Point out that nowhere in your description did you say that the woman was planning a birthday party for a little boy. Students figured this out by making inferences based on what you did say. Clues such as *birthday cake* and *toy fire trucks,* combined with what students know about birthdays, led them to make accurate inferences.

Help students to see that they make inferences all the time. Ask them to think about their day and recall an inference they made. Help students increase their awareness of how often they make inferences. Ask them to write down three inferences they make in the next few days in their Reading Notebooks.

Teaching Approach

Ask students to jot down a definition for *inference* in their Reading Notebooks.

Making Inferences

Read aloud the top of page 48 in the *Reader's Handbook*. Discuss the definition of *inference* presented there. Be sure students understand that an inference involves combining what you see or read with what you already know.

A Plan for Making Inferences

Now talk about the importance of making inferences when reading. Explain that authors often do not tell readers everything they need to know about a character or an event. Write the following on the board: *Read between the lines*. Help students understand that means to take what an author tells them about something and use what they already know to *infer*, or read between the lines, to figure out what the author isn't telling readers. There is a good reason why authors don't tell their readers every detail: having to make inferences makes reading more fun, and it pulls readers into the selection and invites them to play a more active role in the reading.

Walk students through the Plan for Making Inferences. Point out that students can think of making inferences as an equation: What I Saw or Read + What I Know Already = What I Infer.

Wrap-up

Finish the lesson by reading the next to last paragraph on page 48. Model how to turn the sample inferences into equations by writing the following on the board:

What I see or read: I see my friend frown and slam the door
+
What I know already: I know that, when people are angry, they often look angry and slam doors.

=

What I infer: My friend is angry.

Have students write an equation in their Reading Notebooks for the storm example in the handbook.

Lesson 4 Making Inferences (continued)

For use with *Reader's Handbook* pages 48–49

Focus

In this lesson, students expand on their understanding of how and why to make inferences when reading.

Getting Started

Open the lesson with a review of what students learned in the previous lesson about making inferences. Display Overhead Transparency 3 and explain the information presented there. Then talk about the inferences students noted in their Reading Notebooks since the previous lesson (see Getting Started on page 80). Ask students:

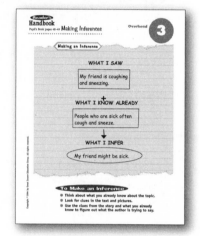

■ Were you surprised by how many inferences you made? Why or why not?

■ What type of inferences did you make the most (such as about people, events, or reading material)?

■ Do you now have a better understanding of the role of inferences?

Invite students to share any additional thoughts. Clarify any remaining questions about how to make inferences.

Teaching Approach

Review the making inferences equation students learned in the previous lesson. Then read aloud the bottom of page 48. Ask students to jot down the inference they would make if they saw a friend sneezing and coughing. Help students see that inferences they make while reading are the same as the inferences they make in life.

Making an Inference

WHAT I SAW

My friend is coughing and sneezing.

$+$

WHAT I KNOW ALREADY

People who are sick often cough and sneeze.

$\downarrow$

WHAT I INFER

My friend might be sick.

Next have students turn to page 49 and look over the inference equation. Compare how this reader made an inference to how students did. Point out the second part of the equation: *What I know already.* Discuss with students the importance of this part.

If students need more instruction on making inferences, model the skill. Demonstrate how to think aloud as you read a paragraph or two from a book in your classroom library. Stop each time you make an inference, and create an inference equation on the board to make your thinking visible.

Wrap-up

Once students seem comfortable with using the skill independently, ask them to read a page or two from something they are reading now. (Making inferences works for both nonfiction and fiction, but for new "users," fiction works best.) Have them follow your model. Then, as a class, talk about what students learned.

Lesson 5 Review and Assess

Check Point

Use the Quick Assess checklist to informally evaluate students' understanding of how to make predictions and inferences. Based on their answers, divide them into two groups. Ask one group to do the Independent Practice on the next page, while the other group completes the guided practice in the *Applications Book and Word Work.*

Quick Assess

Can students

- ☑ name two essential reading skills?
- ☑ explain how to make a prediction?
- ☑ state the two parts that make up an inference?

Guided Practice

For students who need reinforcement on how to make predictions and inferences, assign pages 17–18 in the *Applications Book and Word Work.*

For students who need more word work, assign page 208 from the *Applications Book and Word Work* on the **short o** sound.

Independent Practice

Ask students who have demonstrated a strong understanding of making predictions and inferences to summarize what they've learned. In their summaries, students should discuss the following:

- What is a prediction?
- Why do readers make predictions as they read?
- What is an inference?
- Why do readers make inferences as they read?

Class Review

Have students pair up. Give each pair a large piece of chart paper to create a Venn Diagram. Have partners brainstorm everything they learned about making predictions and making inferences on the back of the chart paper. Then have pairs list their ideas in the Venn Diagram. Remind them that if the fact is about predictions only, they should write it in the Prediction circle. If the fact is about making inferences only, they should write it in the Inference circle. If the fact is true about both making predictions and making inferences, they should write it where the two circles intersect.

Test Book

Use the short-answer and multiple-choice tests on pages 16–17 to assess students' understanding of the material presented in this week's lessons.

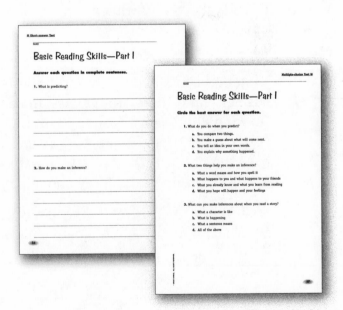

Basic Reading Skills—Part II

Goals

Here students explore three more essential skills to help them become active readers. Students will learn the importance of

- ☑ drawing conclusions as they read
- ☑ comparing and contrasting as they read
- ☑ evaluating as they read

Background

Help students connect this week's lessons to their prior knowledge by asking them to

- explain what *basic reading skill* means
- describe what thinking skills they use when they read
- talk about ways they want to improve their reading skills

Opening Activity

 To get students motivated and build background for this unit, divide the class into three groups. Assign each group one of the following: Drawing Conclusions (pages 50–51), Comparing and Contrasting (pages 52–53), and Evaluating (pages 54–55). Ask the groups to look over the pages in the *Reader's Handbook* that focus on their essential reading skill. They should try to answer these questions.

- What is the definition of our skill?
- What, if any, graphic organizers will we use with the skill?
- What does the art tell us about the skill?

After groups complete the activity, have them share what they learned. Give each of the three groups chart paper. Have groups compile a master list about their reading skill to present to the class.

Weekly Plan

Lessons	Summary
1. **Drawing Conclusions**	Work with students as they learn how to draw conclusions when reading.
2. **Comparing and Contrasting**	Explore with students how and why to compare and contrast when they read.
3. **Evaluating**	Help students begin exploring the basic reading skill of evaluating.
4. **Evaluating** (continued)	Enhance students' understanding of how and why to make evaluations as they read.
5. **Review and Assess**	Informally assess students to decide if more guided practice is needed with drawing conclusions, comparing and contrasting, and evaluating. Then give an assessment.

Lesson Materials

	Components	Pages
Plan	*Teacher's Guide and Lesson Plans*	86–97
Teach	*Reader's Handbook* *Overhead Transparencies*	50–55 4, 5, 6
Practice	*Applications Book and Word Work*	19–21, 209
Assess	*Test Book*	18–19

Lesson 1 Drawing Conclusions

For use with *Reader's Handbook* pages 50–51

Focus

Here students learn how to draw conclusions when reading.

Getting Started

Explain that in this lesson students will learn how to draw conclusions. Use Overhead Transparency 4 to support your teaching.

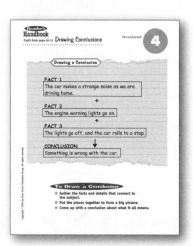

 Describe the following scenario to students: *Imagine you are driving in a car. Behind you comes an ambulance with its sirens blaring. Cars pull to the side as the ambulance, followed by two police cars, passes by. Next, you come to two cars on the side of the road. What do you think happened?*

Ask students to explain how they came up with their ideas. To understand what happened, students had to pull together information and draw conclusions.

Teaching Approach

Read aloud the top of page 50 of the *Reader's Handbook*. Point out that drawing conclusions often requires readers to put together a number of facts, much like putting together a jigsaw puzzle.

Read aloud the scenario presented at the bottom of page 50. Have students jot down their conclusions and share them as a class. Then point students to the illustration on page 51 and work with them to examine the steps one reader took to draw conclusions.

◀ **Drawing Conclusions** ▶

FACT 1

The car makes a strange noise when my mom starts it up.

\+

FACT 2

The engine warning lights go on.

\+

FACT 3

The lights go off, and the car rolls to a stop.

CONCLUSION ⬇

Something is wrong with the car.

Once students have a general understanding of how to draw conclusions, move on to talking about the importance of drawing conclusions when reading. Just like predicting and making inferences, drawing conclusions pulls readers deeper into their reading by requiring them to take an active role in the reading process.

Model drawing conclusions by reading aloud a brief selection from a book in your classroom library. First, draw a blank organizer similar to the one above on the board. Read aloud the selection once without stopping. Then reread it, this time thinking aloud as you focus on the facts you pull together to draw a conclusion. Write each fact in the organizer. Continue your Think Aloud as you pull the facts together to draw a conclusion. Write the conclusion in the organizer. Discuss your Think Aloud with the class.

Wrap-up

Ask students to use their Reading Notebooks to practice drawing conclusions with paragraphs in the handbook. Ask students to make a chart similar to the one on Overhead Transparency 4. Good excerpts to use are from *The Great Kapok Tree* (p. 346), *Spotlight on Cody* (p. 347), and *Stone Fox* (p. 324).

Lesson 2 Comparing and Contrasting

For use with *Reader's Handbook* pages 52–53

Focus

In this lesson, students learn how and why to compare and contrast when they read.

Getting Started

Begin the lesson with a quick review of the three basic reading skills students have explored so far: predicting, making inferences, and drawing conclusions. Then introduce the lesson by making a number of comparison statements, such as the following:

■ Our classroom is smaller than the gymnasium.

■ Today is colder than yesterday.

■ My sister and I both love to read.

Ask students what these statements have in common. Help them see that they are all statements of comparison and contrast. In each one you are describing how two things are either similar or different. Explain that statements such as these are examples of another basic reading skill: comparing and contrasting. Ask students to make a list of three comparisons between this year's classroom and last year's classroom. Invite students to share their comparisons.

Teaching Approach

Have students read page 52 of the *Reader's Handbook*. Ask them to provide examples of similarities and differences among themselves and their siblings or friends. Show Overhead Transparency 5 as an example of a way to organize their thoughts. Challenge students to think of ways they are both alike and different from one another. Help them see that comparisons can involve both similarities and differences at the same time.

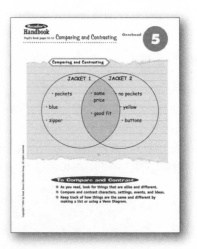

Venn Diagram

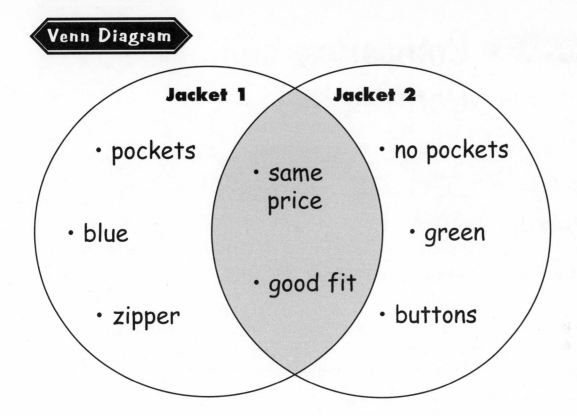

Jacket 1

Jacket 2

- pockets

- blue

- zipper

- same price

- good fit

- no pockets

- green

- buttons

Walk students through the Venn Diagram on page 53. Talk about why this is a useful tool for keeping track of comparisons.

Talk about how readers use comparing and contrasting to better understand what they read. Lead them to see that when readers make comparisons, they become more involved in what they are reading. As the class discovered about predicting, making inferences, and drawing conclusions, comparing and contrasting helps readers better understand, remember, and enjoy what they read.

Wrap-up

Have students draw a blank Venn Diagram in their Reading Notebooks. Then have them choose two characters from a story the class read recently. Tell students to use their Venn Diagrams to keep track of the similarities and differences between the two characters. Invite students to share their diagrams with a partner. Can students use their partners' diagrams to describe how the characters are alike and different? If not, have students add more information to their diagrams.

⬤ Lesson 3 ⬤ Evaluating

For use with *Reader's Handbook* page 54

Focus

In this lesson students will begin exploring the basic reading skill of evaluating.

Getting Started

Although students make judgments all the time, they probably rarely stop to consider the thinking process behind these evaluations.

 Bring in two brands of American cheese or another food product. Label one *Product A* and one *Product B*. Tell students that they are going to act as food taste-testers to determine which brand tastes better. Give students an evaluation guide such as the one below:

Taste Testing Form

1. **Which product looks better?** _____ **Why?** _____

2. **Which product tastes better?** _____ **Why?** _____

3. **Would you ask your parents to buy Product A?** _____
   Why or why not? _____

4. **Would you ask your parents to buy Product B?** _____
   Why or why not? _____

Comments:

Take a class poll to see which product most students preferred. Point out that students used two essential thinking skills to fill out their forms: comparing and contrasting and evaluating.

Remind students that whenever they choose one thing over another based on qualities like taste or looks, they are making comparisons. Next, ask students what they know about making evaluations. Write their ideas on the board. Explain that in this lesson they will learn why evaluating is one of the five essential reading skills.

Teaching Approach

Read aloud the top paragraph on page 54 of the *Reader's Handbook*. Discuss the definition of evaluating. Invite a volunteer to explain what it means to give an opinion. Be sure students understand that opinions are personal judgments, not facts, and that people often have different opinions about the same thing. Reinforce this concept by reviewing students' opinions of the two products. Point out that while everyone tasted the same two items, not everyone shared the same opinion. Use Overhead Transparency 6 to show how students can organize their thoughts on a Web. Ask students to make a Web for the product they preferred in the middle and their reasons on the outside.

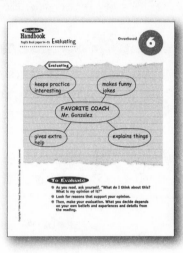

Once students have a general idea of what it means to evaluate, have them read the next paragraph on page 54 independently. Work as a class to list additional situations in which students make judgments. List their ideas on the board. Ask students to explain what they base their evaluations on. List the criteria next to the corresponding item. To help students realize how often they make judgments, ask them use their Reading Notebooks to keep track of three evaluations they make the rest of the day. They will return to this activity in the next lesson.

Return to the opening activity. Help students see that once they compared the two items, they used the comparisons to make judgments about, or evaluate, which product tasted and looked better. Make clear that many times students will find themselves using more than one reading skill as a time.

Wrap-up

Finish the lesson by asking students to work in small groups to create an evaluation form, similar to the taste testing form, for judging a current TV show or movie. Have groups first brainstorm a list of characteristics people would use to evaluate the show or film. Encourage groups to use their lists as a guide for developing their evaluation forms. After students complete the activity, have groups share and compare their forms. Talk about similarities and differences among their evaluation questions. If possible, have students exchange evaluation forms and answer the questions.

Lesson 4 Evaluating (continued)

For use with *Reader's Handbook* pages 54–55

Focus

In this lesson, students expand on their understanding of how and why to make evaluations as they read.

Getting Started

Have students take out their lists of evaluations from the previous lesson. Then talk about what they evaluated in the past day. Have students get in pairs to share what they evaluated. Lead a discussion by asking the following questions.

■ Were you surprised by the judgments you made over the course of the day? Why or why not?

■ What type of evaluations did you make the most (such as about people, events, or food)?

■ What were the most interesting things you learned about how you make judgments? Explain.

Teaching Approach

Remind students that using a graphic organizer can help them evaluate. Review the Web on page 55 of the *Reader's Handbook*. Explain that this is an example of how one student evaluated his or her coach.

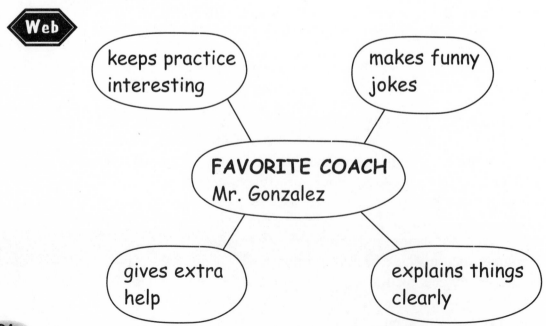

Purpose of the Web

Talk about the purpose of the Web. Ask students, "How can a Web like this help you evaluate someone or something?" Point out that sometimes when students make an evaluation, especially in school, they need to support their evaluation with reasons. A Web helps you make judgments and lets you list reasons to support them.

When to Evaluate

Next, read aloud or have student volunteers read aloud the rest of page 55. Discuss how and why readers make evaluations as they read. Point out that the most common type of evaluation readers make when they read is whether they enjoyed the reading or not. Explain that readers also make judgments about characters or plot events or whether they believe information presented in nonfiction texts. Invite students to list other times readers make evaluations about what they read.

Model how readers make evaluations by thinking aloud as you read a brief excerpt from a book in your classroom library. After reading, think aloud as you make a judgment about an aspect of the selection. Create a Web to illustrate your reasons for your evaluation. Clarify any questions students have about evaluating.

Wrap-up

Provide the class with a variety of short readings, including picture books, poems, and newspaper articles. Have students choose a piece to read and evaluate. After students read their selection, have them create a Web in their Reading Notebooks. Ask them to use their Webs to answer the following: *What do I think about this? Why?*

After students complete the activity, have them share their evaluations with others who read the same selection. Remind students that evaluations are based on personal opinions, so there is no one correct answer.

Lesson 5 Review and Assess

Check Point

Use the Quick Assess checklist to informally evaluate students' understanding of how to draw conclusions, compare and contrast, and evaluate. Based on their answers, divide them into two groups. Ask one group to do the Independent Practice on the next page while the other group completes the guided practice in the *Applications Book and Word Work*.

Quick Assess

Can students

- ☑ name three basic reading skills?
- ☑ describe how to draw a conclusion?
- ☑ explain how to compare and contrast?
- ☑ explain how to make evaluations?

Guided Practice

For students who need reinforcement on the basic reading skills, assign pages 19–21 in the *Applications Book and Word Work*.

For students who need more word work, assign page 209 from the *Applications Book and Word Work* on the **short i** sound.

Independent Practice

Ask students who have demonstrated a strong understanding of the basic reading skills to apply their knowledge to two kinds of ice cream. Have them design a poster based on these activities about their two flavors.

■ Draw a conclusion on how a friend reacts to the two ice cream flavors.

■ Compare and contrast the two flavors.

■ Evaluate the two flavors of ice cream.

Class Review

Divide the class into two teams. Explain that you will give Team 1 a clue about one of the five basic reading skills. If they guess it correctly, they will earn 2 points. If they do not guess correctly, the other team can "steal" and earn 1 point for the correct answer. Explain that teams will have 30 seconds to discuss their answer and then one representative will state their final response. Make clear that some clues will have more than one answer; teams must give all possibilities in order to earn their points. Clues include:

■ I am a basic reading skill. (Teams need to list all five.)

■ Readers use me to answer the question, "What do I think about this?" (evaluate)

■ "Read between the lines." (making inferences)

■ Using me is like putting together a jigsaw puzzle. (drawing conclusions)

■ Venn Diagrams work well with me. (comparing and contrasting)

■ Readers use me to ask the question, "What happens next?" (predicting)

Test Book

Use the short-answer and multiple-choice tests on pages 18–19 to assess students' understanding of the material presented in this week's lessons.

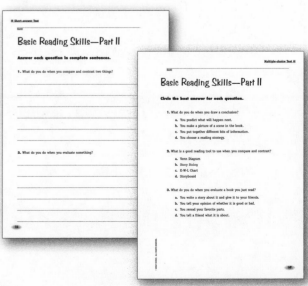

Being an Active Reader

Goals

Here students explore ways to become more active readers. Students will learn to

- ☑ read actively
- ☑ make six kinds of notes: mark, react, ask questions, draw pictures, make things clear, and predict
- ☑ look for places to write notes while reading

Background

Help students connect these lessons to their prior knowledge by asking them to

- ▨ describe what they do when they read
- ▨ tell what they know about taking notes

Opening Activity

Ask students to draw a picture that illustrates what they think of when they hear the word *active*. Invite volunteers to share their drawings with the class. Talk about what it means to be active. Create a class list of favorite activities. Then, talk about what all these have in common. Help students see that being active requires them to *do* something.

Explain that in this unit students will learn how to become active readers. Point out that good readers don't just move their eyes across the page, but instead they are constantly *doing* something, such as asking questions and making predictions. Based on what they learned from the class discussion, what do students think it means to be an active reader? Have students work with a partner to come up with a definition to share with the class.

Weekly Plan

Lessons	Summary
1. **Mark and React**	Teach students how to take notes that focus on marking up and reacting to the text.
2. **Ask Questions and Create Pictures**	Explore with students two more types of notes—asking questions and drawing pictures.
3. **Make Things Clear and Predict**	Help students use notes to clarify and predict.
4. **Where to Write Notes**	Work with students as they explore three places to write notes when they read.
5. **Review and Assess**	Informally assess students to decide if more guided practice is needed on being an active reader. Then take an assessment.

Lesson Materials

	Components	Pages
Plan	*Teacher's Guide and Lesson Plans*	98–109
Teach	*Reader's Handbook*	56–63
	Overhead Transparencies	7
Practice	*Applications Book and Word Work*	22–23, 210
Assess	*Test Book*	20–21

Lesson 1 Mark and React

For use with *Reader's Handbook* pages 56–57

Focus

Here students learn how to takes notes that focus on marking up and reacting to the text.

Getting Started

Read aloud the top of page 56 in the *Reader's Handbook*. Talk about how reading actively is like joining in a game. Ask students, "How are these two activities alike?" Then explain that one way active readers stay involved in their reading is by taking notes. Explain that there are six kinds of notes active readers make as they read:

- ■ Mark or Highlight
- ■ React
- ■ Ask Questions
- ■ Create Pictures
- ■ Make Things Clear
- ■ Predict

Encourage a student to play a game of tic-tac-toe on the board with you. Allow two more students to play while you point out that it is a game of marking a move and reacting to it. Explain that marking and reacting are also kinds of notes they can take while reading. Show students Overhead Transparency 7 and highlight the mark and react notes.

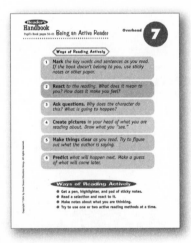

Teaching Approach

Before going into more detail on kinds of notes to take, discuss with students the importance of taking notes. Have students help you make a list of reasons to take notes. Then, remind them that if the book is not their own, they will have to make their notes on another piece of paper or on sticky notes.

Mark

Tell students that the first type of notes they will explore involves marking up or highlighting parts of their reading. Explain that one of the trickiest parts about note-taking is deciding what part of a selection to mark. Point out that if students mark up the whole piece, their notes won't be very helpful. Instead, students need to focus their notes to match their purpose. For example, if they want to learn more about a character, they might circle or underline words and sentences that talk about the character.

Next, explore with students how one reader marked up important parts from a selection. Read aloud the selection on the bottom of page 56. Then talk about the sticky note. Point out that different readers will take different notes about the same reading passage. Model this by giving students the same paragraph from a book you are reading in class. Ask them to mark what is important. Compare their notes when they finish.

React

Ask students what it means to react. Can students give examples of what happens when people react? Help students understand that "to react" means to respond to something. Active readers constantly react to their reading.

Next, read aloud the excerpt on page 57. Model how readers react to a selection by thinking aloud and reacting as they read. Then talk about the sticky notes one reader made in reaction to the selection. Again, remind students that every reader will react differently to what he or she reads. Point out that taking notes on their reactions helps readers make connections to a selection, and making connections is one of the steps in the After Reading stage of the reading process.

Wrap-up

Have students read an excerpt from elsewhere in the handbook that you pick out. Pass out three or four sticky notes to everyone in the class. Ask students to use them to make notes about their selections. Remind them to focus their notes on marking key words or passages and for reacting to what they read. After completing the activity, have students share and compare their notes with partners.

Lesson 2 Ask Questions and Create Pictures

For use with *Reader's Handbook* pages 58–59

Focus

In this lesson, students will explore two more types of notes active readers make while reading—asking questions and drawing pictures.

Getting Started

Choose a historical figure your class is familiar with. Allow them to ask yes or no questions until they figure out the name of the person. Then have them draw a picture of this person. Encourage them to add details to help people identify him or her. Explain to students that they just used two types of note-taking skills to clarify information. Tell them they will learn how to do this when reading.

Teaching Approach

Review with the class why readers make notes as they read. Remind them that marking up the text, reacting, asking questions, and drawing pictures all help readers play an active role in their reading.

Ask Questions

Read aloud the top of page 58 in the *Reader's Handbook*. Ask students, "What other questions might readers ask as they read?" List students' questions on a large piece of chart paper. These might include:

■ Why is the character acting this way?

■ What does the author mean by this?

■ What does this word mean?

■ What will happen next?

Keep the chart paper up throughout the rest of the lesson. Encourage students to add to the list as more questions arise.

Next, read aloud the excerpt on page 58. Model how to ask questions as you read. Then discuss the two sample questions. See if your students can come up with their own questions about the selection. Make clear that asking questions encourages readers to keep reading to find answers.

Create Pictures

Once students understand the purpose of asking questions, move on to the next type of notes—creating pictures. Ask students if they ever draw pictures of what they read. How do students think drawing pictures would help them read more actively?

Read aloud the top of page 59. Point out that drawing pictures can help students better understand and remember what they read.

Have students close their eyes while you read the excerpt on page 59. Ask them to create pictures in their minds as you read. After you finish the Read Aloud, have students draw pictures of what they "saw." Then have the students compare their drawings to each other's and to the sample in the handbook. Talk about the similarities and differences among the pictures. Make clear that readers will often draw different pictures of the same selection because different readers "see" what they read in different ways. Also, stress that students don't have to be strong artists, as long as they understand their drawings.

Wrap-up

Ask students to read another excerpt from *the Reader's Handbook*. Give each student three or four sticky notes. Have them ask questions about their reading on the sticky notes. Encourage them to use the list of questions the class generated as a guide. Then ask them to draw a picture of the selection. After students complete the activity, discuss how different students take different notes about the same reading. Did students find it easy or difficult to ask questions and create pictures as they read?

Lesson 3 Make Things Clear and Predict

For use with *Reader's Handbook* pages 60–61

Focus

This lesson focuses on using notes to clarify and predict while reading.

Getting Started

Put students into groups of three. Give two students a paragraph from a novel you may be reading in class. Have student A read the paragraph out loud very quickly, making it difficult to understand. Student B will read along silently. Then have student B explain, or make clear, what was read to student C. Have all the students predict what will happen next. Explain that this lesson will be about the last two types of notes that active readers make while reading: notes that make things clear and notes for predicting.

Teaching Approach

Ask students what they do when they come across something they don't understand in a piece of writing. Do they skip it? Do they reread? Bring students back to the opening activity and point out that in order to understand they had to pause and revisit the reading. Explain that one way active readers help themselves figure out what is confusing to them is to take notes.

Make Things Clear

Read aloud the top of page 60 in the *Reader's Handbook*. Talk about why it is a good idea to stop every page or two to write down what is happening so far. By doing this, students will not only better understand what they read, but they will remember more as well. Then have students read the excerpt from *Tornado* independently. Point out how one reader made things clearer.

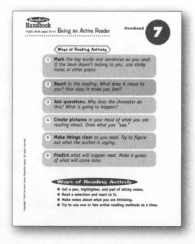

Taking notes to clarify can be more difficult for some students to understand than the other notes they have learned about so far. Perform a Think Aloud in which you focus on making things clear as you read. Use Overhead Transparency 7 for additional support.

Predict

Review what students learned about making predictions earlier in the handbook. Remind them that predicting is a basic thinking and reading skill. Explain that active readers use predicting as another way of making notes while reading. Discuss why making predictions helps readers play an active role in their reading. Remind students that predicting what will happen next makes readers want to keep on reading to find out what really does happen. Prove this by reading the opening paragraph of a mystery or a "cliff-hanger" and allowing students to predict what happens next. Students will want you to keep reading!

Read aloud the top of page 61. Then have students follow along as you read aloud the excerpt from *Tornado*. Talk about the two sample predictions. Do students agree with them? What do students think will happen next? Invite volunteers to share their predictions. Remind students that the purpose of making predictions is not to always be correct, but to get more actively involved in the story. Explain how it is OK to change predictions as you read.

Wrap-up

Finish the lesson by asking students to summarize out loud or in writing what they've learned about the six types of notes. You might have them write their ideas in journal form or divide them into small groups and ask them to discuss their ideas with each other.

Take time now to review with students all of the kinds of active reading notes you have introduced.

■ Mark or Highlight
■ React
■ Ask Questions
■ Create Pictures
■ Make Things Clear
■ Predict

Be sure students understand that they don't have to use them all and that it is okay to rely on one or two kinds of notes most of the time.

Lesson 4 Where to Write Notes

For use with *Reader's Handbook* pages 62–63

Focus

In this lesson, students will learn three places to write notes as they read.

Getting Started

Review with students what they learned about writing notes as they read. Remind them that sometimes they will not be able to write their notes in the book itself. What other places could they write their notes? List their ideas on the board. Talk about the pros and cons of each idea. Explain that in this lesson they will explore three places to jot down their reactions, questions, predictions, and drawings as they read.

Teaching Approach

Review with students the six types of notes active readers use:

- Mark or Highlight
- React
- Ask Questions
- Create Pictures
- Make Things Clear
- Predict

Use Sticky Notes

Explain that sticky notes can be helpful when readers cannot write in the book itself. Point out that, even when readers can write in a book, sticky notes can be a more effective way of taking notes because they stick out from the side of the selection and make it easier for readers to find their notes. Remind students to place their sticky notes close to the passage to which they refer.

Read aloud the first excerpt from *Tornado* on page 62. Ask a volunteer to tell what type of note the reader created to go with this passage. Give a sticky note to each student and have each make a different note for this passage.

After writing their notes, invite students to share what type of note they chose to use. Talk about why they did so.

Write on the Page

Explain to students that for brief pieces of writing, taking notes right on the page can be very helpful. Make clear, however, that students must never mark books that do not belong to them. For their own books, students can mark important, interesting, or confusing passages by circling, highlighting, or underlining them. Point out that students can also take notes in the margins. Show students an example of a book you have marked up.

Have another volunteer read aloud the second excerpt from *Tornado* on page 62. Point out the two ways one reader marked up the piece.

Write in a Notebook

Ask students to pull out their Reading Notebooks. Review with students what they learned about keeping a Reading Notebook. Point out that a Reading Notebook is one good place to take notes. Explain that readers write notes in a notebook for a variety of reasons.

- If readers do not have sticky notes and the book is not their own, they can make notes in their notebooks.
- Making notes in a notebook keeps all the notes in one spot.
- Students can review and add to their notes in their notebooks.

Read aloud the top of page 63. Talk about the importance of writing down the title and page number when making notes. Point out that if students just write a note but don't include what it refers to, the note won't be helpful when students return to it for review. Then have students read the excerpt on page 63 independently and study the model notes shown there.

Wrap-up

Ask students to take out their Reading Notebooks. Have them choose an excerpt elsewhere in the handbook. Tell students to write notes in the Notes section of their Reading Notebooks. Remind them to include page numbers next to each note. Have students use all six types of notes they learned about in this unit.

Lesson 5 Review and Assess

Check Point

Use the Quick Assess checklist to informally evaluate students' understanding of the ways to be an active reader. Based on their answers, divide students into two groups. Ask one group to do the Independent Practice on the next page, while the other group completes the guided practice in the *Applications Book and Word Work*.

Quick Assess

Can students

- ☑ explain what active reading is?

- ☑ describe three or four kinds of notes to make while reading?

- ☑ tell three places to write notes while reading?

Guided Practice

For students who need reinforcement in how to be an active reader, assign pages 22–23 in the *Applications Book and Word Work*.

For students who need more word work, assign page 210 from the *Applications Book and Word Work* on the **short u** sound.

Independent Practice

Ask students who have demonstrated a strong understanding of "Being an Active Reader" to make a summary poster of what they've learned. Give students a copy of a reading passage they have never seen and ask them to glue it in the middle of the page. Their poster can be similar to Overhead Transparency 7. Their posters should show the following:

■ The six types of notes active readers make while reading

■ Three places they can write notes while reading

Class Review

Have students work in pairs to create an acrostic for *Active Reading*. Explain that an acrostic uses the letters of a word to begin each line. Next to each letter, another word or phrase is written that begins with the same letter. For example:

> *D* evoted
> *O* nly wants to be loved
> *G* ood friend

Give each pair a piece of chart paper. Explain that to create an acrostic, pairs should first write the phrase *Active Reading* down the left side of the page, one letter per line. Then pairs need to find a word or phrase about active reading that begins with each letter in *Active Reading*. Write this word or phrase next to the corresponding letter.

Test Book

Use the short-answer and multiple-choice tests on page 20–21 to assess students' understanding of the material presented in this week's lessons.

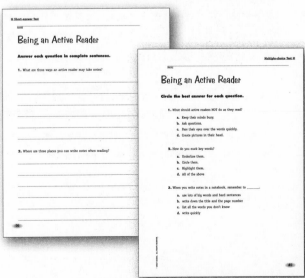

Ways to Be a Good Reader

Goals

Here students explore specific suggestions they can use to improve their reading habits. In these lessons, students will learn the importance of

- ☑ choose a quiet reading place
- ☑ make time for reading every day
- ☑ select a good book by previewing it
- ☑ make a plan to read daily

Background

Help students connect this week's lessons to their prior knowledge by asking them to

- ▪ discuss where and when they read
- ▪ describe their favorite reading spot
- ▪ tell how they choose a book to read

Opening Activity

Ask students to visualize their favorite spot to read. Then have them draw or use magazine and newspaper cut-outs to create a collage that represents their reading place. Encourage students to include both pictures and words in the collage and to use their art as a way of exploring their thoughts and feelings about reading.

Have students share their "reading place" with the class. Students will benefit by seeing where their classmates read. You might want to have students create a "reading corner" in class that is decorated with their drawings and collages.

Weekly Plan

Lessons	Summary
1. **Find a Reading Place**	Work with students to understand the characteristics of a good reading place.
2. **Find Time for Reading**	Consider with students the best way to find time for reading and the importance of creating a daily reading plan.
3. **Choose a Good Book**	Explore with the class the process of choosing a good book.
4. **Preview a Book**	Support students as they practice previewing a book.
5. **Review and Assess**	Informally assess students to decide if more practice is needed. Then give an assessment.

Lesson Materials

	Components	Pages
Plan	*Teacher's Guide and Lesson Plans*	110–121
Teach	*Reader's Handbook*	64–67
	Overhead Transparencies	7
Practice	*Applications Book and Word Work*	24–27, 211
Assess	*Test Book*	22–23

Lesson 1 Find a Reading Place

For use with *Reader's Handbook* page 64

Focus

Here students learn the characteristics of a good reading place.

Getting Started

Divide the class into small groups. Encourage students to explain how their reading place drawing or collage represents their reading spot and how it helps them concentrate on what they're reading or studying. Then have each group create a list of characteristics of a good reading place.

Teaching Approach

Use the list of good reading place characteristics and discuss with students the importance of each item. Ask, "How can the characteristics we've listed here help you be a better reader?"

Next, direct students' attention to page 64. Read aloud the introductory paragraph at the top of the page. Then explain that, although students can read just about anywhere, it is still a good idea to designate one place in school or at home as their special reading spot. This is a good opportunity to describe your reading place to the class.

Next, have students read silently the list at the bottom of the page.

◀ **What a Good Reading Place Has** ▶

✔ good light
✔ peace and quiet
✔ comfortable chair
✔ pen, pencil, or highlighter
✔ sticky notes or a notebook

Discuss the importance of each item on the list. Use these questions to assess students' comprehension of the material.

■ Why is it important to find your own special reading place?

■ What items should you place in your reading spot?

■ Why are good light and peace and quiet important when you're reading?

■ What should students do if they can't find a particular reading spot at home?

If you haven't done so already, have students help you set up a reading corner in your classroom. Place a few chairs, or a few large pillows, in the corner. If possible, use a bookcase or flip-chart to screen the reading area from the rest of the classroom.

Wrap-up

Ask students to read silently the rest of page 64. Then have them take out their Reading Notebooks and make a list of the items they'd like to place in their own reading spot. Ask students to share their work with a partner and to feel free to make changes to their own lists after their discussion.

Lesson 2 Find Time for Reading

For use with *Reader's Handbook* page 65

Focus

In this lesson, students will consider the best way to find time for reading and the importance of creating a daily reading plan.

Getting Started

Begin the lesson by asking students to write their schedule on a typical school day. Distribute blank schedules and show students how to fill in the individual columns. The schedules you give students might look something like this.

◤ **Day of the Week** ◢ _____

Time Before School	Activities
7:00–7:30 A.M.	
7:30–8:00 A.M.	
8:00–8:30 A.M.	
Time After School	**Activities**
3:00–3:30 P.M.	
3:30–4:00 P.M.	
4:00–4:30 P.M.	
4:30–5:00 P.M.	
5:00–5:30 P.M.	
5:30–6:00 P.M.	
6:00–6:30 P.M.	
6:30–7:00 P.M.	
7:00–7:30 P.M.	
7:30–8:00 P.M.	

Model for students how to fill in the activities column and give them time to complete the task.

Teaching Approach

Discuss students' daily schedules. Ask them to calculate which activities they spend the most time on and to make a note of them in the margins of the schedule. Then direct students' attention to page 65.

Read aloud the first paragraph on the page. Then pause to discuss. Ask students, "Why is it important to spend a little time reading each day? How is the reading you do for fun different from the reading you do for school?"

Continue reading the second and third paragraphs. Point out that good readers make an effort to do at least 20 to 40 minutes of fun reading every day. Have students look at their schedules to see how this compares with the amount of time *they* spend reading.

Next, work with students to set up a personal daily reading plan. Distribute another blank schedule to all students and ask them to create schedules that allow for 30 minutes of reading either before or after school. If students are having trouble fitting reading time into their schedules, consider reserving one 30-minute period per week for free reading.

Time After School	Activities
3:00–3:30 P.M.	*Walk home.*
3:30–4:00 P.M.	*Eat snack while reading.*
4:00–4:30 P.M.	*Play outside.*

Wrap-up

Ask students to summarize what they've learned thus far about how to be a good reader. Discuss key points from "Find a Reading Place" and "Find Time for Reading."

Lesson 3 Choose a Good Book

For use with *Reader's Handbook* page 66

Focus

Explore with students the process of choosing a good book. Present three general characteristics students should consider when making their book selections.

Getting Started

In an earlier lesson, students wrote the steps they follow when making a peanut butter and jelly sandwich. Repeat the activity here, but this time have students write the process they go through when selecting a book. Ask students to imagine themselves at a bookshelf in the library. Then have them list what they do first, second, third, and so on. Students might include some or all of the following steps on their lists:

■ I skim the titles.

■ I look for words that interest me.

■ When I come to a good title, I look at how thick the book is.

■ I look at the art.

■ I read the author's name.

■ I read the back cover.

■ I read the first sentences.

Teaching Approach

This lesson focuses on helping students choose a good book for them—an art many of them haven't yet mastered.

How to Choose a Book

Focus on what the majority of readers do first when selecting a book. See how many read the title first or how many judge the thickness of the spine before anything else. Then explain to students that the purpose of this lesson is to teach them what they should think about when choosing a book to read.

What's in a Book?

Ask students to turn to page 66. Read aloud the introductory paragraph and the paragraph under the head "What's in a Book." Walk students through the part that explains how to choose a good book. Pause along the way to see if they want to add to the instructions.

Choosing a Book

What It Looks Like
- size of the print
- number of pages
- pictures or drawings

What It's About
- topic or subject
- kind of book (novel, biography, poetry)
- your interest in the topic

How It's Written
- long or hard words
- lots of long sentences

Howdy partner!

Work with students to apply what they've learned about selecting books. Take small groups of students to the classroom library and go through the steps of choosing a book. Help students understand that the process takes just a minute or two. Then have students return to their desks with their selections and begin previewing.

Wrap-up

Finish the lesson by asking students to summarize out loud or in writing what they've learned about choosing a book. Pull out five or six choices of books you may read out loud to the class. Have the class help you go through the process of choosing a good book.

Lesson 4   Preview a Book

For use with *Reader's Handbook* page 67

Focus

In this lesson, students will learn a four-step plan they can follow when previewing a book.

Getting Started

Write the following question on the board: *Where does an armadillo live?* Then pull out any book that you have covered and fixed so you can see only one paragraph, which has nothing to do with armadillos. Tell a student to read the paragraph and answer the question. When the students realize they cannot answer the question, have them figure out what they could have done first to prevent them from using the wrong book.

Teaching Approach

Ask the class, "Why do you think it's important to preview a book before you begin reading?" Help students understand that previewing before reading is like watching a preview of a movie before going to see it at a movie theater. A preview whets your appetite or interest and helps you know what to expect.

Why to Preview a Book

The process of previewing involves choosing the book you think might be interesting, forming an opinion of it, and then starting to read it. Explain that if you don't spend time previewing, you may find out a book is too hard, not interesting, not what you want, or too easy.

Point out that previewing also helps a reader call up everything he or she knows about a subject. By doing so, the reader is ready and can more easily make connections to the reading. The result is that the reader will get more out of a reading because he or she is prepared and ready to read.

Where to Look

Next, ask students to brainstorm a list of the elements they might look at when previewing a book.

Have students turn to page 67 and read the paragraph and four tips at the top of the page. Discuss the importance of knowing what types of books interest students most and then searching for those subjects when choosing a book. Also stress how helpful it can be to talk to others. Children this age are highly influenced by their peers, so ask a couple of your students to report on their favorite books.

Now, have students examine the steps in How to Preview a Book.

How to Preview a Book

1. **Look at the front and back cover.**
  - **What is the book about?**
  - **How interesting does it look?**

2. **Look at the first page or two.**
  - **How does the book start?**
  - **What's the writing like?**
  - **Are the words easy or hard to read?**

3. **Look at the table of contents.**
  - **What do the chapter titles tell you?**
  - **How is it organized?**

4. **Flip through the pages.**
  - **How long is the book?**
  - **What do the pages look like?**

Also model how to use the Five Finger Test with a book from your classroom library. Have students hold up a finger for each word they don't know on one page. If five fingers are up, it is too hard, and they should choose another book. Show students how to do this a few times.

Wrap-up

Display Overhead Transparency 7. Have students decide which of the ways to read actively will be most effective for them. If there are parts that students don't understand, you may need to review those specific sections in the handbook.

Lesson 5 Review and Assess

Check Point

Use the Quick Assess checklist to informally evaluate students' understanding of the ways to be a good reader. Based on their answers, divide them into two groups. Ask one group to do the Independent Practice on the next page, while the other group completes the guided practice in the *Applications Book and Word Work*.

Quick Assess

Can students

☑ identify the characteristics of a good reading place?

☑ list four things to look for when choosing a book?

☑ explain two things to do when previewing a book?

☑ tell how to become a better reader?

Guided Practice

For students who need reinforcement in how to be a good reader, assign pages 24–27 in the *Applications Book and Word Work*.

For students who need more word work, assign page 211 from the *Applications Book and Word Work* on the **short e** sound.

Independent Practice

Ask students who have demonstrated a strong understanding of "Ways to Be a Good Reader" to summarize what they've learned by making a short picture book. In their books, students should discuss the following:

■ the characteristics of a good reading place

■ the importance of creating a daily reading plan and sticking with it

■ how to choose a good book

■ the best way to preview a book

Class Review

Divide the class into small groups. Give each group a piece of posterboard and ask them to create a "Ten Ways to Be a Good Reader" poster for their school library. Groups should begin by drafting their lists and discussing the merit of each point. Then the group secretary can write the list on the posterboard as the other students in the group create eye-catching illustrations to add to the final product. When they've finished, ask groups to present their work to the rest of the class.

Test Book

Use the short-answer and multiple-choice tests on pages 22–23 to assess students' understanding of the material presented in this week's lessons.

How to Read Aloud

Goals

Here students explore the value of reading aloud. Students will learn how to

- ☑ prepare for reading aloud
- ☑ read aloud with friends and classmates
- ☑ read aloud without mistakes in a smooth and interesting way

Background

Help students connect this week's lessons to their prior knowledge by asking them to

- ■ describe times when they've read aloud
- ■ discuss the challenges of reading aloud

Opening Activity

Find an audio book you think students might enjoy. Have students listen to the first chapter of the book. Ask, "What did you notice about the speaker's voice? What did the speaker do to get your attention? What is your opinion of this Read Aloud? What might the speaker have done to improve the work?" Audiobooks with great kid-appeal include:

- ■ *Dominic* by William Steig (performed by Peter Thomas, 165 minutes, full-length cassette)

- ■ *Revolting Rhymes and Dirty Beasts* by Roald Dahl (performed by Alan Cumming, 60 minutes, full-length cassette)

- ■ *Three Little Pigs and Other Fairy Tales* by various authors (performed by Boris Karloff, 53 minutes, full-length cassette)

Weekly Plan

Lessons	Summary
1. **Why Read Aloud?**	Work with students to understand the reasons for reading aloud.
2. **Tips for Reading Aloud**	Explain tips for reading aloud.
3. **How to Prepare for Reading Aloud**	Guide students through the process of preparing to read aloud.
4. **Practice Reading Aloud**	Support students as they practice reading aloud.
5. **Review and Assess**	Informally assess students to decide if more guided practice is needed for reading aloud. Then give an assessment.

Lesson Materials

	Components	Pages
Plan	*Teacher's Guide and Lesson Plans*	122–133
Teach	*Reader's Handbook*	68–71
	Overhead Transparencies	7
Practice	*Applications Book and Word Work*	28–29, 212
Assess	*Test Book*	24–25

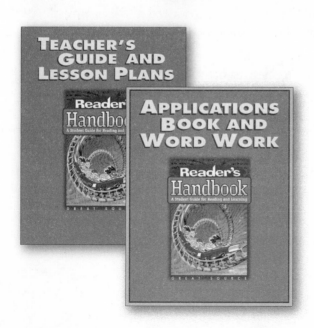

Lesson 1 Why Read Aloud?

For use with *Reader's Handbook* page 68

Focus

In this lesson, discuss various reasons for reading aloud and how it can improve reading fluency. Present three fun ways to read aloud.

Getting Started

Write five to eight social studies or science facts on slips of paper. Have a volunteer choose a slip and act out the fact using no words. The other students must guess what is being acted out. Discuss how this information could have been relayed easier. Students will probably say that reading the slip out loud would have relayed the information more easily.

Teaching Approach

Reading aloud can actually help some students process the information in a text—particularly those who are auditory rather than visual learners.

After your introduction, ask students to turn to page 68. Have a volunteer read aloud the first two paragraphs on the page. Emphasize to students that learning how to be a careful listener is an important part of learning to read aloud. Have a student summarize what he or she just heard.

Next, direct students' attention to the chart on the bottom of the page. Discuss the items one at a time. Pause after each one to be sure students understand what each one is telling them to do. Use the comprehension questions on the next page to assess their understanding.

Read with a Buddy

Have students get together with a partner and take turns reading aloud a selection from the handbook or *Applications Book and Word Work*. Have students talk about things they liked when their partners read aloud. Then ask these questions:

■ How does "read with a buddy" work?

■ In what ways could reading with someone else improve your understanding of the material?

■ What do you think is easiest about reading with a buddy? What would you say is most difficult?

Perform a Reading

Have a volunteer read out loud a page from the class novel. Then discuss how it went with these questions:

■ What is difficult about reading in front of a class?

■ Why should you read aloud the material several times before reading it to the class?

Record What You Read

Ask a student to read a new paragraph from his or her science book into a tape recorder. Then ask these questions:

■ What is the purpose of recording what you read aloud?

■ What should you do once you've made a recording of your Read Aloud?

■ In what ways can reading aloud help you be a better reader?

Wrap-up

Give students an opportunity to make a three-page flip book of the ways to read aloud.

Lesson 2 Tips for Reading Aloud

For use with *Reader's Handbook* page 69

Focus

In this lesson, students will learn several tips they can use to improve their performance during a Read Aloud.

Getting Started

Begin by asking a volunteer to summarize what the class has learned thus far about reading aloud. Then discuss students' responses to the audiotape they listened to in the opening lesson. Ask various students to retell the story they heard and then comment on the quality of the reading.

Teaching Approach

Spend the first part of your lesson discussing listening strategies students can use during a Read Aloud.

Take Notes During a Read Aloud

Explain to the class that taking notes during a Read Aloud can help them process what they've heard and retain key details. Then teach one or two graphic organizers students might use for their Read Aloud notes. Two organizers that work well as note-taking tools during a Read Aloud are a Story String and Key Word Notes. Model for students how to use a Story String during a fiction Read Aloud of a common story, such as "The Three Little Pigs."

Story String   "THE THREE LITTLE PIGS"

1. Three pigs leave home to build their own homes.

2. A wolf comes and blows down the house of straw, but the pig escapes.

3. The wolf goes to the house of sticks, but the pig gets away.

4. The wolf tries to blow down the house of bricks, but can't.

5. The wolf goes down the chimney, but the three pigs catch him.

6. The three pigs live happily ever after.

Key Word Notes

Key Words or Topics	Notes
Students can write key words here. These include repeated words and words the reader emphasizes through intonation.	Have students write quick notes about the key words here.

Key Word Notes work well when listening to a Read Aloud. Have students divide a notebook page into two columns, with the right-hand column larger than the left. Show them how to do this by reading aloud a page from their social studies books.

Three Tips for Reading Aloud

After you finish your discussion on listening, ask students to turn to page 69 and read the introductory paragraph. Explain that you'd like to spend the rest of the lesson working on the three tips students can follow when reading aloud.

1. Be clear and accurate.

Have a volunteer read the bulleted points in this column. Point out that practice is essential when reading aloud. Even the best readers skip or stumble over words on a first reading. Students will notice, however, that the passage will be easier to read on the second or third time through.

2. Read smoothly.

Read the bulleted points in this section. Explain how to use commas and periods as pause-points when reading aloud.

3. Be interesting.

Finish by discussing how important it is to read expressively, using gestures and facial expressions as needed. Model the difference between reading with expression and reading in a monotone.

Wrap-up

Ask students to think carefully about what they learned from page 69. Then ask them to do a one-minute quickwrite on the topic of "How to Read Aloud."

Lesson 3 How to Prepare for Reading Aloud

For use with *Reader's Handbook* page 70

Focus

Here students learn how to prepare for reading aloud.

Getting Started

Review the reasons students read aloud and how it can help build confidence and fluency and—in some cases—improve their understanding of the material. Then display Overhead Transparency 7 and discuss with students how active readers are also active listeners. Show students which of the active reading characteristics listed apply to reading aloud.

Teaching Approach

Next, direct the class to read silently the first paragraph on page 70. Explain the importance of preparing for a Read Aloud whenever possible. Reiterate that reading aloud well comes only with practice.

Preparing

Have students think about how they usually prepare for reading aloud. Direct them to imagine they've been asked to read aloud a page or unit from their social studies text. How would they prepare?

Work with the class to make a list of preparation techniques on the board. See the sample list on the next page.

Preparation Techniques

1. Always start with a silent reading of the passage.

2. Look for the most important parts to help decide what to stress.

3. Practice reading key parts with expression.

4. Practice reading aloud the rest of the selection.

5. Read aloud the entire selection, with emphasis, at least two times.

Direct students' attention to the third sentence on page 70: "Everyone needs to prepare." Then point out details on the page that support this main idea. If students were to read the passage aloud, they would modulate their voices to draw attention to these key ideas.

Wrap-up

As a way of helping students reflect upon what they've learned, ask students to prepare a Read Aloud using the techniques. Allow students to make a recording of a book they are currently reading in class. Assign each student a few pages from a chapter and record them in order.

Lesson 4 Practice Reading Aloud

For use with *Reader's Handbook* pages 68–71

Focus

In this lesson, students will practice reading aloud both fiction and nonfiction selections.

Getting Started

Ask students to thumb through the *Applications Book and Word Work* and find one passage they'd like to practice reading aloud. Encourage students to look at several fiction, nonfiction, and poetry passages before making a selection. Ask them to mark the passage with a sticky note so that they can share their choices with the rest of the class.

Teaching Approach

Once students have each chosen a passage, have them use the reading process to help them read and respond to the selections. Stress to students that their Read Alouds will be a lot stronger if they have a solid understanding of the passages.

Ask students to write notes about their passage either on a Main Idea Organizer (for nonfiction), a Story String (for fiction), or a Double-entry Journal (for poetry). Students' goal here is to find the essential words, phrases, and sentences in the writing so that they know the parts to emphasize when they read aloud.

Practice Reading Aloud

Work with small groups of students and support them as they practice reading aloud. Offer encouragement to those who stumble or mispronounce words, directing them to a dictionary or a class pronunciation guide as needed.

When students are ready, ask volunteers to read aloud their passages, with expression. Once everyone has had a chance to read, discuss the class's work. Have students say what they'll do differently when it comes time for their next oral reading.

Summing Up

Finish the unit with a discussion of what students have learned about reading actively. Review the following basic reading skills:

- Predict
- Make Inferences
- Draw Conclusions
- Compare and Contrast
- Evaluate

Then discuss what active readers do before, during, and after reading a selection. Ask students to turn to page 71. Have a volunteer read the page aloud and then ask other volunteers to summarize the information on the page.

Wrap-up

Ask students to review the "Being an Active Reader" section (pages 56–63) of the *Reader's Handbook*. Have them note techniques that they plan to use to improve their reading skills. Then ask them to add their own active reading techniques that they've used in the past to the list. Have students share their work with a partner and then discuss as a class.

Lesson 5 Review and Assess

Check Point

Use the Quick Assess checklist to informally evaluate students' understanding of what's involved in reading aloud. Based on their answers, divide them into two groups. Ask one group to do the Independent Practice on the next page while the other group completes the guided practice in the *Applications Book and Word Works*.

Quick Assess

Can students

- ☑ name two tips for reading aloud?

- ☑ explain what it means to read clearly, accurately, smoothly, and interestingly?

- ☑ tell how to prepare for reading aloud?

Guided Practice

For students who need reinforcement in reading aloud, use pages 28–29 in the *Applications Book and Word Works*.

For students who need more word work, assign page 212 from the *Applications Book and Word Works* on the **letter y** as a vowel.

Independent Practice

Invite students who have clearly mastered the art of reading aloud to practice reading aloud in groups. Before they begin, work with students to choose an appropriate selection. Then ask:

■ What is your purpose for reading this selection?

■ What did you notice on your preview?

■ What do you predict the selection will be about?

■ What difficulties do you except when it's your turn to read aloud?

Class Review

Work as a class to prepare an audiotape of a short story, folktale, or fairy tale that they can share with the students in a younger grade. Before you begin, choose a selection with plenty of characters so that most of the students have a chance to participate. Then ask students to write notes on what they might do to plan for the Read Aloud. Have your readers practice their roles while the remainder of the class creates a booklet of illustrations the audience can thumb through as they listen to the performance.

Finish the activity with a discussion of the challenges readers faced. Discuss strategies for overcoming these challenges and encourage students to apply them the next time they read aloud.

Test Book

Use the short-answer and multiple-choice tests on pages 24–25 to assess students' understanding of the material presented in this week's lessons.

WEEK 10

Understanding Letters and Sounds

Goals

Here students read about letters and sounds. This week's lessons will teach them to

- ☑ figure out what sounds letters make
- ☑ decide how many syllables a word has
- ☑ figure out a word they don't know

Background

Help students connect this week's lessons to their prior knowledge by asking them to

- ■ brainstorm a list of consonants and vowels
- ■ name consonant and vowel sounds
- ■ tell what they do to figure out the number of syllables a word has
- ■ explain the procedure they follow when they come to a big word that they can't pronounce or define

Opening Activity

Read the above list of unit goals to the class. Then ask students to bring from home a shoebox or index-card-sized file box. Invite them to decorate their boxes as they like. Then explain that students will use these "unfamiliar word" boxes this year to keep track of words they don't know. Make available a stack of index cards. When you hear a child stumble over a word, or when you see that the child has misspelled a word, ask him or her to write it on the card and drop it in the box. Offer weekly practice in using the words. Once students have mastered a word, have them remove it from the box. Later in the year, you might have students drop in words they're having trouble defining and then invite them to do some dictionary work with their cards in hand.

Weekly Plan

Lessons	Summary
1. **How Letters Make Sounds**	Present information on letters of the alphabet and how letters make sounds.
2. **Sounds and Spelling**	Explore the relationship between sounds and spelling.
3. **Syllables**	Discuss the importance of knowing how to break long words into several smaller syllables.
4. **Figuring Out Big Words**	Present a three-step plan that students can use to figure out the meaning of big words.
5. **Review and Assess**	Informally assess students to decide if they have an understanding of the material. Then give an assessment.

Lesson Materials

	Components	Pages
Plan	*Teacher's Guide and Lesson Plans*	134–145
Teach	*Reader's Handbook* *Overhead Transparencies*	74–81 9
Practice	*Applications Book and Word Work*	30–34, 213
Assess	*Test Book*	26–27

Lesson 1 How Letters Make Sounds

For use with *Reader's Handbook* pages 74–77

Focus

Here students focus on the letters of the alphabet and their individual sounds.

Getting Started

Open with an activity designed to spot-check students' phonemic awareness. Show students the pronunciation guide found in a dictionary. Explain how the vowels have different sounds. Write your name on the board using the pronunciation guide as a model.

Pronunciation Guide

		ī	pie	ōō	boot
ă	rat	îr	pier	ŭ	cut
ā	ray	ŏ	pot	ûr	urge
âr	rare	ō	toe	th	thin
ä	father	ô	paw	*th*	this
ĕ	pet	oi	boy	hw	whoop
ē	be	ou	out	zh	vision
ĭ	it	ŏŏ	took	ə	about

Then ask students to write their names on the board following the same process. Have each student sound out the letters of his or her name, as in /k-ay-t-ee/. Remind the class that at this point you're interested in hearing *sounds,* not syllables.

Teaching Approach

Read aloud the introductory paragraph on page 74 and explain the comparison between letter sounds in a word and building blocks in a tower. Then tell students that in this lesson they'll learn how sounds are put together to form words. They'll also learn that if they know the sounds a letter makes, they can figure out how to say even the most difficult words.

Setting Goals

Next, ask students to preview pages 77. Have them read the headings to get a sense for what the unit will be about. Then ask them to write in their Reading Notebooks their goals for learning letters and sounds. Write general class goals on the board when they finish.

Teaching about Our Language

Start off by asking questions about the English language.

■ How many letters are there in the English alphabet?

■ How many consonants are there, and how many vowels?

■ What letter can be both a consonant and a vowel?

■ What is the difference between uppercase and lowercase letters?

From this discussion you can gauge students' understanding of the language and phonics and their phonemic awareness. The purpose is not to make them into linguists but rather to engage their minds on the building blocks of language.

Next, ask students to read the Alphabet Chart on page 75. Ask them to note in particular the placement of **y**. Explain that **y** is a vowel when there are no other vowels in the syllable or it is at the end of a word.

Read aloud the text under "How Letters Make Sounds." Explain that while most consonants have only one sound, there are a few exceptions. The chart on page 76 outlines some of those exceptions.

After students study the Consonant Sounds Chart, have them turn to page 77 and read through the Vowel Sounds Chart.

Discuss clusters such as /**sh**/, /**th**/, /**ch**/, and /**br**/. Invite students to brainstorm words that contain these blends in both the beginning and end positions.

Wrap-up

Ask students to turn to pages 428–432 in the Almanac and review other vowel and consonant sounds. Give each student a consonant or cluster and have them come up with tongue twisters. Here are some examples.

■ Charlie Cheetah chewed chocolate cherries.

■ Many mumbling mice are making music at midnight.

■ The big black bug bled blue-black blood.

⬭ Lesson 2 Sounds and Spelling

For use with *Reader's Handbook* page 78

Focus

In this lesson, students will explore the relationship between sounds and spelling.

Getting Started

One of the chief challenges young learners face is memorizing the many exceptions to spelling rules in English. Explain to students that while there are 44 different sounds in the English language, there are *more than* 44 spellings that represent those sounds. For an example, show how many letter combinations the **long e** sound can make, such as in *fee, key, sea, we,* and *chief.* Then ask students to work in pairs to come up with as many words they can think of with the **long o** sound. You may have to explain that a long vowel makes the sound of the name of the letter.

Teaching Approach

Ask students to read silently the explanatory text at the top of page 78. Then have them study the **long a** chart in the middle of the page.

◆ Spellings of Long a ▶

same	play	hey
wait	break	weigh

The point here is to make students aware of the variety of ways to spell the **long a** sound, not to have students learn them all by heart.

Next, ask students to read the text under the chart and think about the sound the letter **s** makes. Explain that, although students know simple consonant and vowel sounds, such as /**s**/ and /**i**/, there are some less common consonant and vowel sounds with which they need to become familiar. Read the following chart with the class. Brainstorm with students more words for this chart of less common sounds.

Less Common Sounds

Consonant Sounds		
ch	church	hitch
wh	where	which
kw	choir	quick

Vowel Sounds		
ä	yard	father
oi	boy	noise
ə	ago	pencil

Supplement the information by explaining and giving examples of silent consonants.

gn	*gn*at	*gh*	*gh*ost
kn	*kn*ife	*mb*	com*b*
wr	*wr*ap	*lk*	tal*k*
tle	cas*tle*		

You also may want to discuss with students the following vowel exceptions:

e = /silent/ as in com*e*   *ough* = /aw/ as in *ough*t
le = /[ə]l/ as in hand*le*   *ea* = /[ĕ]/ as in h*ea*d
ul = /[ə]l/ as in awf*ul*

Reinforce your teaching on vowels and consonants by reviewing with students the more common phonograms (a vowel sound plus a consonant sound) in English. See pages 431–432 in the handbook for a more complete list of phonograms. These include

Phonogram	-ay	-am	-ail	-at	-ill	-ing	-ip	-out	-uck
Example	pay	jam	pail	cat	sill	ring	sip	about	duck

Wrap-up

Broaden students' understanding of sounds and letters by doing a number of word sorts. For example, ask students to sort these words.

day	say	game	save
neigh	take	lay	sleigh

Encourage them to organize the words by their letter patterns.

Lesson 3 ▶ Syllables

For use with *Reader's Handbook* page 79

Focus

Here students explore the importance of knowing how to break long words into several smaller syllables.

Getting Started

Model for students how to clap the syllables of a word such as *dai • sy*. For it, they need to clap twice. Have them clap syllables for the names of objects in the room. Challenge students to think of words with three or more syllables, such as *syl • la • bles.*

Teaching Approach

Teaching syllabification can improve students' reading and spelling skills. Students can use their knowledge of syllabication to help them break apart words into their smaller components.

There are plenty of syllabication rules in English. Unfortunately, there are also plenty of exceptions to these rules. Here is a list of key syllabification rules, along with a note about exceptions. Please note these rules are not discussed at length in the handbook.

Syllabification Rules

Rule 1. VCV   A consonant between two vowels is broken after the first vowel (*bro • ken*).

Rule 2. VCCV   Divide two consonants between vowels, as in *pic • ture*. This rule does not apply if the consonants are blends or digraphs.

Rule 3. Affixes   Prefixes always form separate syllables (*un • able*). Suffixes form separate syllables if they contain a vowel (*plant • ing*).

Rule 4. Compounds   Always divide compound words between the two words (*school • house*).

Direct students to page 79. Read aloud the explanatory text at the top of the page. Then have students study the Syllable Chart.

Syllable Chart

One-syllable Words
dog
plant
make

Two-syllable Words
din • ner
flow • er
gi • ant

Three-syllable Words
Sat • ur • day
dan • ger • ous
im • por • tant

Four-syllable Words
tel • e • vi • sion
in • ter • est • ing
un • u • su • al

Five-syllable Words
ex • am • i • na • tion
un • be • liev • a • ble
dis • a • bil • i • ty

Six-syllable Words
un • nec • es • sar • i • ly
ir • reg • u • lar • i • ty
im • prob • a • bil • i • ty

Explain to students that learning about syllables can help
them break apart long words they don't recognize, as well as
help them spell.

Wrap-up

Expand your lesson on syllables by asking students to do a word
sort based on the number of syllables in it. Give pairs of students
ten minutes to come up with as many words in each syllable group
as possible. For a variation, limit the subject the words are about.

Lesson 4 Figuring Out Big Words

For use with *Reader's Handbook* pages 80–81

Focus

Here students will learn a three-step plan they can follow when decoding long words.

Getting Started

Begin by asking students to illustrate a "how-to" plan that they currently use when they come to a word they don't understand. Some may show they guess and go, while others may show they sound out the word or consult a dictionary. Then tell the class that the purpose of this lesson is to teach them a three-step plan they can follow when they get stuck on a word.

Teaching Approach

Ask students to turn to page 80 in the *Reader's Handbook*. Have them read silently the explanatory text at the top of the page, including the *international* example.

Then write the handbook's three-step plan on the board and walk students through the individual steps.

Plan for Figuring Out Big Words

1. Look for little words and sounds.

2. Look for parts you know.

3. Put it all together.

1. Look for Little Words and Sounds

Remind students that longer words can be divided into syllables. Explain that if they divide a word into syllables, or little words, they might be able to recognize one or more of the little words (or chunks) contained in a long word.

■ *hand • ker • chief*

■ *ad • ver • tise • ment*

2. Look for Parts You Know

Next, students should try to put together a few of the chunks to see if they make familiar words. Point out the *international* example and explain how putting together two chunks can yield the word *nation,* which may be more familiar to students. For practice, have students divide the following words into syllables and then combine chunks to create words with which they are familiar:

ev • ery • bod • y

trav • el • ing

dif • fer • ence

pic • nick • ing

3. Put It All Together

Have students turn to page 81 and read the text. Once again, discuss the *international* example. Then have a volunteer explain the meaning of *interrupt* or *interfere.* Write the following sentence on the board and discuss how context clues can help students determine what it means:

The Olympics are an international sports event.

Offer additional practice as needed. Show Overhead Transparency 9 in anticipation of questions about using context clues. Students will learn more on the subject in a future lesson.

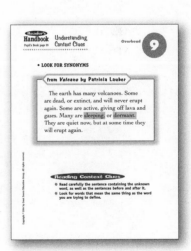

Wrap-up

List several challenging words on the board and have students define what each means. Explain that you are looking only for the most general definitions, as in "I know that *international* has something to do with countries because I see the smaller word *nation*." Words you might use for the activity include:

- literature
- performance
- satisfactory
- representative
- government
- noticeable
- obedience

Lesson 5 Review and Assess

Check Point

Use the Quick Assess checklist to informally evaluate students' understanding of letters and sounds. Based on their answers, divide them into two groups. Have one group do the Independent Practice with a word set you've chosen beforehand. Ask the other group to do the guided practice in the *Applications Book and Word Work*.

Quick Assess

Can students

- ☑ tell how sounds are made?
- ☑ describe how to break words into syllables?
- ☑ explain a plan to figure out big words?

Guided Practice

For students who need reinforcement in letters and sounds, use pages 30–34 in the *Applications Book and Word Work*.

For students who need more word work, assign page 213 from the *Applications Book and Word Work* on the **long *a*** sound.

Independent Practice

Ask students who have demonstrated a strong understanding of the material discussed in the lesson to write their own word list for the consonants listed on page 76 or the vowels on page 77. Ask them to think of an example for each sound. Then have them present their work to the class or to a small group of students.

Class Review

Post a syllable chart on the board, similar to the one on page 79. Then ask students to hunt in the handbook for words that have one, two, three, four, and five syllables. Have students race against each other, or have groups compete to see which group can find the most words.

Then review the steps for figuring out big words. Ask, "What steps should you follow when you come to a big word?" Have students name each step (pages 80–81) and discuss how it works.

Test Book

Use the short-answer and multiple-choice tests on pages 26–27 to assess students' understanding of the material presented in this week's lessons.

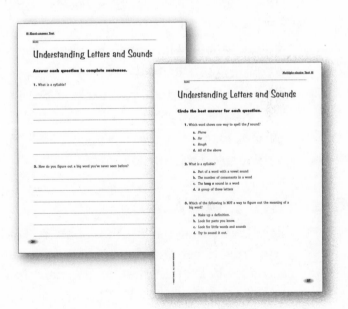

**WEEK 11**

Understanding Words and Word Parts

Goals

Here students explore the various word parts and how to use them to figure out a word's meaning. They will also learn about confusing word pairs. This week's lessons will help them

☑ break down words into prefixes, suffixes, and root words

☑ determine which meaning of a homophone is correct

☑ identify confusing word pairs

Background

Help students connect this week's lessons to their prior knowledge by asking them to

■ talk about what they do when they come across an unfamiliar word

■ consider what they already know about prefixes, suffixes, and root words

■ think about words that confuse them because they sound or are spelled alike

Opening Activity

Read the above list of unit goals to the class. Then work with students to set their own goals for reading this section of the *Reader's Handbook*. Explain that in the next few units they will focus on ways to improve their vocabulary. Ask students to get into pairs and discuss the following questions. "What are your personal goals for learning how to figure out the meaning of new words? What do you feel you need improvement on? What would you like to learn more about?" Have the class list their goals in their Reading Notebooks. At the end of the lesson, students can decide which goals they've met and which they need to spend more time on.

Weekly Plan

Lessons	Summary
1. **Prefixes and Suffixes**	Help students learn how to use prefixes and suffixes to figure out new words.
2. **Roots**	Strengthen students' understanding of root words and how they can help to determine the meaning of unfamiliar words.
3. **Homophones**	Explore homophones with students and help them learn how to choose the correct one.
4. **Confusing Word Pairs**	Work with students as they explore ways to make sense of other confusing word pairs.
5. **Review and Assess**	Informally assess students to decide if more guided practice is needed with words and word parts. Then give an assessment.

Lesson Materials

	Components	Pages
Plan	*Teacher's Guide and Lesson Plans*	146–157
Teach	*Reader's Handbook*	82–89
Practice	*Applications Book and Word Work*	35–39, 214
Assess	*Test Book*	28–29

Lesson 1 Prefixes and Suffixes

For use with *Reader's Handbook* pages 82–84

Focus

Here students will learn how to use prefixes and suffixes to help them learn new words.

Getting Started

Access students' prior knowledge of word parts by asking questions such as:

■ Have you ever heard of word parts?

■ If so, what do you know about them?

■ Here is a word that can be broken into parts: *unwrapped*. Can you identify its three parts?

 Help students see that *unhappy* includes the root word *happy* and the prefix *un-*. Post on the board a chart of prefixes, root words, and suffixes. Then ask students to put the different parts together to see how many words they can form.

Prefixes	Root word	Suffixes
un	read	able
pre	made	ed
re	view	ing

Teaching Approach

Write *happy* next to the word *unhappy* on the board. Ask a volunteer to explain the difference between the two words. Help students see that adding the prefix *un-* completely changes the meaning of the original word. Explain that by learning the meaning of common prefixes, including *un-,* students will improve their vocabulary and have an easier time figuring out unfamiliar words.

Kinds of Words and Word Parts

Walk students through page 82 of the *Reader's Handbook*. Look over the chart. Explain that students will explore all five types, starting with prefixes and suffixes. Then use the example on the bottom of the page to illustrate how knowing word parts can help readers determine a word's meaning.

Prefixes

Write the following prefixes on the board:

un, tri, re, micro

Challenge students to think of words that begin with each of these prefixes. List their ideas next to the corresponding prefix. Have volunteers explain the meaning of each word. Point out to students that the word parts you wrote on the board are called *prefixes*. Point out that the word *prefix* has the prefix *pre*. Explain that it is something you "fix" before a word.

Read aloud the top of page 83. Walk students through the list of prefixes. Encourage students to memorize the meaning of the most common prefixes.

Suffixes

Explain that while prefixes come at the beginning of a word, suffixes come at the end. Can students name any suffixes? List their ideas on the board.

Next, walk students through the Kinds of Suffixes list on page 84. Point out that the suffixes are grouped into three types:

1. Suffixes that make nouns
2. Suffixes that make verb forms
3. Suffixes that make adjectives

To improve students' recognition of these common suffixes, have them work in small groups to come up with additional examples for each suffix listed on page 84 on large chart paper. Display their work for use as a reference for suffixes.

Wrap-up

Have students make flash cards to help them memorize the most common prefixes and suffixes. Pass out ten index cards to each student. Have students look over pages 83–84 and 438–439 of the handbook and choose ten prefixes and suffixes. Have students write the prefix or suffix on the front of the card and the definition on the back. Ask them to work in pairs to "quiz" each other.

 **Lesson 2** Roots

For use with *Reader's Handbook* page 85

Focus

In this lesson, students will learn about root words and how they can use them to determine the meaning of unfamiliar words.

Getting Started

 Access students' prior knowledge by asking them what they know about root words. Remind them that they used root words in the previous lesson. Brainstorm any root words students can remember from the last lesson or know offhand. List their thoughts on the board. Keep the list up and add to it as you work with students throughout the lesson.

Teaching Approach

Direct students to the top of page 85. Be sure students understand why knowing a few root words will help them figure out the meaning of many words while reading. Do students recognize the role prefixes, suffixes, and roots play in helping readers improve their vocabulary?

Teaching Specific Roots

Next, discuss with students the Kinds of Roots list on page 85. Read aloud each root, its meaning, and the examples. Try to come up with more examples as you go through the list.

Kinds of Roots

Root	Meaning	Examples
div	separate	divide, division
gram	write	grammar, telegram
magn, mega	big	magnificent, megaphone
mem	remember	memory, memo
multi	many	multimedia, multicultural
port	carry	transport, import
tele	far	telescope, telephone
therm	heat	thermos, thermometer

Learning Root Words

Tell students you don't expect them to memorize all of the roots. By spending time on roots word, you will help students become familiar with them. They will very likely take notice of them more in the future.

Point out that while it would be quite difficult to memorize every root, memorizing the most common, just as they did with prefixes and suffixes, will help students figure out the meaning of unfamiliar words.

Kinds of Roots

Root	Meaning	Root	Meaning
astro	star	*phon*	sound
bio	life	*port*	carry
dict	speak, tell	*scrib, script*	write
min	small	*spect*	see
ped	foot	*struct*	build, form

Pass out eight index cards to each student and have them create root word flash cards. Have students work in pairs to quiz each other on the roots. Challenge students to include examples for each root.

Wrap-up

Give each student, or pair of students, an article or page from the newspaper. Tell students they need to find three new words with a prefix, suffix, or root mentioned in the past few lessons. Challenge students to write their new words on a large chart and come up with the meanings using what they know about word parts. Have students share their new words with the class.

tele-phone

tele = far

Lesson 3 Homophones

For use with *Reader's Handbook* pages 86–87

Focus

In this lesson, students explore homophones and learn how to choose the correct one.

Getting Started

Read the following sentence aloud: *I eight for cookies at school and a hole pizza two.* Then write it on the board. Ask students if they can spot four misspelled words (*eight, for, hole, two*). If students have trouble, help them by pointing out that *eight* should be spelled *ate*. Have volunteers find the remaining three and give the correct spellings. Ask students then to write and illustrate both sentences. Explain to students that these are homophones, and the pictures show how important it is to understand them.

Teaching Approach

Based on the opening activity, ask how students would define a homophone. Then have a volunteer read aloud the top of page 86. Make clear that, even though the words sound alike, they are spelled differently have different meanings.

Review the definitions students provided. Compare them to the actual definition from the handbook. Then talk about how students decide which homophone to use. Make clear that because homophones have different meanings, students need to choose the homophone that fits with the rest of the sentence. Write the following on the board:

Week or *weak*?

1. I felt so _____ when I was sick.

2. Our class is going on a field trip next _____.

Perform a Think Aloud to illustrate how you decided which word to choose. For example: *I know that* week *means "seven days," so that would make the most sense with sentence number 2. I know that* weak *means "feeling not very strong," so that would make sense with sentence number 1.*

Once your students have a basic understanding of what homophones are, discuss the Common Homophones listed on pages 86–87.

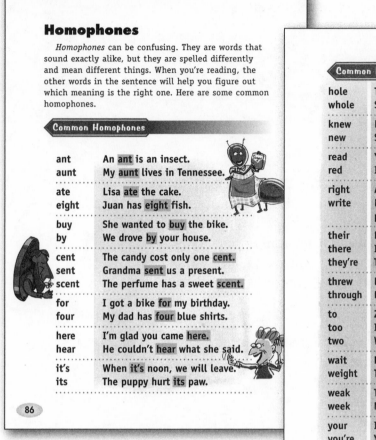

Common Homophones

Homophones

Homophones can be confusing. They are words that sound exactly alike, but they are spelled differently and mean different things. When you're reading, the other words in the sentence will help you figure out which meaning is the right one. Here are some common homophones.

Common Homophones

ant	An ant is an insect.
aunt	My aunt lives in Tennessee.
ate	Lisa ate the cake.
eight	Juan has eight fish.
buy	She wanted to buy the bike.
by	We drove by your house.
cent	The candy cost only one cent.
sent	Grandma sent us a present.
scent	The perfume has a sweet scent.
for	I got a bike for my birthday.
four	My dad has four blue shirts.
here	I'm glad you came here.
hear	He couldn't hear what she said.
it's	When it's noon, we will leave.
its	The puppy hurt its paw.

86

Words and Their Meaning

Common Homophones, continued

hole	There's a hole in my sock.
whole	She ate the whole pizza!
knew	He knew the answers on the test.
new	She has a new soccer ball.
read	Yesterday I read my book.
red	I like my red shirt.
right	All her math homework was right.
write	Did you write your name on your paper?
their	Do you like their shoes?
there	I put the book over there.
they're	They're coming to the party.
threw	He threw the ball across the street.
through	Her dad drove through the tunnel.
to	Zack went to the museum.
too	I wanted to go too.
two	We saw two baby pandas.
wait	Please wait for me by the door.
weight	The nurse wrote down my weight.
weak	The little puppy was weak.
week	Next week is my piano lesson.
your	I like your hair.
you're	You're the best speller I know!

87

Help students get a handle on the list by having them review it on their own and decide which homophone pairs they already use correctly. Then have students write the five most confusing pairs for them in their Reading Notebooks. Talk with students about what they could do to help them remember the different meanings of the most confusing pairs.

Wrap-up

Have students work in pairs to enhance their understanding of the different meaning of homophones. Begin by asking students to exchange lists of their five most confusing homophone pairs. Have partners create "quizzes" for the five words, similar to the fill-in-the-blank exercise you presented earlier in the lesson. After students take the quiz, have partners check and discuss their answers. If students still are unsure of any of the words' meanings, ask them to add the words to their word boxes.

Lesson 4 Confusing Word Pairs

For use with *Reader's Handbook* pages 88–89

Focus

In this lesson, students will explore ways to make sense of other confusing word pairs, including words that sound almost alike or are spelled very similarly.

Getting Started

Review what students have learned so far about ways to understand unfamiliar or confusing words. Remind students that homophones are words that sound alike but are spelled differently and have different meanings. Point out that homophones are not the only type of word pairs readers find confusing. Illustrate this by writing the following two words on the board:

> *desert* and *dessert*

Then write these definitions on a separate part of the board:

1. food eaten after a meal
2. a hot, dry, sandy place

Ask students to jot down the two words and the number of the definition that matches each word. Did everyone match *desert* with definition 2 and *dessert* with definition 1? Explain that word pairs such as these can be confusing for readers. Can students think of other confusing word pairs?

Teaching Approach

Read aloud the first paragraph on page 88. Point out the two most common reasons readers get confused about word pairs.

1. The words are spelled almost the same.
   Examples: *angel, angle; advice, advise; trail, trial*

2. The words sound almost alike.
   Examples: *accept, except; capital, capitol; metal, medal*

After discussing the reasons why some words are often confused with one another, review with students the Confusing Word Pairs list on pages 88–89.

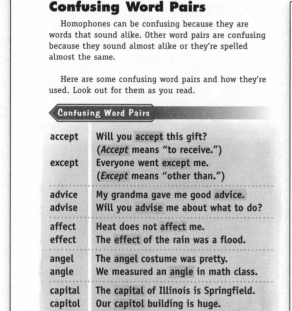

Confusing Word Pairs

Confusing Word Pairs

Homophones can be confusing because they are words that sound alike. Other word pairs are confusing because they sound almost alike or they're spelled almost the same.

Here are some confusing word pairs and how they're used. Look out for them as you read.

Confusing Word Pairs

accept	Will you accept this gift? (*Accept* means "to receive.")
except	Everyone went except me. (*Except* means "other than.")
advice	My grandma gave me good advice.
advise	Will you advise me about what to do?
affect	Heat does not affect me.
effect	The effect of the rain was a flood.
angel	The angel costume was pretty.
angle	We measured an angle in math class.
capital	The capital of Illinois is Springfield.
capitol	Our capitol building is huge.
chose	He chose a good movie. (*Chose* is past tense of *choose*.)
choose	I choose to play the violin. (*Choose* is present tense.)

88

Words and Their Meaning ■

Confusing Word Pairs, continued

desert	The desert is a hot, sandy place.
dessert	She wanted cake for dessert.
lay	He will lay the blanket on the bed.
lie	We will lie down and rest soon.
loose	The button on her coat is loose.
lose	Don't lose your lunch box today!
metal	The car is made of metal.
medal	He won a medal in the Olympics.
quiet	People should be quiet in the library.
quite	She was quite a good dancer.
quit	He wanted to quit studying.
sit	She will sit in the back seat.
set	Lauren set the table last night.
than	I'm older than she is.
then	Brad will go to the pet store first and then to the grocery store.
though	We will come, though we'll be late.
through	The highway goes through town.
trail	Did you walk along the trail?
trial	The robbers will go on trial tomorrow.
weather	The weather is cloudy and cool.
whether	Do you know whether the Cubs won?
were	Were you finished with dinner?
where	Where did you put my coat?

89

Have pairs of students take turns reading each word pair and sample sentence. Ask them to quiz each other on the pairs. Talk about which pairs are most problematic for students. Then have students list the top five most confusing word pairs. Come together as a class and invite volunteers to share their personal lists. Talk about why those words are so confusing and ways students can learn to keep them straight. Have students add unfamiliar words to their word boxes.

Wrap-up

Have students reflect on their learning in their Reading Notebooks. Ask these questions:

1. What was the most useful thing I learned in this unit?

2. What am I still confused about?

3. How will I use what I learned here the next time I read?

Lesson 5 Review and Assess

Check Point

Use the Quick Assess checklist to informally evaluate students' understanding of words parts and confusing word pairs. Based on their answers, divide them into two groups. One group can do the Independent Practice on the next page and the other group can do the guided practice in the *Applications Book and Word Work*.

Guided Practice

For students who need reinforcement understanding words and word parts, use pages 35–39 in the *Applications Book and Word Work*.

For students who need more word work, assign page 214 from the *Applications Book and Word Work* on the **long o** sound.

Independent Practice

Students who demonstrate a strong understanding of word parts, homophones, and confusing word pairs can apply their knowledge as they read a copy of a page from a social studies or science textbook. Ask students to do the following as they read:

◼ Circle any prefixes.

◼ Underline any suffixes.

◼ Highlight any homophones or words from their Confusing Word Pairs list.

Class Review

Offer students two creative ways to review what they learned:

1. Students can work independently to draw pictures illustrating five or six confusing word pairs, including homophones.

2. Students can work in small groups or on their own to create word collages. Provide students with magazines and pieces of chart or construction paper. Collages can include words with prefixes and/or suffixes, homophones, and other confusing word pairs. Students might also add photos of confusing words to their collages.

Test Book

Use the short-answer and multiple-choice tests on pages 28–29 to assess students' understanding of the material in this week's lessons.

WEEK 12

Learning New Words and Using a Dictionary

Goals

Here students find ways to learn new words. They will also learn about the parts of a dictionary and how to use it effectively. This week's lessons will teach them to

☑ start a Word Notebook

☑ use new words

☑ use a dictionary

☑ identify the features of a dictionary

Background

Help students connect to this week's lessons by asking them to

■ review what they learned about words and word parts in the previous lesson

■ describe what they know about using a dictionary

■ tell what they do currently when they come to a new word

Opening Activity

Read the above list of unit goals to the class. Then explain that in this unit students will be introduced to a five-step plan for learning new words as well as how to use a dictionary. Have students choose five words that they most want to learn from their word boxes or Reading Notebooks. Point out that one of their goals for the unit will be to use what they learn to figure out the meaning of these words. If students cannot come up with five words on their own, flip through a current reading selection for words with which students might have difficulty.

Weekly Plan

Lessons	Summary
1. **Learning New Words**	Present a five-step plan for learning and remembering new words.
2. **Exercise Your Word Skills**	Explore with students six ways to improve their word power.
3. **Using a Dictionary**	Teach students how to use a dictionary to help them learn about words, including what words mean and how they are spelled.
4. **Using a Dictionary** (continued)	Work with students to further explore the key features of a dictionary.
5. **Review and Assess**	Informally assess students to decide if they have an understanding of what they have learned. Then give an assessment.

Lesson Materials

	Components	Pages
Plan	*Teacher's Guide and Lesson Plans*	158–169
Teach	*Reader's Handbook* *Overhead Transparencies*	90–97 8
Practice	*Applications Book and Word Work*	40–44, 215
Assess	*Test Book*	30–31

Lesson 1 Learning New Words

For use with *Reader's Handbook* pages 90–94

Focus

Here students learn a five-step plan for learning and remembering new words.

Getting Started

Review what students have learned so far about figuring out the meaning of new words. Be sure the discussion includes learning about word parts, homophones, and confusing word pairs. Then review what students do currently when they come across new words. Ask students to illustrate their current procedure for learning new words. Allow students to share their drawings and then talk about which techniques work best for students so far and why. Explain that students will learn a five-step plan for learning new words.

Teaching Approach

Talk with the class about the importance of learning new words and in becoming a word collector. Here you'll discuss some ways they can do that.

1. Write It Down

Tell students that the first step in the plan is to write down the new word in their word boxes or notebooks. Read aloud the text under "Write It Down" on page 90. As a class, talk about the sample Word Notebook. Be sure students look at this as a model for keeping track of new words.

> **Word Notebook**

English Class—May 4
from <u>The Kid in the Red Jacket</u>

<u>fidgeting</u>, p. 7

<u>emotions</u>, p. 8

2. Look It Up

Read aloud page 91. Talk briefly about using a dictionary. Point out the entry word and definition. Be sure students know that entries in a dictionary are in alphabetical order. Point out, too, that a dictionary can help them spell.

◀ **Word Notebook** ▶

> English Class—May 4
> from <u>The Kid in the Red Jacket</u>
>
> <u>fidgeting</u>, p. 7—moving around nervously
>
> <u>emotions</u>, p. 8

3. Write the Definition

Walk students through the third step in their plan. Talk about why it is always a good idea for students to put information in their own words. Explain that this step will help them remember the word.

4. Say It Aloud

Make clear to students that saying the word aloud will help them remember it. Talk about how a dictionary entry can help students learn how to pronounce words correctly.

5. Use Your New Word

The final step is done after students have learned the new word. Talk about the three examples. Can students think of other ways they can use new words? Make clear that the more they use the new words, the more quickly the words will become part of their everyday vocabulary.

Wrap-up

Have students pick a word they don't know, or hand out a word. Ask students to follow the five-step plan for learning the new word. Have students use the terms section of their Reading Notebook to keep track of the five steps.

Lesson 2 Exercise Your Word Skills

For use with *Reader's Handbook* page 94

Focus

In this lesson, students will explore six ways to improve their word power.

Getting Started

Just as football players have to practice throwing and catching a ball, readers need to practice using their new word skills in order to really understand them. Brainstorm with students ways they can improve their vocabulary. Start off the list by suggesting an online word-a-day site as a part of their morning routine. Then list students' ideas on the board. Keep the list up throughout the lesson and add to it as new ideas come up.

Teaching Approach

Start by reminding students of the similarities between exercising for physical activities and exercising for mental activities, such as learning new words.

Read

Walk students through each of the six ways to build vocabulary listed on page 94. Talk about why students think reading exercises word skills. Tell students you want them to be word-wise and curious about words. By looking at and playing with words, students can expand their vocabulary.

Search for Synonyms and Antonyms

Explain how looking for synonyms and antonyms improves vocabulary. First, remind students that *synonyms* are words with similar meanings, and *antonyms* are words with opposite meanings. Mention to students that they can use a thesaurus to look up synonyms for words.

Collect Interesting Words

Have another student read how to collect interesting or fun words. Point out that words that are spelled the same forward and backward are called *palindromes*. List a few palindromes on the board, such as *noon, radar, Otto,* and *eve*. Add others to the list if you can.

Learn a Word a Day

Continue the lesson by reading aloud the next way to build word power. Talk about places students can look for new words. Point out that this activity is very much like the students' word boxes. Explain that whether students choose to use their word boxes or their Reading Notebooks to keep track of new words, the important point is for students to collect, learn, and ultimately use their new words.

Hunt for Homophones

Have students read the paragraph about homophones on page 94. Remind students that homophones are words that sound alike but are spelled differently and have different meanings. Have student volunteers provide examples of homophones.

Play Word Games

Read aloud the last way to exercise word power—word games. Talk about other kinds of word games, such as word searches and secret codes. Then review the six ways of building word skills with the class. You might use questions such as these to get the discussion going:

■ Which do you think will be most helpful? Why?

■ Which do you think will be most challenging? Why?

■ Which do you think you will use most often? Why?

Wrap-up

End the lesson by supplying students with a variety of word games, such as crossword puzzles, word searches, and secret codes. Invite students to work in pairs to complete the games. Challenge students to create their own crossword puzzles or secret codes using words from their spelling lists or other words of their choice.

Lesson 3 Using a Dictionary

For use with *Reader's Handbook* page 95

Focus

Here students learn how to use a dictionary to help them understand about words, including what they mean and how they are spelled.

Getting Started

Create a Web for the term *dictionary* on chart paper.

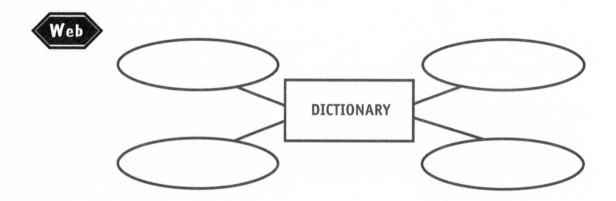

Web

DICTIONARY

Ask students to brainstorm words or activities they associate with dictionaries. Fill in the cluster with students' ideas. If the class needs help getting started, you might use prompts such as:

■ What do you find in a dictionary?

■ Why do people use a dictionary?

■ What does a dictionary entry include?

Keep the Web up throughout the next two lessons. Add to it as students work and learn more about using a dictionary.

Teaching Approach

Explain that in this lesson students will focus on what a typical dictionary entry includes. Discuss what students have learned already about the importance of using a dictionary for learning new words. Review the five-step plan for learning new words. Point out that steps two, three, and four all require a dictionary. Once students understand how much readers rely on dictionaries, ask students to return to the sample dictionary entry on page 91 in the handbook.

Sample Dictionary Entry

from *The American Heritage Children's Dictionary*

fidget *verb* To move in a nervous or restless way: *I fidgeted in my seat while waiting to give my presentation to the class.*
fidg•et (**fĭj′ĭt**) *verb* fidgeted, fidgeting

Explain the main parts of the entry. Point out the following:

1. Dictionary entries show the word's correct spelling and its part of speech.
2. Dictionary entries also tell what the word means. Point out that often a word has more than one meaning. Talk about ways students can decide which definition to choose.
3. Dictionary entries tell how to split a word into syllables. Review what students learned about syllables previously in the handbook.
4. Dictionary entries show how a word is pronounced. Explain that dictionaries generally include a pronunciation guide to help readers understand the different symbols. Pass around a dictionary for students to see a pronunciation key up close. Choose a few entries to demonstrate how the pronunciation key will help someone figure out how to say the word.

Wrap-up

Provide students practice using a dictionary entry. Have students choose a word from their personal list of unfamiliar words. Ask them to use a dictionary to find three things.

■ what the word means

■ how to pronounce it

■ how to split it into syllables

Remind students to follow the five-step plan for learning new words. Students should write the definition in their own words and write a sentence using the word to help them remember it more easily.

Lesson 4 Using a Dictionary (continued)

For use with *Reader's Handbook* pages 96–97

Focus

Here students will further explore the key features of a dictionary.

Getting Started

Have students reflect on their previous experiences using dictionaries by providing the following prompts for them to answer.

■ The easiest thing about using a dictionary is . . . because . . .

■ The hardest part about using a dictionary is . . . because . . .

Teaching Approach

Pass out dictionaries to the class and have students preview them. Their preview should focus on the unique features of a dictionary, as well as their purpose for using it. Then discuss the previews. Add new information to the Web. At this point it should be clear to students that a dictionary is one long alphabetical list.

Next, direct students' attention to the sample dictionary page on page 97. Use the information on page 96 to help explain the key features. Point to each item on Overhead Transparency 8.

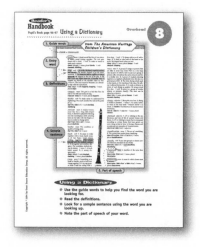

1. Guide Words

Have students put his or her finger on the words at the top of the dictionary page. Explain that these are called *guide words*. Point out that the first guide word, *clank,* is also the first word defined on the page, and *classroom* is the last entry on the page. Lead students to see that guide words help readers decide if the word they are looking for is on the page. Only words that fall between the guide words in alphabetical order will be on that page. Show students how *chair* will come before this page and *click* will come after. Ask students to come up with other *c words* that will fall before, on, or after the sample page.

2. Entry Words

Have students find an entry word on the Overhead Transparency. Make clear that this is the word being defined. Entry words are normally in boldface type to make it easier for readers to find them. Ask students how many entry words they see on the page. Help them see that the words are in alphabetical order.

3. Definitions

Have students look over the definition of *clap*. Ask them to compare it to the definition of *fidget* on page 91. Highlight that while *fidget* has one definition, *clap* has many. Explain that often words have more than one meaning and that each one is listed and numbered.

4. Sample Sentences

Words with multiple meanings often include sample sentences to help readers decide which meaning they want. Read aloud the first two definitions for *clash* and the sample sentences. Talk about how the sample sentences help readers better understand the two meanings.

5. Part of Speech

Remind students why the part of speech is included in the entry. Explain that some words can be used as more than one type of speech. Have students return to *clash* on page 97. Point out that *clash* can be used as a verb and as a noun.

Wrap-up

Give each student an index card. Have students choose another unfamiliar word from their word boxes or Reading Notebooks. Ask students to write a sample dictionary entry for it. Students can use this checklist as they work:

■ Does my entry word stand out from the rest of the entry?

■ Do I use my own words to write a definition of the word?

■ Do I include all the definitions for the word?

■ Does my sample sentence match the definition?

■ Do I include the part of speech?

Lesson 5 · Review and Assess

Check Point

Use the Quick Assess checklist to informally evaluate students' understanding of how to learn new words and use the dictionary. Based on their answers, divide them into two groups. Have one group do the Independent Practice on the next page. Ask the other group to do the guided practice in the *Applications Book and Word Work*.

Quick Assess

Can students

☑ explain a way for learning new words?

☑ list ways to use new words?

☑ describe the parts of a dictionary?

Guided Practice

For students who need reinforcement in learning new words and using the dictionary, use pages 40–44 in the *Applications Book and Word Work*.

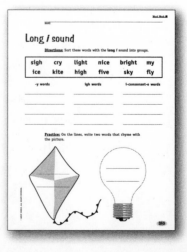

For students who need more word work, assign page 215 from the *Applications Book and Word Work* on the **long i** sound.

Independent Practice

Ask students who have demonstrated a strong understanding of the material discussed in the lesson to design a dictionary page for the rest of the unfamiliar words they chose at the beginning of the week. Their page will have guide words and should be in alphabetical order. Remind students to use the five-step plan for learning new words.

Class Review

Bring in five or six different dictionaries. Divide the class into groups and give each group a different dictionary. Explain that while most dictionaries include the same basic information, many dictionaries have special features that set them apart from others. Ask each group to preview its dictionary. Have each group look for ways its dictionary compares to the sample dictionary page on page 97 of the handbook. Have groups list other interesting features they find in their dictionaries. After groups complete their preview, ask them to share and compare what they discovered with the rest of the class. Talk about what features are standard and what features vary from dictionary to dictionary.

Test Book

Use the short-answer and multiple-choice tests on pages 30–31 to assess students' understanding of the material presented in this week's lessons.

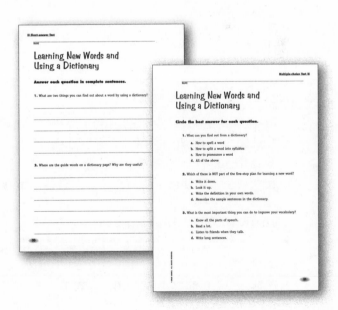

Context Clues and Vocabulary Questions

Goals

Here students use context clues to determine the meaning of unfamiliar words. They will also learn techniques for answering vocabulary test questions. This week's lessons will teach them to

- ☑ use different kinds of context clues to figure out unknown words
- ☑ answer different types of vocabulary questions on tests

Background

Help students connect this week's lessons to their prior knowledge by asking them to

- ■ explain what they do when they come to a word that they don't know
- ■ tell how they feel about answering vocabulary questions on tests

Opening Activity

Read the above list of unit goals to the class. Then ask, "If you had a treasure, where would you hide it?" Have students draw a treasure map detailing where to find their treasure in the school building. Invite students to share their maps. Talk about the purpose of treasure maps.

Write the phrase *context clues* on the board. Ask students what they know about this phrase. Explain that context clues are like treasure maps; they provide clues for helping readers find the treasure—in this case, the meaning of an unfamiliar word.

Weekly Plan

Lessons	Summary
1. **Synonyms and Antonyms**	Present information on how to use synonyms and antonyms to figure out the meaning of unfamiliar words.
2. **Surrounding Sentences and Definitions**	Explore two more types of context clues—surrounding sentences and definitions.
3. **Examples and Repeated Words**	Teach students the last two types of context clues—examples and repeated words.
4. **Answering Vocabulary Questions**	Present strategies students can use for tackling vocabulary test questions.
5. **Review and Assess**	Informally assess students to decide if they have an understanding of the material. Then give an assessment.

Lesson Materials

	Components	Pages
Plan	*Teacher's Guide and Lesson Plans*	170–181
Teach	*Reader's Handbook* *Overhead Transparencies*	98–109 9, 10
Practice	*Applications Book and Word Work*	45–49, 216
Assess	*Test Book*	32–33

Lesson 1 Synonyms and Antonyms

For use with *Reader's Handbook* pages 98–100

Focus

Here students learn about context clues and how to use synonyms and antonyms to figure out the meaning of unfamiliar words.

Getting Started

Hold up a picture of a small mouse. Ask students to help you list as many words to describe the mouse as possible. Encourage the use of words with the same meaning (*tiny, small*). Keep a list of their words on the board. When you have about 20 words, ask the students to help you organize them into groups with the same meaning. Some groups may be *small, fast, furry,* and *gross.* After the words are grouped, add another more difficult word with the same meaning to the bottom of the list. Ask students what they think each word means. Explain that they are using the words on the list as clues to figure out the meaning of the new word.

Allow students about five minutes to draw a picture of an animal that is the complete opposite of the mouse. Help them come up with a list of words to describe the animal before they draw it. For example *big, slow, hairless,* and *beautiful.*

Teaching Approach

Talk about why readers can be compared to detectives. Be sure students understand that, when they rely on the context in which a word is used to find the meaning, they are like detectives in search of clues.

Next, walk students through the sample passage on page 98 of the handbook. Think aloud to model how readers can use context clues to find the meaning of *infinitesimal.* Then read aloud the list of the six kinds of context clues. Explain that students will learn about all six kinds of clues in the next few lessons.

1. Synonyms

Ask a volunteer to define *synonym*. Explain that synonyms make excellent context clues because they have the same meaning as the unfamiliar word. Model how to use synonyms as context clues by thinking aloud as you read aloud the excerpt on page 99. Focus your Think Aloud on how to use the synonym *sleeping* to figure out what *dormant* means. Ask a volunteer to use the same approach to figure out the meaning of the word *extinct*. If the volunteer needs help, encourage him or her to look for its synonym in the sentence. Use Overhead Transparency 9 to support your instruction.

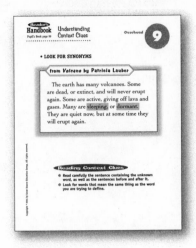

2. Antonyms

Next, review what students know about antonyms. Remind them that antonyms are words that have opposite meanings. Strong readers use antonyms as clues to a new word's meaning. Invite a student volunteer to read aloud the excerpt on page 100. Can students find an antonym for *slob* that will help them understand its meaning? If students have trouble, ask them to focus their "detective work" on the last paragraph.

Wrap-up

Have students read independently in a library book for five to ten minutes. Tell them to keep track of all the words they don't know. Ask them to be detectives and look for context clues that give synonyms or antonyms for the words they didn't know. Ask volunteers to share the new words and talk about any context clues they find.

Lesson 2 · Surrounding Sentences and Definitions

For use with *Reader's Handbook* pages 101–102

Focus

In this lesson, students will explore two more types of context clues—surrounding sentences and definitions.

Getting Started

Put a difficult word on the board and ask if students know what it means.

> circumference

Then put the word in a sentence and ask if they know the meaning now.

> The <u>circumference</u> measured 12 feet.

If they still don't know the meaning of the word, add a sentence before and after it.

> The dodge ball game was played in a small area. The <u>circumference</u> measured 12 feet. It is better to play in a circle that has a circumference of at least 30 feet.

Explain to students what the clues are for finding the meaning of the word.

Teaching Approach

Explain that students will have to look more carefully for word meanings with these types of context clues.

Surrounding Sentences

Read aloud the top of page 101. Next, have a volunteer read *Your Pet Hamster.* Ask the rest of the class to follow along, paying attention to clues that will help them figure out the meaning of *hoarders.* Make clear that the second sentence, *They like to store food,* begins to explain the unfamiliar word. The rest of the paragraph provides additional clues. Challenge students to use the clues in the paragraph to come up with a definition for *hoarders.*

174

Definitions

Review what the class discussed about using definitions as context clues. Ask students where they are more likely to find this type of context clue—in information books or stories? Discuss their answers. Then read aloud the top of page 102. Point out that definitions are more common in textbooks and other types of nonfiction. Then read aloud the excerpt from *Rain Forest Secrets*.

Ask students to look for the two definitions in the excerpt. Invite volunteers to provide definitions for *greenhouse effect* and *transpire* based on the information in the excerpts. Then read aloud the bottom of page 102. Discuss what students think about this type of context clue. Clear up any questions they might have about this and any of the other context clues they have explored so far.

Wrap-up

End the lesson by having students work in pairs to read a page from a social studies or science textbook. Ask partners to highlight unfamiliar words and then use context clues to determine their meaning. Make sure they state whether they got the meaning from a definition or a surrounding sentence.

Lesson 3 Examples and Repeated Words

For use with *Reader's Handbook* pages 103–104

Focus

Here students explore the last two types of context clues—examples and repeated words.

Getting Started

Put students into pairs and give each student a vocabulary term that they have learned this year. Explain that one student is going to pretend he or she is from Mars and does not understand much English and the other student must explain the term to the alien without saying the actual term. The alien must try and guess what the person speaking English is describing. When finished, have the students switch roles and complete the activity with the other term.

When the activity is over, bring the class together to discuss the different techniques students used to get the alien to say the word. See how many students say they kept repeating things or how many tried to give examples. Tell them these are the next two context clues.

Teaching Approach

Review the context clues that have been discussed with students already. Explain that here they will learn two more types of context clues.

Example Clues

Read aloud the first paragraph on page 103. Then talk about the signal words students should look for (*for example, such as, including, like,* and *especially*). Next, read aloud the excerpt from *Discovery Works*. Ask students to focus on clues that will help them determine the meaning of *wetlands*. After reading, talk about the examples listed for *wetlands*: *swamps, marshes,* and *bogs*. Point out the signal word *include*. Then ask students what they think wetlands are. Use Overhead Transparency 10 for additional support.

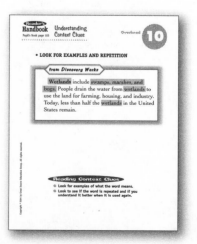

Repeated Words

Review what students predicted they will learn about using repeated words as context clues. Read aloud the top of page 104 of the handbook to begin to find out. Next, have a volunteer read aloud the excerpt on page 104. Ask the class to pay attention to how often *genius* is repeated and how they can use this repetition to determine its meaning.

Explain that repeating a word in a selection is often not enough context for figuring out its meaning. Instead, repeated words are combined with one of the five other kinds of context clues. Review the five other kinds of clues. Then ask students which type the author used in this excerpt. Can students tell that the antonym *stupid* provides important information about the meaning of *genius*?

Wrap-up

Type out a list of 6–12 sentences that all have an unfamiliar word. Try to write sentences that incorporate the six types of context clues. Leave the unfamiliar word out of the sentences when you show them to the students. Tell them their task is to come up with the missing word and to explain which context clue helped them come up with the word. Here are some sample sentences.

■ People thought that a pot of gold was a symbol of good luck. The word _____ means a sign. (symbol)

■ Henry jogged, or _____, to the bus stop. (ran)

■ Meg's twin sister was always _____, unlike Meg, who was always serious. (funny, laughing)

Lesson 4 ▸ Answering Vocabulary Questions

For use with *Reader's Handbook* pages 105–109

Focus

Here students learn strategies for tackling vocabulary questions.

Getting Started

Tell students that in this lesson they will learn ways to answer vocabulary questions. Talk about their past experiences with vocabulary questions. What do students do currently when they work on these types of questions? Ask students to reflect on these questions in their Reading Notebooks.

- What do I think when I see a vocabulary question?
- What strategies do I use when I answer this type of question?
- How well do my strategies work?
- How would I like to improve how I answer a vocabulary question?

Teaching Approach

Explain that there is more than one type of vocabulary test question. Each type of question requires a slightly different approach.

Definition Questions

Explain that some questions ask students to pick the best definition. Go over the sample question on page 105 of the handbook. Use the text at the bottom of the page to help with your instruction. Point out the importance of knowing the meaning of common prefixes and suffixes for answering vocabulary test questions.

Synonym Questions

Discuss what students learned about using synonyms to help them figure out the meaning of new words. Explain that they can use the same strategies for answering synonym test questions. Walk them though the sample question on page 106. Invite a student volunteer to think aloud as he or she answers the question.

Antonym Questions

Review with students the tips for answering antonym questions on page 107 of the handbook. Talk about the three steps for attacking the questions. Include these steps in your Think Aloud as you model how to answer antonym questions.

Paragraph Questions

Explain to students that paragraph questions are one of the most common types of vocabulary test questions. Pair students to work through the sample question on page 107.

Come together as a class and talk about this type of vocabulary test question. Point out that test questions like these show how important it is for students to know how to use context clues. Can students tell which type of context clue they used to answer the sample question?

Wrap-up

Break students into groups of four or five. Assign each group one of the four types of vocabulary test questions they explored in this lesson. Ask groups to create another sample question to present to the class. Have groups give the rest of the class time to try to answer the question on their own. Then ask groups to provide the correct answer and the steps test-takers would take to find it.

Lesson 5 ▸ Review and Assess

Check Point

Use the Quick Assess checklist to informally evaluate students' understanding of how to use context clues and answer vocabulary test questions. Based on their answers, divide them into two groups. Have one group do the Independent Practice on the next page while the other group does the guided practice in the *Applications Book and Word Work.*

Guided Practice

For students who need reinforcement in using context clues and answering vocabulary test questions, use pages 45–49 in the *Applications Book and Word Work.*

For students who need more word work, assign page 216 from the *Applications Book and Word Work* on the **long u** sound.

Independent Practice

Ask students who have demonstrated a strong understanding of the material discussed in the lesson to apply their knowledge to a page or two of a reading selection. Have students identify four or five unfamiliar words in the passage. Encourage students to try to use context clues to determine each word's meaning. Ask students to identify which of the six types of context clues they used for each word.

Class Review

Have students work in small groups to create a Context Clues Chart, such as the one below.

Kind of Context Clue	Definition	Sample Sentence

Have groups list the six types of clues and provide brief definitions of each. Challenge groups to make up sample sentences to illustrate each context clue. Remind them that some types of context clues require more than one sentence. Invite groups to share and compare their charts. Students might copy the chart in their Reading Notebooks to refer to as needed.

Test Book

Use the short-answer and multiple-choice tests on pages 32–33 to assess students' understanding of the material presented in this week's lessons.

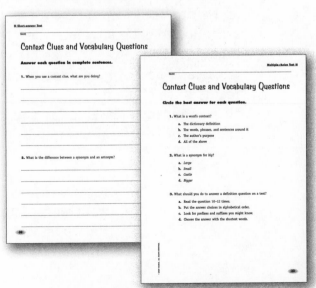

Understanding Paragraphs

Goals

Here students learn the basic characteristics of a paragraph and how to identify a paragraph's subject. In this week's lessons, students will learn to

- ☑ define a paragraph and a topic sentence
- ☑ recognize paragraph signals
- ☑ find the subject of a paragraph

Background

Help students connect this week's lessons to their prior knowledge by asking them to

- ■ name the characteristics of a paragraph
- ■ discuss why writers use paragraphs
- ■ consider how paragraphs can help a reader
- ■ consider how you can tell where a paragraph begins and where it ends

Opening Activity

Take two or three paragraphs from the same page of a book and write each sentence on large strips of paper. Give a sentence to each student. Then tell the class they need to organize themselves into as many groups as paragraphs you cut apart. Do not give a lot of direction. When the class is ready, have students explain their reasoning. Note the way they grouped themselves as you complete this exercise toward the end of this week's lessons.

Weekly Plan

Lessons	Summary
1. **What Is a Paragraph?**	Explore with students the chief characteristics and standard organization of a paragraph.
2. **Paragraph Signals**	Discuss paragraph signals and what they mean.
3. **Finding the Subject**	Help students understand the importance of finding the subject of a paragraph.
4. **Finding the Subject** (continued)	Work with students to find the subject of sample paragraphs.
5. **Review and Assess**	Informally assess students to decide if more guided practice is needed about paragraphs. Then give an assessment.

Lesson Materials

	Components	Pages
Plan	*Teacher's Guide and Lesson Plans*	182–193
Teach	*Reader's Handbook* *Overhead Transparencies*	112–115 11
Practice	*Applications Book and Word Work*	50–52, 217
Assess	*Test Book*	34–35

Lesson 1 What Is a Paragraph?

For use with *Reader's Handbook* page 112

Focus

Here students will explore the chief characteristics of a paragraph, as well as how a paragraph is organized.

Getting Started

Bring in all the makings of a sandwich (bread, turkey, lettuce, tomato, mustard, and cheese). Tell the class you are going to make a sandwich for lunch. Put it together in the wrong way—the cheese and turkey on the outside with the mustard on top. Ask your students if this is okay. Help them realize it has all of the pieces but is organized wrong. Then show them a paragraph that is out of order. Discuss how this paragraph seems to them.

In a well-constructed paragraph, the sentences work together to explore a single idea. Then, in the writing as a whole, the *paragraphs* work together to build a clear and interesting piece of writing. Most paragraphs contain the following three parts:

1. a subject
2. a main idea (either stated or implied)
3. details that support the main idea

In addition, most paragraphs contain a sentence that tells (or strongly suggests) the focus or topic of the paragraph. This sentence is usually called the *topic sentence*.

Teaching Approach

Explain to students that in the next four lessons they'll be exploring paragraphs—what they are, how they are constructed, what they look like, and what a reader can learn from them. Then offer some background information about paragraphs, and ask students to work with you to write a class definition of *paragraph*.

Next, post the following terms on the board: *topic sentence, main idea, supporting details.* Work with students to define these terms. Refer them to the Elements of Nonfiction section of the *Reader's Handbook*.

◄ Key Paragraph Terms ►

Topic sentence   page 202
Main idea   page 197
Supporting details   page 202

Next, direct students' attention to page 112 and have them read the first two paragraphs silently. Ask again, "What is a paragraph?" Modify the definition on the board as needed. Have students tell you about each paragraph. Tell them to imagine what page 112 would be like if it were all one paragraph. Lead students to see how paragraphs break down information and make it easier to take in the material.

Next, have students study the illustration at the bottom of the page. Explain how a paragraph is like a table with four legs. Ask, "What is a topic sentence?"

Wrap-up

Finish the lesson with a Read Aloud of the third paragraph on page 112. Focus attention on these points:

■ Many paragraphs begin with a topic sentence.

■ The other sentences in a paragraph give details about the topic.

Lesson 2 Paragraph Signals

For use with *Reader's Handbook* page 113

Focus

Here students will learn two paragraph signals.

Getting Started

Gather two sample paragraphs from all types of texts: novels, essays, newspaper articles, textbooks, and so on. Have pairs of students examine the two samples. Then have them compare the paragraphs and note characteristics they have in common. Draw a Venn Diagram on the board and have students use it to make their comparisons. Make sure students notice the different ways to signal the start and end of a paragraph.

Venn Diagram

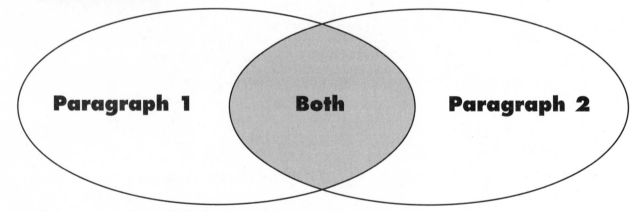

Teaching Approach

Show the students a full page of text that you put together that has no paragraph signals. Have students comment on it. Overall they should say that the page looks hard to read. Then explain to students that writers signal where a paragraph begins and where it ends. The purpose of these signals is to let readers know when the topic shifts or changes. They also break down the information into easier chunks to understand.

Recognizing Paragraph Signals

Next, write the term *indent* on the board. Have students define what it means. Then tell the class, "Indenting lets you know where each new paragraph begins. Writers indent a paragraph by moving the first line four or five spaces to the right." Show students the same copy with indentations this time.

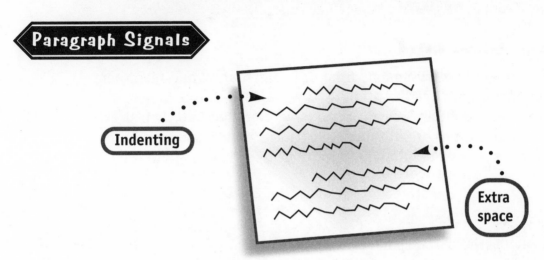

Paragraph Signals

Indenting

Extra space

Take the copy you have already shown twice and show it again, but with extra white space added. Talk about what the extra space does to the page. Ask a volunteer to read aloud the text on the top half of the page. Ask, "Why might a writer leave extra white space between two paragraphs?"

Importance of Paragraph Signals

Remind students that the sentences in a paragraph should all relate to a single idea. It's up to the reader to figure out what that idea is. Make the point that paragraphs organize ideas. Paragraph signals are a kind of courtesy the writer uses to help readers understand.

Wrap-up

Ask students to create a Key Word Notes organizer in their Reading Notebooks and then define the following terms:

■ paragraph

■ extra space

■ indent

Encourage students to add to their definitions as they make their way through the lessons to come.

187

Lesson 3 Finding the Subject

For use with *Reader's Handbook* page 114

Focus

Here students will learn how to find the subject of a paragraph.

Getting Started

Choose five or six paragraphs from different sources and read them aloud. After each one, have students write down the first word that comes to mind on a piece of paper. Have them hold up their pages. Discuss similarities and differences between their responses. Lead students to understand many times their free responses are the subjects of the paragraphs.

Teaching Approach

Display Overhead Transparency 11. Read aloud the text as students follow along.

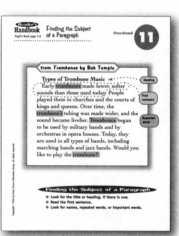

How to Find the Subject

Talk through the steps of finding the subject of a paragraph. Ask, "Why do you need to figure out the subject of a paragraph? How do you do it?"

Next, have students turn to page 114. Ask them to read silently the text under "Finding the Subject." Discuss what they learn from the reading. Then post on the board three places students should look to find clues about the subject of a paragraph:

■ the title or headings

■ the first sentence

■ names, repeated words, or important words

Process of Finding the Subject

Discuss the remainder of the information on page 114. Have students draw in their notebooks a Process Notes Organizer to list the steps involved in finding the subject of a paragraph. Students' organizers should look something like the following:

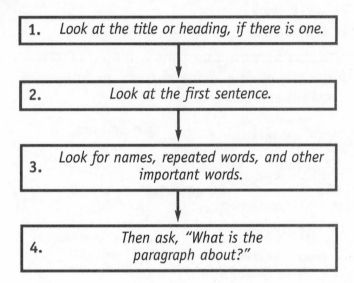

Process Notes

1.	Look at the title or heading, if there is one.
2.	Look at the first sentence.
3.	Look for names, repeated words, and other important words.
4.	Then ask, "What is the paragraph about?"

Wrap-up

For a final activity, ask students to return to the paragraphs and Venn Diagram they completed in a previous lesson. Ask partners to work together to find the subject of the two paragraphs. Remind students to follow the steps outlined in their Process Notes Organizer. Reiterate the importance of asking themselves the question, "What is this paragraph mostly about?" Then explain to students that, in the lesson that follows, they'll put together everything they've learned in order to find the subject of a paragraph from an informational book.

Lesson 4 Finding the Subject (continued)

For use with *Reader's Handbook* pages 114–115

Focus

In this lesson, students practice finding the subject of
a paragraph.

Getting Started

Model for students how to brainstorm a subject. Put the term
"winter" in the middle of a Web and come up with eight to ten
words that relate to winter.

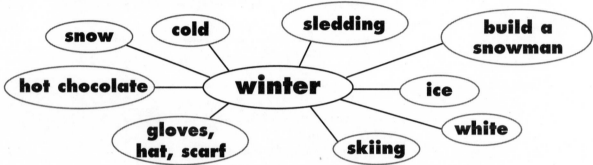

Point out that you could make two paragraphs from these terms,
one about things to do in winter and one about what winter is like.
Give students the term *summer* and have them make a Web. Then
ask them to divide the terms into two or three possible paragraphs.

Teaching Approach

Review where students should look when trying to figure out the
subject of a paragraph:

- ■ the title or headings
- ■ the first sentence
- ■ names, repeated words,
  important words

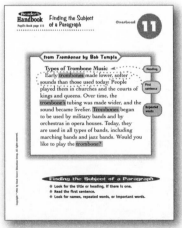

Point out these items to students with
your finger on Overhead Transparency 11.
Be sure students know *where* to look.

After your review, ask students to turn to
page 115 of the *Reader's Handbook*. Point
out the excerpt from *Trombones* at the top of the page. Explain that
you'd like students to use the reading process to read the paragraph.

Identifying the Subject

When students finish reading, work with them to identify the subject (trombones) of the paragraph. Be sure students note the title of the book and the heading of the paragraph and that the word *trombone* is repeated several times in the paragraph's body.

Help students understand that most writers do not directly state the subject of a paragraph (as in "This paragraph is about dogs."). Instead, they leave clues and expect readers to draw their own conclusions.

Read aloud the discussion on the second half of page 115. Explain that most of the time it's easy to figure out the subject of a paragraph. Assign several paragraphs from various library books for students to examine. Choose paragraphs in which the subject is relatively easy for students to find. For example, you might assign one or more of the following excerpt paragraphs from the handbook:

- page 138 (how moths and butterflies look)
- page 164 (Franklin's experiment)
- page 224 (plants making food)
- page 226 (plants using food)

Wrap-up

Ask students to thumb through the notes they made about paragraphs in their Reading Notebooks. Ask, "What questions do you have about paragraphs? Why is it important to be able to find the subject of a paragraph?" Then explain that once students know how to find a paragraph's subject they need to learn how to find its main idea.

Bring back the sentence strips from the opening activity on page 182. Have the class organize themselves again, this time thinking about what they learned about paragraph terms and signals.

Lesson 5 Review and Assess

Check Point

Use the Quick Assess checklist to informally evaluate students' understanding of the characteristics of a paragraph. Use their answers to help you divide them into two learning groups. Have one group do the Independent Practice on the next page while the other group completes the guided practice in the *Applications Book and Word Work*.

Quick Assess

Can students

- ☑ find the topic sentence in a paragraph?
- ☑ explain two signals used to mark the start of a paragraph?
- ☑ state three places to look for the subject of a paragraph?

Guided Practice

For students who need reinforcement in understanding paragraphs, use pages 50–52 in the *Applications Book and Word Work*.

For students who need more word work, assign page 217 from the *Applications Book and Word Work* on the **long e** sound.

Independent Practice

Choose from a class text a paragraph with a clear topic sentence, an obvious subject, and a stated main idea. Then divide your independent learners into small groups. Ask group members to work together to read and then analyze the paragraph. Then have a group secretary record key information from the paragraph, including:

■ the subject

■ the topic sentence

■ signal words

You may decide to have students return to this Independent Practice during the next unit, "Finding the Main Idea."

Class Review

Have students use the writing process to help them write a paragraph about a topic of general interest, such as "My Favorite Birthday Party." Work with the class on writing a good topic sentence and three supporting details. Use a Main Idea Organizer like the one below.

Subject		
Main Idea		
Detail 1	**Detail 2**	**Detail 3**

Test Book

Use the short-answer and multiple-choice tests on pages 34–35 to assess students' understanding of the material presented in this week's lessons.

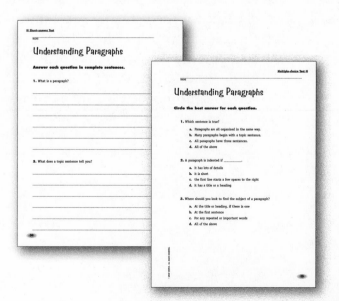

Finding the Main Idea

Goals

Here students explore how to find the main idea of a paragraph. In particular, they'll learn to

- ☑ identify where the main idea is in a particular paragraph
- ☑ differentiate between a stated and implied main idea
- ☑ use tools to separate details from the main idea
- ☑ follow a plan to find the main idea

Background

Help students connect this week's lessons to their prior knowledge by asking them to

- ▮ recall characteristics of a paragraph
- ▮ explain how to find the subject of a paragraph
- ▮ differentiate between the subject and the main idea of a paragraph

Opening Activity

Before class begins, type two or more paragraphs that have either stated and implied main ideas and at least three supporting details apiece. Then jumble the sentences in the paragraphs. Have students work in small groups to reorder the sentences in the paragraphs. Ask students to try putting the main idea sentence at the beginning and ending. Help students see that the order in which the sentences in a paragraph are arranged can affect the overall meaning of the writing.

Weekly Plan

Lessons	Summary
1. **Main Idea in First Sentence**	Discuss the importance of finding the main idea of a a paragraph. Model a paragraph in which the main idea appears in the first sentence.
2. **Main Idea in Last Sentence**	Help students find the main idea in the final sentence.
3. **Implied Main Idea**	Discuss implied main idea and how to find one in a paragraph.
4. **Plan for Finding the Main Idea**	Present a four-step plan for finding the main idea of a paragraph.
5. **Review and Assess**	Informally assess students to decide if guided practice is needed for finding the main idea of a paragraph. Then give an assessment.

Lesson Materials

	Components	Pages
Plan	*Teacher's Guide and Lesson Plans*	194–205
Teach	*Reader's Handbook*	116–123
	Overhead Transparencies	3, 12, 13
Practice	*Applications Book and Word Work*	53–56, 218
Assess	*Test Book*	36–37

⬤ Lesson 1 ⬤ Main Idea in First Sentence

For use with *Reader's Handbook* pages 116–117

Focus

In this lesson, students discuss the importance of a main idea and learn that sometimes the main idea is in the first sentence of a paragraph.

Getting Started

Open the lesson with a review. Discuss the term *paragraph* and ask students to volunteer its characteristics. Help them recall the following facts about paragraphs:

■ A paragraph usually has three parts: the subject, main idea, and supporting details.

■ Some paragraphs begin with a topic sentence, which identifies the subject of the writing.

■ The sentences in the body of the paragraph support the main idea.

■ Writers indent the first line of a new paragraph four or five spaces in order to signal the beginning of that paragraph.

■ Sometimes they leave extra space between paragraphs to show that the subject is changing.

 Divide the class into groups of four or five. Give them a topic sentence that will state the main idea in the first sentence. Ask the students to come up with detail sentences to complete the paragraph. Allow them to share their paragraphs with the class.

Teaching Approach

After you define *main idea* and help students understand the difference between the subject and main idea, begin building awareness of how readers go about finding the main idea.

Stated Main Idea

Read aloud the first and second paragraphs on page 116 of the *Reader's Handbook*. Explain to students that sometimes an author will state the main idea directly. Other times, the reader will have to make inferences about the main idea. Tell the class that in this lesson and the one that follows, they will learn how to find the *stated* main idea of a paragraph.

How to Find the Main Idea

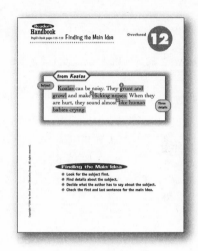

Display and then discuss Overhead Transparency 12, "Finding the Main Idea of a Paragraph." Have students apply what they learned to the paragraph from *Koalas* on page 117. Ask, "What is the subject of the paragraph? What is the main idea? Where is the main idea in this paragraph?" If students have a different main idea, ask, "What is the author saying about koalas?" Point out that the first sentence carries the main idea. Then, help students understand how the other two sentences in the paragraph all relate to (support) the main idea that koalas are noisy animals.

Wrap-up

Draw a Main Idea Organizer on the board. Have students do the same in their Reading Notebooks. Ask them to write the main idea and three details from *Koalas* in the organizer. Spot-check to be sure students understand the relationship between a main idea and its supporting details. Here is an example of what their notebooks should look like.

Main Idea Organizer

SUBJECT	Koalas	
MAIN IDEA	Koalas can be noisy.	
DETAIL	**DETAIL**	**DETAIL**
They grunt and growl.	They make clicking noises.	They cry out loud like babies.

Lesson 2 Main Idea in Last Sentence

For use with *Reader's Handbook* pages 118–119

Focus

Students explore how to find the main idea in the last sentence.

Getting Started

Write this list on the board.

1. I went to the beach.
2. I built a sand castle and played in the water.
3. The sun was shining.
4. The waves were big and fun.
5. _____

Tell students you need help filling in a final sentence to sum up the list of details. Guide them to say something like, "I had a great time at the beach." Explain this is the main idea in the last sentence. Have students work in pairs to create their own list of detail sentences. Then they can trade papers and fill in the last sentence—or the main idea.

Teaching Approach

Begin by asking students to read the first paragraph on page 118. Then read aloud the second paragraph, emphasizing the need to think about the subject of the paragraph. Explain that the location of the main idea won't always be immediately apparent. This is why students read first for the subject and then ask, "What is the author saying about the subject?"

Next, ask students to read the paragraph from "Out of Sight, Out of Mind" on page 119. Emphasize that students should watch for clues about the subject.

Find the Subject

When students finish, ask, "What is the subject of the paragraph?" Students should be able to say that the subject is frog eggs. Then ask, "What is the author saying about frog eggs?" Ask students to state the main idea in their own words. Then have them reread the paragraph in search of a sentence that reflects the main idea. Students should note that the final sentence is a statement of the main idea: "Laying many eggs, then, is an adaptation that helps frogs survive as a species."

Find the Main Idea

During the second half of the lesson, have students get together in small groups to complete a Main Idea Organizer for the frog eggs paragraphs. Ask them to use their own words to restate the author's main idea and supporting details. For example, here is a model of a Main Idea Organizer about the paragraph on frog eggs.

Main Idea Organizer

SUBJECT	*Frog eggs*		
MAIN IDEA	*In order to survive as a species, frogs lay many eggs.*		
DETAIL *They lay thousands of jelly-covered eggs.*	**DETAIL** *Some eggs become food for other animals.*	**DETAIL** *Some tadpoles hatched from frog eggs become food for snakes.*	**DETAIL** *Only a few eggs survive to develop into adult frogs.*

Wrap-up

Ask groups to present their organizers to the class. Then discuss the ways in which the details support the main idea. Have a student summarize the process of how to find the main idea in the last sentence.

Lesson 3 Implied Main Idea

For use with *Reader's Handbook* pages 120–121

Focus

Here students will learn to find an implied main idea in a paragraph.

Getting Started

Write two sentences on the board. One will use the word *implied* correctly. The other one will use it wrong. See if students can figure out the sentence that uses it correctly. Then, ask students to define the word as best they can. Help them understand that *implied* means "understood without being directly stated."

Teaching Approach

Explain that not every paragraph students read will have a clearly stated main idea. Ask, "What do you think you should do if there is no main idea statement? How can you figure out the main idea?"

Remind students what it means to make an inference. Direct them to reexamine pages 48–49 of the handbook to review this thinking skill. Then present Overhead Transparency 3 and review the steps for making an inference. Students will need this important skill when looking for a paragraph's main idea.

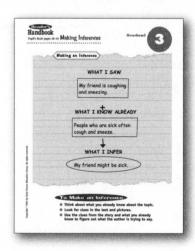

Finding an Implied Main Idea

Have students turn to page 120 and follow along as you read aloud the first paragraph. Ask what it means to be a detective in search of clues in a paragraph: "What sorts of clues would you expect to find?" Discuss with students how they need to be like detectives and use the clues they find.

Using Details as Clues

Have students read the paragraph on page 120. Ask students, "Who or what is the subject of the paragraph?" (Booker T. Washington) "What do the authors want us to know about Booker T. Washington?" Create a Web on the board. Write "Booker's Trip to School" in the center. Have students suggest the details that belong on the spokes. Then ask again, "What is the main idea of this paragraph?"

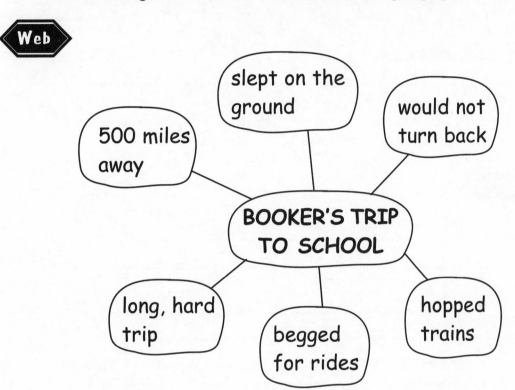

Explain that each of the details listed on the Web are the author's clues about the main idea. Point out that even though the author never comes right out and says so, it is clear that the message here is that Booker T. Washington would overcome any obstacle to get an education.

Wrap-up

Select another paragraph from the book on Booker T. Washington— or from another biography—and ask students to read for the main idea. If you think students will benefit, walk them through once again the process of finding clues and then inferring the main idea.

Lesson 4 Plan for Finding the Main Idea

For use with *Reader's Handbook* pages 122–123

Focus

In this lesson, students will review a four-step plan they can follow when searching for the main idea of a paragraph.

Getting Started

Discuss with students the term *plan*. Ask how many of them have plans for things. Let them share their plans. Choose a math concept they have all mastered and ask them to write a plan for solving this type of problem on a Process Notes Organizer.

Process Notes

1.

2.

3.

4.

Teaching Approach

Direct students' attention to the Plan for Finding the Main Idea. Have students read the plan slowly and carefully, taking notes as they go.

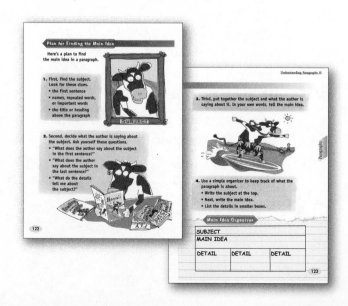

Step 1

Ask, "What is Step 1 about? What do you need to do to complete it?" Remind students of the importance of looking for clues about the subject and main idea in the title or heading, the first sentence, and in names, repeated words, or important words.

Step 2

Point out the three bulleted questions and explain that the third question is the one students will ask themselves if they think the paragraph has an implied main idea.

Step 3

Read aloud Step 3 and explain how important it is for students to be able to restate a main idea in their own words. Tell the class that forming a restatement can actually help them better understand what the author is saying.

Step 4

Finish the lesson by reading aloud Step 4. Help students understand that creating a graphic organizer such as the one shown can make it easier for them to understand and remember what they've read.

Main Idea Organizer

SUBJECT		
MAIN IDEA		
DETAIL	DETAIL	DETAIL

After they restate the main idea, students should look for the details in the paragraph that support the main idea. Remind the class that not every paragraph detail will support what the author is saying. Students might find a detail that relates to the subject but doesn't directly support the main idea.

Wrap-up

Divide the class into three groups. Assign each group a paragraph from a library book or textbook. Ask each group to read its paragraph and then complete a Main Idea Organizer that group members will present to the class.

Lesson 5 Review and Assess

Check Point

Use the Quick Assess checklist to informally evaluate students' understanding of how to find the main idea of a paragraph. Use their answers to the checklist's questions to divide them into two groups. Ask the first group to do the Independent Practice on the next page. Have the other group do the guided practice in the *Applications Book and Word Work*.

Guided Practice

For students who need reinforcement finding a paragraph's main idea, use pages 53–56 in the *Applications Book and Word Work*.

Quick Assess

Can students

- ☑ tell two common places to find the main idea in a paragraph?

- ☑ explain what a main idea is?

- ☑ describe the steps readers can follow to find the main idea of a paragraph?

- ☑ explain one tool to use to help find the main idea?

For students who need more word work, assign page 218 from the *Applications Book and Word Work* on long and short vowels.

Independent Practice

Students who clearly understand how to find or infer the main idea of a paragraph can practice their newfound skills with a paragraph you choose ahead of time. Distribute copies of the paragraph to the group. Then have students analyze the paragraph by following the handbook's plan to find the main idea. When they finish, students can create a Main Idea Organizer that reflects their understanding of the paragraph.

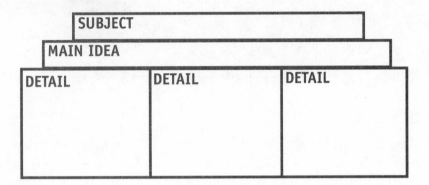

Main Idea Organizer

SUBJECT		
MAIN IDEA		
DETAIL	DETAIL	DETAIL

Class Review

Have students return to the paragraph they wrote in the previous lesson, or have them start over by writing a new paragraph. Assign a topic (such as "My Favorite Birthday Party") and have students construct a main idea sentence they can use in their paragraphs. Then ask them to write three details that support their main idea sentence. Invite small groups of students to read their work aloud.

Test Book

Use the short-answer and multiple-choice tests on pages 36–37 to assess students' understanding of the material presented in this week's lessons.

Short-answer Test

Finding the Main Idea

Answer each question in complete sentences.

1. What is the difference between a paragraph's subject and its main idea?

2. Where are two places the author often gives the main idea?

Multiple-choice Test

Finding the Main Idea

Circle the best answer for each question.

1. What does the main idea of a paragraph tell?
   a. The subject
   b. What the author says about the subject
   c. How you feel about the subject
   d. The most important details

2. How can you find the main idea of a paragraph?
   a. By reading the first sentence.
   b. By reading the last sentence.
   c. By putting together all the details.
   d. All of the above

3. A Main Idea Organizer helps you keep track of _____.
   a. the subject, the main idea, and the details
   b. what you already know about the subject
   c. your questions about the main idea
   d. the number of words

Kinds of Paragraphs

Goals

Here students explore various types of paragraphs, including narrative, descriptive, persuasive, and expository. This week's lessons will teach them to

- ✓ identify four different kinds of paragraphs
- ✓ explain the differences in kinds of paragraphs
- ✓ use tools to keep track of information in paragraphs

Background

Help students connect this week's lessons to their prior knowledge by asking them to

- ■ review characteristics of a paragraph
- ■ name various paragraph signals
- ■ discuss how to find the subject and main idea of a paragraph

Opening Activity

Gather sample paragraphs from a variety of media, including newspapers, magazines, advertisements, journals, and real-world writing, such as instructions, announcements, and, recipes. Write the following paragraph purposes for writing on the board:

- ■ to tell a story
- ■ to describe
- ■ to give an opinion
- ■ to give information

Have students sort sample paragraphs by category of purpose. Use the activity to introduce the notion that not all paragraphs share a common purpose and that identifying a possible purpose can help students read and respond to a paragraph.

Weekly Plan

Lessons	Summary
1. **Narrative Paragraphs**	Work with students as they explore the characteristics and purpose of narrative paragraphs.
2. **Descriptive Paragraphs**	Introduce and discuss descriptive paragraphs.
3. **Persuasive Paragraphs**	Help students define and then distinguish persuasive paragraphs from other kinds of paragraphs.
4. **Expository Paragraphs**	Discuss expository paragraphs and then review the four types of paragraphs.
5. **Review and Assess**	Informally assess students to decide if more guided practice is needed on the four kinds of paragraphs. Then give an assessment.

Lesson Materials

	Components	Pages
Plan	*Teacher's Guide and Lesson Plans*	206–217
Teach	*Reader's Handbook* *Overhead Transparencies*	124–128 12
Practice	*Applications Book and Word Work*	57–60, 219
Assess	*Test Book*	38–39

Lesson 1 Narrative Paragraphs

For use with *Reader's Handbook* pages 124–125

Focus

Help the class recognize the characteristics of narrative paragraphs, as well as what they are used for and where students might expect to find them.

Getting Started

Ask students to get into pairs. Choose a paragraph example in a fictional piece and a nonfiction piece on the same general topic. Have the pairs read each paragraph and discuss how they are different. Help them understand that one is giving information about the topic and the other is telling a story about the topic.

Then give students the topic "party." Tell them to write about this subject in a short paragraph. At the end of the lesson, they will identify the kind of paragraph it is.

Teaching Approach

List the four types of paragraphs on the board:

■ Narrative

■ Descriptive

■ Persuasive

■ Expository

Introduce each type of paragraph in a sentence or two. Then explain that here students will study narrative paragraphs, which tell a story.

Kinds of Paragraphs

Reinforce your teaching by asking students to examine the diagram on page 124 of the *Reader's Handbook*. Have students read about each type of paragraph. Then ask a volunteer to summarize what the class has learned about the four types.

Narrative Paragraphs

Next, direct students to turn to page 125. Read aloud the explanation of narrative paragraphs at the top of the page. Emphasize that a narrative paragraph tells a story about people, places, or events. Then ask students to use the reading process to help them read the narrative paragraph from *The Gold Cadillac*.

When students finish, ask these questions:

■ Who or what is the paragraph about?

■ What happened in this paragraph?

■ How did you feel as you were reading the paragraph?

Then ask students to read silently the explanation of narrative paragraphs in the middle of the page. Emphasize that this narrative paragraph tells about a series of events.

Tell the class that when they read a narrative paragraph, it's important for them to track the sequence of events the author describes. This will help them understand the story. Walk students through how to use Summary Notes.

> **Summary Notes**

- The family waited a long time for the father.
- The police had given him a ticket for speeding.
- They put him in jail.
- After the judge came, the father paid the ticket and left.

Wrap-up

Share another narrative paragraph with students. Choose a second excerpt from Mildred Taylor's *The Gold Cadillac* or a paragraph from a novel the class has enjoyed. Work with students to create Summary Notes that retell the events described in the paragraph.

Lesson 2 Descriptive Paragraphs

For use with *Reader's Handbook* page 126

Focus

Here students will continue their exploration of paragraphs, focusing in particular on descriptive paragraphs.

Getting Started

Have students list all of the words that describe their home. You may want to review what an adjective is and come up with a list of words that describe the school building. Then have students draw a picture of their home on the other side of the paper. Encourage them to use the correct colors. Allow students to stand up and show their pictures. The rest of the class can offer adjectives to describe the home.

Teaching Approach

Explain to students that the words describing their home can be put into a paragraph. This would be a descriptive paragraph.

Understanding Descriptive Paragraphs

Begin your discussion of the characteristics of descriptive paragraphs. Explain to students that in a descriptive paragraph the sentences work together to present a single, clear picture of a person, place, thing, or event. Ask students to recall descriptive paragraphs they've read in the past. What were they about? Students might recall biographical or autobiographical writing, newspaper profiles, travel brochures, and so on.

Explain to students that descriptive paragraphs are not something they can skip because "nothing happens." Descriptive paragraphs tend to be very important in stories, because they can help tell more about characters or where a story takes place.

Reading a Descriptive Paragraph

Ask students to use the reading process to help them read and respond to the excerpt from Jon Scieszka's novel. When students finish reading, have them make a list of the details they noticed in the excerpt. Explain to students that details in a descriptive paragraph often appeal to one or more of the five senses: sight, hearing, smell, taste, and touch. In the case of the Scieszka paragraph, the details all appeal to the sense of sight.

Using a Web

Direct students' attention to the Web at the bottom of page 126. Ask the class to examine the details in the circles and then look back at the paragraph to see where they came from.

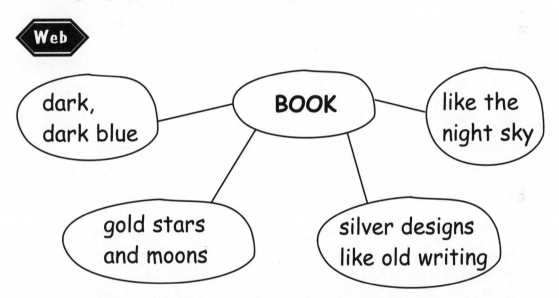

Help students understand that a Web is an all-purpose note-taking tool that readers can use to keep track of key details, organize information, and brainstorm ideas. A Web works very well for keeping track of the details given in a descriptive paragraph.

Wrap-up

Choose a dry or dull paragraph for students to read and respond to or make it up. Ask students to add descriptive details to make it more interesting. Then have students share their new paragraphs.

> *We went to the beach. We watched the dolphins swim in the water. The sailboats were sailing. Johnny made a sandcastle. A wave hit it. The sandcastle disappeared. The beach was fun.*

Lesson 3 Persuasive Paragraphs

For use with *Reader's Handbook* page 127

Focus

In this lesson, students will explore the characteristics and purpose of persuasive paragraphs.

Getting Started

Make a list of "not-so-popular" topics to give to students. These can be issues such as year-round school, an earlier start time for school, an hour of homework each night, shorter lunch periods, and so on. Have students get in pairs and assign each pair a topic. Partners then take turns presenting opposite sides of their topic to each other. Allow each student a few minutes to discuss his or her side of the issue. After both students talk, explain that they were persuading each other.

Teaching Approach

Ask students what they think it means to persuade. Help them understand that to persuade is to urge someone to perform an action or adopt a belief about something.

Understanding Persuasive Paragraphs

In persuasive writing, the author gives an opinion (or strong feeling) about a subject and then tries to convince the reader that the opinion is valid. Good persuasive writers include several supporting points to solidify their arguments.

1. The Main Idea

A persuasive paragraph may or may not contain a stated main idea. Review with students how to find the stated main idea of a paragraph by checking the first and last sentences and asking, "What is the author saying about the subject?" Then display Overhead Transparency 12 and review the procedure shown there.

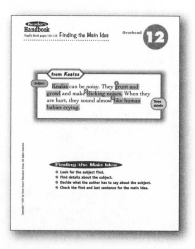

2. Support for Author's Opinion

Have students turn to page 127 of the handbook. Read aloud the explanation at the top of the page, and reiterate that a persuasive paragraph gives the author's opinion. Have students read the excerpt from *What We Can Do About Litter,* searching for the writer's opinion as they go. Students should note that the writer's opinion appears in the final sentence of the paragraph:

> To help reduce garbage and litter, do not buy things that have more wrapping than is really needed.

Then remind the class that a good writer will also include details (in the form of facts and examples) in support of his or her opinion. Ask students to return to the paragraph they just read and note the numbered details. Have volunteers explain how each of the details supports the author's opinion.

Using Summary Notes

Summary Notes work well with a persuasive paragraph. Explain to students they can use this type of organizer to record important ideas and their supporting details. Have students examine the Summary Notes at the bottom of page 127 and the instructions for creating this type of organizer in the Reading Tools section of the handbook.

Summary Notes

AUTHOR'S OPINION
We should not buy things with too much wrapping.
1. Many things come with extra wrapping.
2. Extra wrapping means more garbage.

Wrap-up

Have students thumb through the Reading Tools section of the handbook in search of another type of organizer that they think might work well with a persuasive paragraph. If students get stuck, have them review information about Main Idea Organizers (page 415) and Webs (page 425).

Lesson 4 Expository Paragraphs

For use with *Reader's Handbook* page 128

Focus

Here students will learn about another type of paragraph—the expository paragraph.

Getting Started

Review the paragraphs students have learned thus far. Create a four-column chart on the board. Ask students to help you write characteristics of the first three paragraphs they learned about.

Kinds of Paragraphs

Descriptive	Narrative	Persuasive	Expository
• tells about (describes) a person, place, or thing • tells a series of events	• tells a story about a person, place, thing, or event	• gives the author's opinion • author wants reader to do or believe something	

Teaching Approach

Begin by telling students that an expository paragraph is a paragraph that explains. It can present information, give directions, or show how to do something. Then offer examples, such as articles from a textbook or reference book, an instruction manual, or—in some cases—writing in a newspaper or magazine.

Expository Paragraphs

Ask students to turn to page 128 in the handbook. Have a volunteer read aloud the paragraph at the top of the page. Then ask students to read the selection from *A Tree Is Growing* and think about what's being explained. Students should understand that "bark" is the subject of the paragraph and that the paragraph gives various facts about an oak tree's bark.

Details in Expository Paragraphs

Next, rewrite the paragraph on the board and then work with students to number each of the four details.

> **from *A Tree Is Growing* by Arthur Dorros**
>
> Bark is the skin of a tree. **1** The outer layer of bark **2** protects the tree. **3** When an oak tree is young, the bark is as smooth as a baby's skin. As the tree grows older, **4** the bark becomes rough and cracked.

Then explain that one way to keep track of details in an expository paragraph is to write them on a Web as you're reading or right after you finish reading.

Web

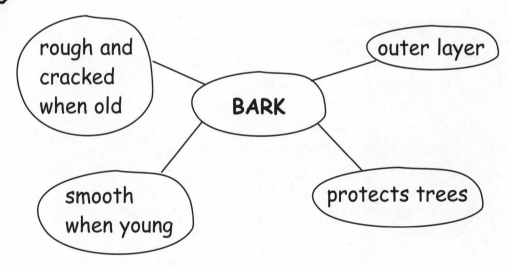

Wrap-up

Review with students the four types of paragraphs they learned about and the two reading tools (Summary Notes and Web) they can use to help them organize key ideas and details. Ask students to search for an example of one of the types of paragraphs discussed and then present what they found to the rest of the class.

Lesson 5 — Review and Assess

Check Point

Use the Quick Assess checklist to informally evaluate students' understanding of the four kinds of paragraphs. Based on their answers, divide them into two groups. One group can do the Independent Practice on the next page while the other group does the guided practice in the *Applications Book and Word Work*.

Quick Assess

Can students

- ☑ list the four kinds of paragraphs?
- ☑ state the purpose of each kind of paragraph?
- ☑ explain tools to analyze different kinds of paragraphs?

Guided Practice

For students who need reinforcement in recognizing different kinds of paragraphs, use pages 57–60 in the *Applications Book and Word Work*.

For students who need more word work, assign page 219 from the *Applications Book and Word Work* on silent letters.

Independent Practice

Place students who have demonstrated a strong understanding of the kinds of paragraphs into four groups. Assign a type of paragraph to each group: narrative, descriptive, persuasive, and expository. Have group members write a brief explanation of their type of paragraph. Students' lists should include information about the following.

■ the purpose of this type of paragraph

■ features that distinguish it from other types of paragraphs

■ what the main idea looks like

■ tools readers can use to track the details in this type of paragraph

Class Review

Write questions (or have students write questions) for a question-answer game show (like Jeopardy!®) about paragraphs. Questions should test students' knowledge of the kinds of paragraphs, in addition to elements of paragraphs such as subject, main idea, and supporting details. Possible questions include the following:

A: Paragraph

Q: What is a group of sentences that tell about a single idea?

A: Main idea

Q: What is the author is saying about the subject?

A: Persuasive

Q: What is a type of paragraph that gives the author's opinion?

Encourage students to return to their handbooks, as needed, during the game.

Test Book

Use the short-answer and multiple-choice tests on pages 38–39 to assess students' understanding of the material presented in this week's lessons.

WEEK 17

How Paragraphs Are Organized—Part I

Goals

In this week's lessons, students learn about paragraphs organized by time, location, and list order. "How Paragraphs Are Organized" will teach them to

☑ look for clues about how paragraphs are organized

☑ use tools to organize paragraph information

☑ understand time order, location order, and list order

Background

Help students connect this week's lessons to their prior knowledge by asking them to

▪ define *paragraph*

▪ explain how to find the subject and main idea of a paragraph

▪ discuss the four types of paragraphs: narrative, descriptive, persuasive, and expository

Opening Activity

Divide students into groups of four or five. Give each group a complete deck of cards. Tell one student in each group to deal out all of the cards to the others. Ask students to pick up the cards in their hands and organize them however they want.

They may ask what game they are going to play. Don't tell them. When students finish organizing, have them share with their groups how they arranged the cards in their hands. Then discuss as a class the ways they came up with (by suit, number, or color). Explain that the game they play will often dictate how to organize the cards. Deciding how to organize also affects words and sentences in paragraphs. Tell students that over the next few weeks they will learn different ways to organize paragraphs.

Weekly Plan

Lessons	Summary
1. **Organizing Paragraphs**	Work with students to understand different methods of arranging details in a paragraph.
2. **Time Order**	Teach students to recognize and analyze time order paragraphs.
3. **Location Order**	Discuss location order paragraphs.
4. **List Order**	Present list order organization and then review the three types of organization students learned in the unit.
5. **Review and Assess**	Informally assess students to decide if they have an understanding of the material. Then give an assessment.

Lesson Materials

	Components	Pages
Plan	*Teacher's Guide and Lesson Plans*	218–229
Teach	*Reader's Handbook* *Overhead Transparencies*	129–135 13, 47
Practice	*Applications Book and Word Work*	61–63, 220
Assess	*Test Book*	40–41

Lesson 1 Organizing Paragraphs

For use with *Reader's Handbook* page 129

Focus

In this lesson, students explore the different methods of arranging details in a paragraph.

Getting Started

Ask students to list the events that have taken place so far this morning in a Story String. Model this by listing the events of your morning on Overhead Transparency 47. Then write on the board the following signal words: *first, then, next, after that,* and *later*. Tell students to use these words as they write each event in a sentence. These words will connect their thoughts. Ask them to exchange papers and read each other's work. This activity introduces one of the most common paragraph organizations: time, or chronological, order.

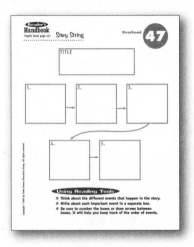

Teaching Approach

After you finish your discussion, explain to students that time order is just one way of arranging details in a paragraph.

Different Kinds of Paragraphs

Writers also can use location order, list order, cause-effect order, and comparison-contrast order. Refer students to the diagram on page 129. Discuss the illustrations on the diagram. Ask questions such as, "What does the map illustration tell you about location order? What does the broken egg illustration tell you about cause-effect order?"

Ways of Organizing Paragraphs

Explain that during the next few lessons, you'll be discussing the various ways a writer can organize details in a paragraph and, in addition, the effect organization can have on a reader. Briefly discuss the five ways to organize a paragraph.

Ways of Organizing Paragraphs

Time Order: The details are arranged in the order in which they occurred. Narrative paragraphs are often organized chronologically.

Order of Location: The details are arranged by place—for example, from left to right or from top to bottom. A paragraph that tells about the roof of a house and then the walls and then the floor and basement is organized by location.

List Order: The details in a paragraph are merely listed, in no particular order.

Cause-Effect Order: The details are arranged to show the result and what caused it. The cause (or causes) may come before the effect is discussed or after.

Comparison-Contrast Order: The details are arranged to show similarities and differences. For example, an expository paragraph might have details that tell how rats are different from mice.

Wrap-up

Encourage students to think about how different things they use each day are organized. Make a list on the board and ask pairs of students to brainstorm the various ways to organize the items. For example, books on a shelf can be organized by height, genre, length, level of difficulty, or the alphabet. Use the items below as topics for students to brainstorm about how to organize them.

■ clothes in a closet

■ shoes

■ class notebook or binder

■ food in a cupboard

■ toys in a playroom

■ stuff in a garage

When students finish, discuss the variety of ways they came up with on how to organize.

Lesson 2 Time Order

For use with *Reader's Handbook* pages 130–131

Focus

Here students will learn to recognize and analyze details arranged in time order.

Getting Started

Post on the board the class schedule for the day, but write it in the wrong order. Ask the students what is wrong with the schedule and have a volunteer put it in the correct order. Explain that it is more useful to everyone when it is in *time order*. Tell students that writers use time order too. This means that the author has told the events in the order in which they occurred.

Teaching Approach

Ask students to think about where they would expect to see a time order paragraph. Suggestions might include in a history book, newspaper, novel, short story, movie review, and so on. Turn to page 130 in the *Reader's Handbook* and read aloud the explanatory paragraph at the top of the page. Then ask the class to read silently the paragraph from *Cyber Space*.

Make sure students notice that the details in this paragraph are arranged by date.

■ In 1876, Bell developed the telephone.

■ In 1880, there were just 33,000 telephones in the world.

■ Ten years later, there were nearly half a million.

Explain to students that one reason authors use time order is that it makes it easy for readers to track a sequence of events.

Next, ask students to read the paragraph in the middle of the page. Tell the class that an author using time order will often leave clues for readers as a way of keeping them oriented in the paragraph. These clues are called *signal words*. They signal changes in time.

Time Clues

- times of the day
- days of the week
- months
- years
- *before*
- *after*
- *then*
- *later*
- *next*
- *first*
- *last*

Discuss the Time Clues list at the bottom of handbook page 130. Ask volunteers to help you add to the list. These might include

- *seasons*
- *decade*
- *during*
- *afterward*
- *immediately*
- *finally*
- *today*
- *tomorrow*
- *next week*
- *yesterday*
- *as soon as*
- *when*

Wrap-up

Finish the lesson by asking students to look at the Timeline on page 131. Have them follow along as you read across the Timeline from left to right.

Timeline

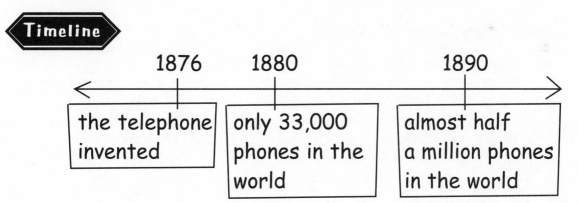

1876 — the telephone invented

1880 — only 33,000 phones in the world

1890 — almost half a million phones in the world

Explain how a Timeline can help readers keep track of details in a paragraph. Encourage students to use it as a During and After Reading tool.

Have students make a Timeline of the big events of the school year to this date. Then give them a paragraph you have prepared about events that took place in the classroom recently. Ask students to pull out the events and add them to their Timelines.

Lesson 3 Location Order

For use with *Reader's Handbook* pages 132–133

Focus

Here students will learn about location order in paragraphs.

Getting Started

Before class draw a quick sketch of the *Stone Fox* excerpt from page 324 of the *Reader's Handbook*. Then tell students you are going to read aloud a passage and they need to draw what they hear. Read the paragraph a few times so students can get all of the information. Put all of their pictures and yours on the board so students can discuss the similarities and differences. The pictures will be fairly similar because the paragraph gives a clear description of the scene.

Teaching Approach

Ask students to define the word *location*. Then ask them to describe the location of their desk for someone else to find.

Introducing Location Order

Ask students what it means when details in a paragraph are ordered by location. Help them understand that an author uses location order to make it easier for readers to visualize (make mental pictures of) a place he or she describes. Write on the board the following methods of organizing location details. Encourage students to add the list as needed.

- north to south
- east to west
- top to bottom
- left to right
- over to under

- inside to outside
- in back of to in front of
- above to below
- side to side
- in a circle

Recognizing Location Order

Explain to students that the location words on the list you've written on the board can be thought of as signal words that indicate a location order paragraph. Encourage the class to watch for them as they read.

Ask the class to follow along as you read the first paragraph on page 132 of the *Reader's Handbook*. Then have students read the excerpt from the novel *Dinosaurs Before Dark*. When they finish, have them name the details the author gives about the view from the tree house. These should include the following:

- *Down below* were the tops of other trees.
- *In the distance* he saw Frog Creek Library.
- Annie pointed *in the other direction*.

Visualizing

Ask students to picture the scene. The author has arranged the details in such a way that it is easy for you to picture Jake looking from one side to another while Annie points the way. Then explain that forming a picture in your mind is called *visualizing*. Good readers visualize what's happening in a story because it makes the story easier to understand and more enjoyable to read.

Wrap-up

Check to see if students have understood what they learned by reading them these sentences from *The Five Little Peppers and How They Grew* by Margaret Sidney. Have students identify the signal words.

So Polly got out an old wooden chair, according to direction, and <u>mounted up on</u> it, with Grandma <u>below</u> to direct. She <u>handed down</u> bowl after bowl, interspersed at the right intervals with cracked teacups and handless pitchers.

Lesson 4 List Order

For use with *Reader's Handbook* pages 134–135

Focus

In this lesson, students will learn about paragraph details that are arranged in list order.

Getting Started

Ask students to make a list of the items they would need to buy at a store if they were throwing a party. Ask each student what he or she thinks is the most important item on the list. Then explain to students that sometimes writers put their facts and examples in a kind of list order, as if they were making a list of items to buy at the grocery store. A writer might use list order if it doesn't matter which detail comes first, which comes second, and so on. Connect that idea to the students saying that different items were the most important.

Teaching Approach

Begin the lesson by reading aloud the information about list order on page 134 of the *Reader's Handbook*. Point out the key sentence in the first paragraph: "Paragraphs organized in list order give lots of details but in no particular order." Help students understand that in the case of list order, the details themselves are far more important than their arrangement. Explain that you can't have a party without a cake and party favors. Both are of equal importance. Next, have students read silently the excerpt from the nonfiction book *Crows! Strange and Wonderful*. Ask them to think about the subject as they read.

Understand the Paragraph

When students finish reading, ask, "What is the subject of the paragraph?" Students should clearly understand that the subject is crows. Next, have them identify the main idea. Explain to students that this paragraph has an implied main idea, which means students will need to make inferences. Show Overhead Transparency 13 as a way of reviewing this process.

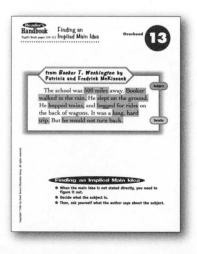

Making a List

Point out the list at the bottom of page 134. Ask a student to explain how creating a list of details can be a helpful way to understand a paragraph.

CROWS
- tease other animals
- make sounds
- can be taught to say words

Finish the lesson by showing the Web on page 135. Remind students what they've learned about this reading tool—that a Web can help them organize information.

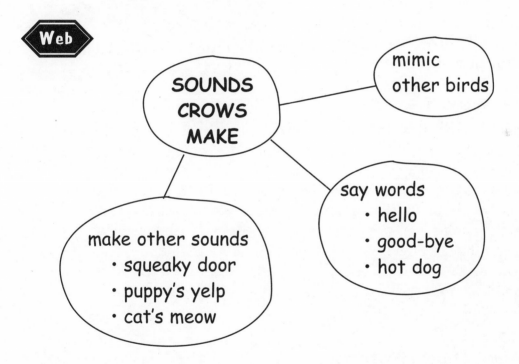

Wrap-up

Review with students the three types of paragraph organization they've learned thus far: time, location, and list order. Pull a handful of paragraphs from different sources. Have each student write *list, location,* and *time* on three index cards in big letters. Read aloud a paragraph of one of these types. Have students hold up the card that says how it was organized. Encourage students to explain why they chose that organization.

Lesson 5 Review and Assess

Check Point

Use the Quick Assess checklist to informally evaluate students' understanding of the three kinds of paragraph organization discussed in the unit. Based on their answers, divide them into two groups. Have one group do the Independent Practice on the next page while the other group does the guided practice in the *Applications Book and Word Work*.

Guided Practice

For students who need reinforcement in understanding how paragraphs are organized, use pages 61–63 in the *Applications Book and Word Work*.

For students who need more word work, assign page 220 from the *Applications Book and Word Work* section on *r*-controlled vowels.

Quick Assess

Can students

- ☑ tell how time order paragraphs are organized?

- ☑ explain the characteristics of a location order paragraph?

- ☑ identify list order paragraphs?

- ☑ describe two tools to use to help keep track of information in various types of paragraphs?

Independent Practice

Students who clearly understand the differences between these three types of paragraph organization can work with a group of students to find their own examples of time, location, and list order paragraphs. Ask groups to analyze the paragraphs they find using the tools discussed in the handbook.

Paragraph Organization

Organization Type	Tool
Time order	Timeline
Location order	Picture (visualizing)
List order	Web

Class Review

Put the students in groups of three. Give a "treasure hunt" list to each group.

■ Give the book and page number of two examples of time order paragraphs.

■ Give the book and page number of an example of location order.

■ Give the book and page number of an example of list order.

Ask students to note where they find their examples and then present their work to the class. Finish by reviewing the characteristics of each of the three types of paragraph organization.

Test Book

Use the short-answer and multiple-choice tests on pages 40–41 to assess students' understanding of the material presented in this week's lessons.

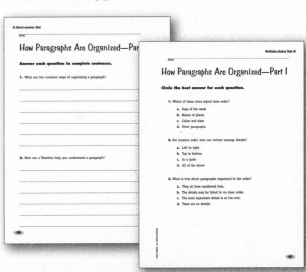

WEEK 18

How Paragraphs Are Organized—Part II

Goals

In this lesson, students learn about cause-effect and comparison-contrast order paragraphs. Here they will learn to

- ☑ recognize two ways writers organize paragraphs
- ☑ explain cause and effect
- ☑ understand comparison-contrast order paragraphs

Background

Help students connect this week's lessons to their prior knowledge by asking them to

- ▪ recall definitions for the following terms: *paragraph, main idea, supporting details*
- ▪ review how to find the subject and main idea of a paragraph
- ▪ retell characteristics of the four types of paragraphs: narrative, descriptive, persuasive, expository

Opening Activity

Read the above list of goals to the class. Then, conduct quick demonstrations of cause and effect and comparison and contrast. For cause and effect, show what happens when you add food coloring to a glass of water (cause). The water turns color (effect). For comparison and contrast, ask students to tell how an apple and an orange or a dog and a cat are alike and different.

Weekly Plan

Lessons	Summary
1. **Cause-Effect Order**	Work with students to understand cause-effect relationships.
2. **Cause-Effect Order** (continued)	Teach students to recognize cause-effect order paragraphs.
3. **Comparison-Contrast Order**	Discuss comparison-contrast order paragraphs.
4. **Comparison-Contrast Order** (continued)	Continue your discussion of comparison-contrast order paragraphs and then review the five types of paragraph organization students have learned.
5. **Review and Assess**	Informally assess students to decide if more guided practice is needed. Then give an assessment.

Lesson Materials

	Components	Pages
Plan	*Teacher's Guide and Lesson Plans*	230–241
Teach	*Reader's Handbook* *Overhead Transparencies*	136–139 5, 36
Practice	*Applications Book and Word Work*	64–66, 221
Assess	*Test Book*	42–43

Lesson 1 Cause-Effect Order

For use with *Reader's Handbook* page 136

Focus

In this lesson, students begin their exploration of cause-effect order of details in a paragraph.

Getting Started

Put the following phrases on the board and ask students to complete the thought.

■ The boy fell down and _____.

■ I kicked the ball and _____.

■ My mom cooked my favorite meal and I _____.

■ The dog barked at the _____.

Tell students that these sentences are cause and effect relationships.

Ask students what they know about the relationship between causes and effects. Explain that paragraphs organized by cause and effect can help readers make connections between a result and the events that preceded it. Present Overhead Transparency 36 to help students visualize what a cause and effect relationship looks like.

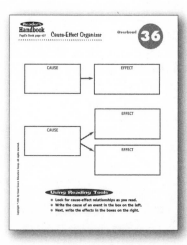

Teaching Approach

Ask students to turn to page 136 of the *Reader's Handbook*. Have a student read aloud the explanatory paragraph at the top of the page. Then ask the class to read silently the paragraph from the nonfiction book *The Super Science Book of Rocks and Soils*.

Begin by asking students to help you create a Main Idea Organizer for the paragraph. This will make it easier for them to see the relationship between the individual details.

Main Idea Organizer

TOPIC	Rocks and ice		
MAIN IDEA	Rocks can be broken by ice		
DETAIL Water expands as it freezes.	**DETAIL** If water gets into a crack and then freezes, it pushes the crack open.	**DETAIL** When the water melts and freezes again, the crack becomes even wider.	**DETAIL** The freezing-melting-freezing cycle can break open the rock.

Explain to students that science and history writers often use cause-effect order to answer the questions *why* or *how*. Point out that the paragraph students just read answers the question, "How can ice break rocks?"

Next, have the class read the explanation for the Cause-Effect Organizer at the bottom of page 136. Ask them to draw a blank organizer in their Reading Notebooks and then work with a partner to add details from the rock-and-ice paragraph to the organizer.

Cause-Effect Organizer

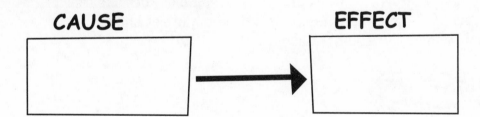

CAUSE   EFFECT

Wrap-up

Finish the lesson by asking students, "How can a Cause-Effect Organizer help you understand details in a paragraph?" Then have the class read silently the information on this tool in the Reading Tools section of the handbook (page 407).

Lesson 2 Cause-Effect Order (continued)

For use with *Reader's Handbook* pages 136–137

Focus

Here students will continue their exploration of cause-effect ordering of details in a paragraph.

Getting Started

Before you begin, review what students have learned thus far about cause-effect order, or have a student summarize characteristics of a cause-effect paragraph. Compare the concept of cause and effect to that of a chain. Write the following events on strips of paper that are 1" by 4".

- ■ I was busy at work.
- ■ I did not have time for lunch.
- ■ I got hungry.
- ■ I ate some pretzels.
- ■ The salt made me thirsty.
- ■ I bought a soda.

Show how each event caused the next event. Then construct a paper chain to visually represent the chain. Have students try to come up with a list of events and causes on their own and make a chain.

Teaching Approach

Ask students to return to the Cause-Effect Organizer they created in the previous lesson and compare it to the organizer shown at the top of page 137 of the handbook.

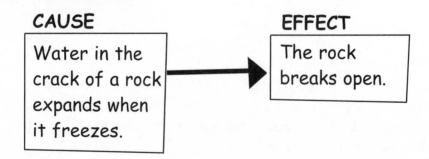

Finding Cause and Effect

Have students look back to the rock-and-ice paragraph to see if they can spot the original sentence reflected in the organizer.

Listing Effects

Next, discuss variations on the standard cause and effect relationship. Help students understand that sometimes a single cause can result in numerous effects, or there can be several effects from a single cause. For an example, draw a Cause-Effect Organizer on the board. Then write *hurricane* in the "cause" section. Brainstorm with students a list of possible effects of a hurricane. Here are some possible students' suggestions.

- property damage
- utility outages
- injury and loss of life
- flooding

Then have students read on their own the explanatory paragraph in the middle of page 137 and the modified Cause-Effect Organizer at the bottom of the page.

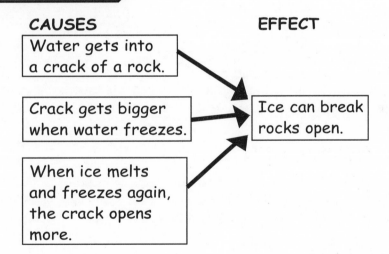

Cause-Effect Organizer

CAUSES → EFFECT

- Water gets into a crack of a rock.
- Crack gets bigger when water freezes.
- When ice melts and freezes again, the crack opens more.

→ Ice can break rocks open.

Wrap-up

Check to see if students understand what they learned by asking them to read this sample paragraph from a science textbook and make a Cause-Effect Organizer.

Snow and Sleet

When the temperature is below freezing, ice crystals form in and above the clouds and fall as snow. When the air warms, the ice crystals can melt and fall as rain. Sleet forms when ice crystals fall through a layer of warm air and melt. Then they pass through a layer of cold air and form into tiny beads of ice, which fall to the ground.

235

Lesson 3 ▸ Comparison-Contrast Order

For use with *Reader's Handbook* page 138

Focus

Here students will learn about comparison-contrast order paragraphs.

Getting Started

Hold up a long sleeve T-shirt with some printing on it. Have students list characteristics about the shirt on the board. Then hold up a short sleeve T-shirt with printing on it. Do the same thing. When both lists are done, review what was written. Circle any descriptions that are the same. Ask students to identify what reading skill they just used.

Direct students to the discussion of comparing and contrasting in the *Reader's Handbook* (pages 52–53) and display Overhead Transparency 5. Discuss how to make a comparison and ask students to brainstorm examples of comparison-contrast relationships.

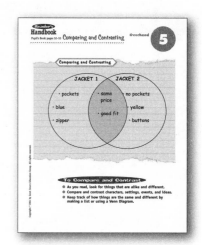

Teaching Approach

Ask student volunteers to name two things that can be compared. Create a Venn Diagram for the example. Work with students to fill in the diagram.

Introducing Comparison-Contrast Order

Explain that writers sometimes use comparison-contrast order to organize paragraphs, especially when they want to highlight the similarities and differences between two or more people, places, things, or ideas. Emphasize that comparing two or more things highlights the similarities and contrasting focuses on the differences.

Identifying Comparison-Contrast Order

Ask students to turn to page 138 of the handbook. Read aloud the paragraph at the top of the page. Then have students read the excerpt from *Ranger Rick*.

After they finish reading, discuss the paragraph as a class. Ask the following questions.

■ What is the topic of the paragraph? (*moths and butterflies*)

■ What is the main idea? (*Moths and butterflies have different characteristics.*)

■ What details does the writer give to support the main idea? (*information about their antennae and body types*)

■ What is being compared? (*how they look*)

Point out the Venn Diagram at the bottom of the page. Ask students to reproduce the diagram in their notebooks and then use it to sort the similarities and differences between moths and butterflies. If you like, ask students to use their prior knowledge of moths and butterflies when completing the organizer.

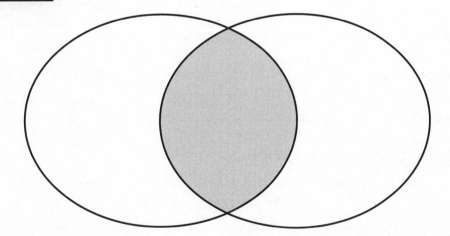

Venn Diagram

Wrap-up

Ask students to write short comparison-contrast paragraphs. Assign a topic, such as how two siblings or two friends are alike and different. Have them create a Venn Diagram at the prewriting stage and refer to it as they write their paragraphs. When students have finished, ask them to share their work with a partner.

Lesson 4 ▸ Comparison-Contrast Order (continued)

For use with *Reader's Handbook* pages 138–139

Focus

In this lesson, continue your discussion of comparison-contrast order. Then review the five types of paragraph organization students have learned about.

Getting Started

Ask students to recall what they know about signal words. Remind the class that authors use signal words to keep the reader oriented in the paragraph. On the board, post a list of signal words students can look for in a comparison-contrast paragraph. Include those shown in the box below.

Signal Words

Comparison		Contrast	
■ like	■ in the same way	■ but	■ although
■ as	■ likewise	■ however	■ different
■ also	■ similarly	■ otherwise	■ on the other hand
■ same		■ yet	■ even though

Teaching Approach

After your discussion of signal words, ask students to return to the Venn Diagrams they created on moths and butterflies. Then have them compare what they wrote to the completed diagram on page 139 in the handbook.

Discuss students' notes in the "both" area. Have them add additional similarities between moths and butterflies.

Wrap-up

Spend the final part of the lesson pulling together what students have learned about arranging details in a paragraph. List across the board the five ways of organizing paragraphs. Then hand out large pieces of paper with the numbered sentences from below written on them. Have students come up one at a time and sort them into the correct categories.

Time Order

1. Details are arranged in order in which they occurred.
2. Narrative writers use this type of arrangement.
3. Expect to see some or all of these signal words: *before, after, then, later, next, first, last.*

Location Order

4. Details are arranged according to place: from left to right, top to bottom, or in a circle.
5. This makes it easy to visualize what authors are describing.

List Order

6. Author gives details in no particular order.
7. The reader can easily remove details from the paragraph and create a list from them.
8. Use a Web to keep track of details in this type of paragraph.

Cause-Effect Order

9. This tells about cause and effect, or why something happens.
10. Use a Cause-Effect Organizer to keep track of details.

Comparison-Contrast Order

11. Comparing means showing how two things are alike; contrasting means showing how they are different.
12. Use a Venn Diagram for comparisons and contrasts.
13. Signal words include *like, as, also, likewise, but, however, different, although,* and *on the other hand.*

Lesson 5 ▸ Review and Assess

Check Point

Use the Quick Assess checklist to informally evaluate students' understanding of the two paragraph organizations discussed in the unit. Based on their answers, divide them into two groups. Have one group do the Independent Practice on the next page while the other group does the guided practice in the *Applications Book and Word Work.*

Quick Assess

Can students

☑ recognize cause-effect order paragraphs?

☑ explain what a comparison-contrast order paragraph is?

☑ identify words that signal a comparison-contrast relationship?

Guided Practice

For students who need reinforcement in understanding how paragraphs are organized, use pages 64–66 in the *Applications Book and Word Work.*

For students who need more word work, assign page 221 from the *Applications Book and Word Work* on diphthongs.

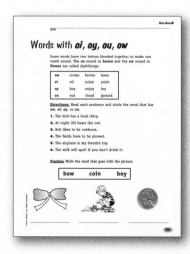

240

Independent Practice

Students who clearly understand the differences between the two paragraph organizations discussed can work in a group to find their own examples of cause-effect and comparison-contrast paragraphs. Ask groups to analyze the paragraphs they find using the tools discussed in the handbook.

▶ **Paragraph Organization** ◀

Organization Type	Tool
Cause-effect	Cause-Effect Organizer
Comparison-contrast	Venn Diagram

Class Review

Divide the class into two large groups. Have one group compare two objects in the classroom and write their ideas on a Venn Diagram. Ask the other group to mix two paint colors (such as blue and yellow) to create a third color. Then ask them to tell what happened on a Cause-Effect Organizer.

When groups have finished, have them trade jobs so that the comparison-contrast group gets to do the cause-effect experiment. Reserve five or ten minutes for a whole-class discussion of the organizers students created.

Test Book

Use the short-answer and multiple-choice tests on pages 42–43 to assess students' understanding of the material presented in this week's lessons.

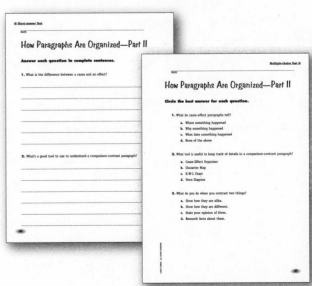

WEEK 19
Reading an Article

Goals

Here students read an article called "Bubble, Bubble, Spittlebug."
This week's lessons will help them learn to

- ☑ recognize the basic parts of an article
- ☑ use the reading strategy of summarizing
- ☑ find the subject and main idea of an article

Background

Help students connect this week's lessons to their prior knowledge
by asking them to

- ■ list places where articles can be found
- ■ talk about what readers can find in articles
- ■ compare articles with other types of text
- ■ discuss the purpose of articles
- ■ tell about articles they have read

Opening Activity

Show the students different places where articles are found, such
as a sports magazine, an Internet website, an encyclopedia, and
the sports page of a newspaper. Divide the class into four groups
and assign each group one of the sources. Give the class the topic
of *baseball*. Each group will search for information on baseball
using its assigned source. When the groups are done, students can
share the information they found.

Weekly Plan

Lessons	Summary
1. **Before Reading: Article**	Work with students as they apply the Before Reading stage of the reading process to reading an article.
2. **During Reading: Article**	Teach students to apply the strategy of summarizing as they read an article.
3. **During Reading: Article** (continued)	Help students to draw a conclusion and make connections as they read an article.
4. **After Reading: Article**	Enhance students' understanding of the After Reading stage of the reading process as they apply it to an article.
5. **Review and Assess**	Informally assess students to decide if more guided practice is needed. Then give an assessment.

Lesson Materials

	Components	Pages
Plan	*Teacher's Guide and Lesson Plans*	242–253
Teach	*Reader's Handbook* *Overhead Transparencies*	142–153 14, 15
Practice	*Applications Book and Word Work*	67–74, 222
Assess	*Test Book*	44–45

Lesson 1 Before Reading: Article

For use with *Reader's Handbook* pages 142–146

Focus

In this lesson, students focus on the Before Reading stage of the reading process as they prepare to read an article.

Getting Started

Gather magazine, newspaper, and encyclopedia articles that have strong visuals, headings, and graphics. Hold up each article and have students state what they think the article is about. Ask students what type of person they think would read each article and why they would read it. Make sure students understand that articles give information on specific topics.

Teaching Approach

Begin by asking students to name the three Before Reading steps. Ask volunteers to discuss how these steps might be applied to reading an article.

A Set a Purpose

Before they read, students need to set a purpose for reading "Bubble, Bubble, Spittlebug." Look at Set a Purpose on page 143 in the *Reader's Handbook*. Ask students if they can answer the questions listed on this page by looking only at the title. See what types of answers they can come up with on their own. Do they have any other questions after reading the title? Then guide them to form specific questions as their purpose for reading.

B Preview

Walk the students through the Preview Checklist on page 143. Show students what to preview with Overhead Transparencies 14 and 15. Using the Preview Checklist, point to where each item is on the overheads. Demonstrate how to use your finger to scan the page for boldface words.

Plan

As a group, read Plan on page 146. Have students add items they learned from the preview. Remind students to use the Preview Checklist to recall what they learned. Write their thoughts on chart paper.

Explain to students that they are almost ready to read the article, but they need to make a plan that will help them fulfill their purpose for reading. To answer their purpose questions with an article, the best reading strategy to use is summarizing. Explain that summarizing will help them focus on the most important information, as opposed to every detail.

Introduce the 5 W's and H Organizer. Tell students that this reading tool will help them focus on important information. When they read the article, they are to look for information to fill the boxes.

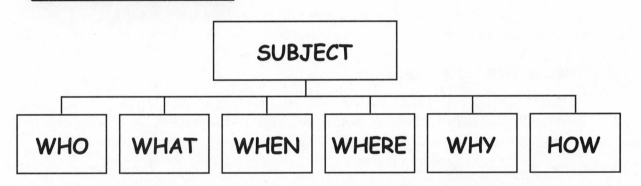

At this point, show students how to take notes in their Reading Notebooks. First, have them write their reading purpose questions. Then have students draw a blank 5 W's and H Organizer like the one above. Tell students they will keep track of the information they learn about spittlebugs by writing the key details in the boxes of their organizers.

Wrap-up

Ask students to share their reading purpose questions and the facts they learned in their previews. Then ask students to show a reading partner how they have set up their Reading Notebooks. Ask students to check their partners' notebooks to see that they have

1. Reading purpose questions

2. 5 W's and H Organizer

Lesson 2 During Reading: Article

For use with *Reader's Handbook* pages 146–149

Focus

Here students will learn how to use the reading strategy of summarizing as they read an article. Students will develop their skills of finding the subject and what the author says about it.

Getting Started

On a large piece of chart paper, set up a blank 5 W's and H Organizer. Choose a topic from social studies class and walk students through the process of filling out the organizer. Then allow students to pick their own topic, such as a sport they play, and ask them to fill out their own 5 W's and H Organizer.

Teaching Approach

Begin by guiding students to see that the two steps of the During Reading stage of the reading process can help them get more from reading an article.

D Read with a Purpose

Remind students of their purpose for reading this article. Students should be ready with their own notebooks and a blank 5 W's and H Organizer.

1. Find the Subject

Use the "Finding the Subject" graphic on page 147 and Overhead Transparencies 14 and 15 to figure out the subject. Help them come to the conclusion that the subject is the spittlebug. Write this word in the center of the organizer.

2. Read and Complete a 5 W's and H Organizer

Now students want to find out what the author says about spittlebugs. By using the 5 W's and H Organizer, you can cover all of the key facts about these insects. Read through the article as a class one paragraph at a time, and ask if any of the 5 W's or H questions are answered. Fill in the organizer as you go.

5 W's and H Organizer

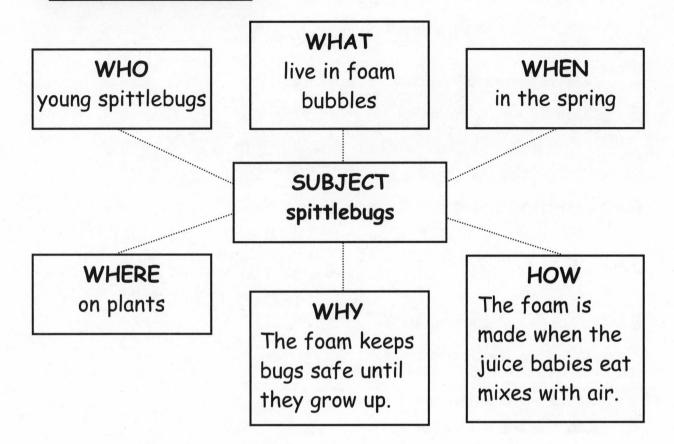

	WHAT live in foam bubbles	
WHO young spittlebugs		WHEN in the spring
	SUBJECT spittlebugs	
WHERE on plants	WHY The foam keeps bugs safe until they grow up.	HOW The foam is made when the juice babies eat mixes with air.

On chart paper, model for students how to complete the organizer. Emphasize that the organizer helps them find what's important in the article and ignore the smaller details. Tell students that using a tool such as a 5 W's and H Organizer can help them better understand what they read.

Wrap-up

Help students see that not all organizers are alike. Different students will understand different things from the article. Show this by having students take the subject of *school* and encouraging them to fill out a 5 W's and H Organizer. Point out that the organizers have many of the same details, but many are different too.

Lesson 3 During Reading: Article (continued)

For use with *Reader's Handbook* pages 149–150

Focus

In this lesson, students will learn how to draw a conclusion and make connections as they read an article.

Getting Started

List on the board all of the things that the students have learned about spittlebugs. Refer to the 5 W's and H Organizer to spark their thoughts. Tell the students that, when they read, they collect a lot of information. They learn all kinds of details about a subject, but they need to draw a conclusion about what was read.

Teaching Approach

D Read with a Purpose (continued)

1. Review

Talk through the steps of the reading process that students have completed. Remind students of their reading purpose when they started reading. Then have students tell you how to make and fill in the graphic organizer from the day before.

2. Draw Conclusions

Tell students that in order to draw a conclusion, they must come up with the main idea of the article. Write the information from the organizer and put it on separate cards. Hold up the subject card (spittlebugs) and tell the students that they can draw a conclusion about the main idea from all of the details. Ask students what conclusions they came to after looking at all of the details in the 5 W's and H Organizer.

Connect

After students have the main idea of the article, explain that it is time to make personal connections. As you read through page 150 of the *Reader's Handbook,* point out the sticky notes. Then have students flip back to the article in their books. In their notebooks have them set up a page with four columns with the following headings: How do I feel about this subject? What do I think about this? How or why is this important to me? and Have I seen or read something like this before? Ask students to read the article in pairs while thinking about these questions. They will fill in their answers as they go.

> Do the bugs ever try to leave before you cover them up?

> Is the white stuff on the tree by my garage this foam?

Wrap-up

 Give two sticky notes to each student. Have them read through the article about spittlebugs and make two more notes on their personal connections. Put all of the sticky notes on the board and go through them with the class. Work on categorizing them into different types of connections. Emphasize that all have value as personal reactions.

Lesson 4 After Reading: Article

For use with *Reader's Handbook* pages 151–153

Focus

In this lesson, students will learn about using the After Reading stage of the reading process with an article.

Getting Started

Ask students what they normally do when they finish reading a book or article. Most of the time, once readers finish the last word of a reading, they probably go on to something else. Explain to students that the moment they "finish" reading is the time they need to look back and reflect on what they read.

Teaching Approach

F Pause and Reflect

This is when readers look back at their original purpose for reading and self-monitor their understanding. Have students return to their reading purpose questions. Ask

■ Can I list three to four facts I learned?

■ Can I tell the main idea in my own words?

■ Are there parts I don't understand?

Point out that, after reading, readers often develop new questions that they want to find out about. For example, students may wonder how the foam helps spittlebugs or where they might find spittlebugs. By thinking back on the reading, new questions and new reasons for reading the article emerge. Then, by rereading even parts of the article, readers can deepen and extend their understanding.

G Reread

Help students see that readers don't always learn everything from a single reading. Good readers "fix up" their understanding by going back and rereading parts of the selection again.

Model the process of rereading by trying to answer the questions on page 151. Then read through the paragraph on page 152 where the answer to Question 1 can be found.

Reread (continued)

When rereading, encourage students to take a fresh look at the selection and use a different reading tool. One useful tool to help in rereading an article is a Main Idea Organizer. Demonstrate to students how to decide which details go in the organizer. Post large cards with the three details in the organizer and three details from the article that are not relevant. Point out the common words in the details and the main idea. This clearly shows students why some pieces of information are in the organizer and some are not.

Main Idea Organizer

MAIN IDEA: Young spittlebugs make foam homes that keep them safe.		
DETAIL	DETAIL	DETAIL
The foam is made from extra plant juices.	The foam protects their bodies.	Most animals keep away from the foam.

 Remember

In order to remember information, students need to make it their own. By sharing what they learned with a partner or writing some notes in their Reading Notebooks, students will have a better chance of remembering what they have read.

Have students get with a partner. Student A in each pair will talk about spittlebugs for one minute. Student B will listen. Then have student B talk for 30 seconds about spittlebugs without repeating anything student A already said. At the end of this 30 seconds, have students write down the main things that they said.

Wrap-up

 Review with students the three steps of the After Reading stage (Pause and Reflect, Reread, and Remember). Have three students or groups of students explain each of the steps to the rest of the class.

Lesson 5 Review and Assess

Check Point

Use the Quick Assess checklist to informally evaluate students' understanding of how to read an article. Based on their answers, divide them into two groups. One group can do the Independent Practice on the next page, and the other group can do the guided practice in the *Applications Book and Word Work*.

Guided Practice

For students who need reinforcement on reading articles, use pages 67–74 in the *Applications Book and Word Work*.

For students who need more word work, assign page 222 from the *Applications Book and Word Work* on beginning consonant clusters.

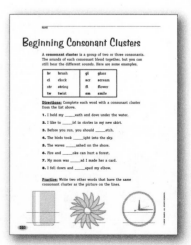

Independent Practice

Have students who demonstrate a strong understanding of the reading process and strategy apply their knowledge of reading to another article. Good choices are those in the magazine *Ranger Rick, National Geographic for Kids,* and *Boys' Life*.

Then ask students to do the following:

■ Write a reading purpose question for the article.

■ Create a 5 W's and H Organizer or a Main Idea Organizer for the article.

Class Review

Put the students in groups of three. Give a "treasure hunt" list to each group. Ask questions such as:

■ What are two things you need to preview in an article?

■ Where do you look to find the subject of an article?

■ What are three reading tools you can use with articles?

Make the questions easy but specific enough that they will have to return to the handbook to find the answers. The questions on the multiple-choice quiz in the *Test Book* can be adapted to make questions.

Test Book

Use the short-answer and multiple-choice tests on pages 44–45 to assess students' understanding of the material presented in this week's lessons.

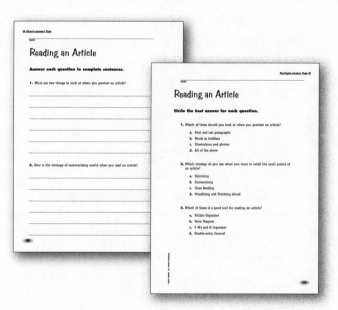

WEEK 20
Reading a Biography

Goals

Here students read an excerpt from a biography of Benjamin Franklin and consider the characteristics of this literary genre. This week's lessons will help students learn to

- ☑ read a biography for key events and details
- ☑ use the reading strategy of note-taking
- ☑ recognize the basic topics in a biography

Background

Help students make a connection between the lesson and what they already know about biographies by asking them to

- ▮ brainstorm characteristics of biographies
- ▮ talk about why people read biographies
- ▮ compare biographies with other types of nonfiction texts
- ▮ discuss biographies they've read in the past or would like to read

Opening Activity

Open the lesson by asking students to imagine they are going to write their own biographies. Have them take out a sheet of paper and then list topics and events they'd want to include when writing their own life stories. When they finish, ask students to volunteer to read aloud their lists. Use the activity to help students understand that most biographies have certain key topics in common, including birth, family, school, work, friends, and so on.

Weekly Plan

Lessons	Summary
1. **Before Reading: Biography**	Work with students as they apply the Before Reading stage of the reading process to a biography.
2. **During Reading: Biography**	Help students learn to apply the reading strategy of note-taking as they read for key events and details.
3. **During Reading: Biography** (continued)	Work with students as they draw conclusions about a biography and forge a connection between the text and their own lives.
4. **After Reading: Biography**	Enhance students' understanding of the After Reading stage of the reading process as they apply it to a biography.
5. **Review and Assess**	Informally assess students' understanding of reading biographies. Finish by giving an assessment.

Lesson Materials

	Components	Pages
Plan	*Teacher's Guide and Lesson Plans*	254–265
Teach	*Reader's Handbook*	154–165
	Overhead Transparencies	16, 17
Practice	*Applications Book and Word Work*	75–82, 223
Assess	*Test Book*	46–47

Lesson 1 Before Reading: Biography

For use with Reader's Handbook pages 154–158

Focus

In this lesson, you'll work with students as they apply the Before Reading stage of the reading process to a biography.

Getting Started

Create a biography corner in your classroom or in the library during one of your visits. Include high-interest biographies of sports stars, celebrities, and famous children. Hand out a biography to each student. Allow them to thumb through the book and write one thing they notice about the work on an index card that stays with the book. Have students pass the book to another student when finished. Allow time for students to look through three to five books. As a class, discuss characteristics of the genre.

Teaching Approach

Help students understand that a biography tells the life story of a real person.

A Set a Purpose

Discuss possible purposes for reading a biography. Then read aloud the information on page 155. Point out the boldface purpose questions. Finish by asking students to jot down their own purpose for reading the Benjamin Franklin biography.

B Preview

Ask students to read silently the Preview Checklist on page 155. Use Overhead Transparencies 16 and 17 to review the items on the checklist. Demonstrate how to skim for key dates and names. Invite students to preview *Benjamin Franklin* on their own.

 **Plan**

Have volunteers take turns reading aloud "Plan" on page 158. Ask students, "What did you learn from your preview of the Table of Contents? What did you learn from your preview of the front and back covers?" Make a list of students' observations on the board.

Explain to students that their next step is to devise a plan that will help them find the information they need while reading a biography. Point out that the best reading strategy to use with this type of literature often is note-taking. In this case, note-taking means writing down facts and details that seem important. Teach students how to use Key Word Notes as support for the strategy.

Key Word Notes

KEY WORDS	NOTES

Direct students' attention to the bottom of page 158. Have them reproduce in their Reading Notebooks the organizer shown. Explain that Key Word Notes helps readers keep track of key details from the reading. In a biography, the left column will include such key topics as *family and friends, school, jobs, major difficulties,* and *achievements.* Taking notes on these topics as they read will help students discover what the person was really like.

Wrap-up

Bring students together to share their reading purpose questions and the information they gleaned from their previews. Double-check that students have recorded the following in their Reading Notebooks.

■ reading purpose questions

■ Key Word Notes

Lesson 2 During Reading: Biography

For use with *Reader's Handbook* pages 158–161

Focus

Here students will learn to apply the reading strategy of note-taking as they read for key events in a biography.

Getting Started

 Set up a Key Word Notes organizer and ask the students to use what they learned in the last lesson to fill in the left column for a biography. This column will include *family and friends, school, hobbies, major difficulties,* and *achievements.* Have students complete the organizer for themselves. When they finish, ask them if they think a category was missing.

Teaching Approach

Read aloud the text on page 159 and then remind students that using Key Word Notes will help them keep track of the key topics.

D Read with a Purpose

Help students understand that reading with a purpose means that they read looking for something. They are looking for information. Like a detective searching for clues, they as readers are searching for answers to their reading purpose questions.

1. Find the Key Topics

First, have students read the excerpt on pages 159–160. Have them list in their notebooks the key topics they find in the reading. These might include family, school, and jobs. Then list students' suggestions for key topics on the organizer on the board.

Key Word Notes

KEY WORDS	NOTES
Family and school	• Father made him leave school at age ten.
Jobs	• First job was in his father's shop. • Later, he owned his own print shop.

2. Find Details about the Person

Next, ask students to read the supporting text on page 161. Explain that one of their purposes is to figure out what the subject of the biography is really like. To do this, they must search for details about his or her personality, likes and dislikes, interactions with others, and so on. Have students continue reading from the biography. Ask them to continue adding to their Key Word Notes about Franklin's personality.

Wrap-up

Ask students to share with a reading partner the notes they made. Once again, point out that no two readers will take exactly the same notes. Different readers will understand different details from the same text.

Then record students' ideas on the organizer on the board. Eliminate key topics that are not supported by details from the selection.

Lesson 3 During Reading: Biography (continued)

For use with *Reader's Handbook* pages 162–163

Focus

In this lesson, students will draw conclusions about a biographical subject and connect what they've read with their own lives and experiences.

Getting Started

As a lesson opener, have students choose some of the key events from the Key Word Notes they made about themselves. Explain that they need to make a Web for each event and write details.

Teaching Approach

 Read with a Purpose (continued)

Begin the lesson by asking students to turn to page 162. Have volunteers read aloud the text at the top of page.

1. Look for Cause and Effect

Explain that good readers think about the events in a person's life that shaped his or her personality. Thinking in terms of cause and effect can help. Then discuss the organizer at the bottom of the page. Have students create a similar organizer in their notebooks.

▶ Cause-Effect Organizer ▶

CAUSE	EFFECT
sorry he bought a whistle	→ made him careful with money

2. Draw Conclusions

Have students draw some initial conclusions about Benjamin Franklin. Ask students, "What have you learned about Benjamin Franklin thus far? What were some important events in his life? How did these events affect his personality?" Use the activity as a warm-up to the Connect step of the reading process.

 **Connect**

After students finish drawing conclusions about Ben Franklin, explain that you'd like them to consider their overall impression of the man. Point out that making a personal connection to the text can help them form their impressions. Invite students to record their responses to the following questions.

■ How do I feel about Benjamin Franklin?

■ Does he remind me of anyone?

■ Have I experienced any of the same things in my life?

Then direct students' attention to page 163. Read aloud the excerpt from the selection and the comment one student made while reading. Have students note their own ideas about Franklin and whether or not they'd like to learn more about him.

> I really like him.
> He knew a lot of
> different things.

Wrap-up

 Divide the class into small groups. Ask one student to act as group secretary. Then invite students to discuss their opinions of biography. Remind the class that, for their opinions to be meaningful, they must be substantiated with facts and details. Encourage students to respond by answering, "I think biographies are _____ because 1) _____ and also because 2) _____." Then share each group's comments with the class as a whole.

Lesson 4 After Reading: Biography

For use with *Reader's Handbook* pages 164–165

Focus

In this lesson, students will learn about the After Reading stage of the reading process and how to use it effectively with a biography.

Getting Started

Invite those who have visited the library corner to share their impressions of the books. Ask, "What would you say is the hardest part of reading a biography? What is the easiest part?" Keep students' comments in mind as you work your way through this lesson.

Teaching Approach

Review the steps of the After Reading stage of the reading process. Ask how these steps might be used with a biography.

F Pause and Reflect

Ask a volunteer to explain the Pause and Reflect step of the reading process. Then have students turn back to their original purpose for reading. Ask students the following questions:

■ Have you found out what kind of life Benjamin Franklin had?

■ Do you now have a clear idea of what he was really like?

G Reread

Remind students that nonfiction usually requires at least two readings because the material may be dense. Ask the class to imagine that they want to find out more about Franklin's interest in science. Explain that they would have to flip through the book looking for information that helps them understand Franklin's science experiments.

Next, ask them to read and take notes on the excerpt at the bottom of page 164. When they finish, have them add their notes to their Key Word Notes. Invite volunteers to share their work.

H Remember

Explain that very often organizing their notes with a different kind of reading tool can help students further process what they've learned. Then ask students to thumb through the Reading Tools section (pages 406–426). Ask them if they can find a tool that will help them keep track of events in Franklin's life.

Guide students to the Timeline. Point out the Timeline in the middle of page 165 and have students summarize the information it contains.

Timeline

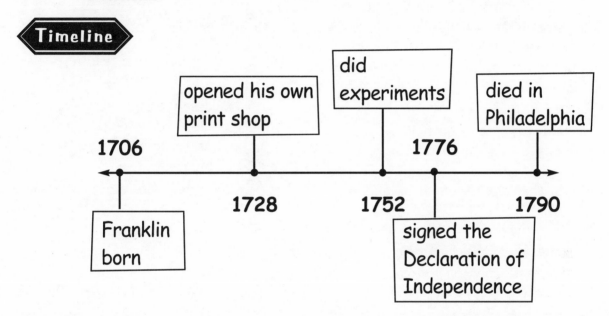

Wrap-up

Finish the lesson by reading aloud Summing Up on page 165. Remind the class of the importance of thinking about the events that shaped the person's life and what he or she was really like. Then review the reading tools that work well with the genre. Give students time to make a Timeline of their life. Have them include five to six important events.

Lesson 5 Review and Assess

Check Point

Use the Quick Assess checklist to informally evaluate students' understanding of how to read a biography. Based on their answers, have students who are proficient do the Independent Practice on the next page. Struggling readers can do the guided practice in the *Applications Book and Word Work*.

Guided Practice

For students who need reinforcement in reading biographies, use pages 75–82 in the *Applications Book and Word Work*.

Quick Assess

Can students

- ☑ explain what a biography is?
- ☑ tell how to preview a biography?
- ☑ explain why looking for cause and effect is helpful when reading a biography?
- ☑ describe and use several kinds of notes that are useful for reading a biography?

APPLICATIONS BOOK AND WORD WORK

Reader's Handbook
A Student Guide for Reading and Learning

GREAT SOURCE

Reading a Biography

Biographies tell the stories of real people and their amazing lives.

Before Reading

Use the reading process and the strategy of note-taking to help you keep track of important information about the subject of a biography.

A Set a Purpose

Your purpose for reading a biography is to learn about the person's life and what he or she was or is really like. Here you will read about Helen Keller. Do you already know about her?

➤ To set your purpose, ask yourself questions about the subject of the biography.

Directions: Ask two questions about a biography called *Helen Keller.*

Purpose question #1: _____

Purpose question #2: _____

Ending Consonant Clusters

The word *sky* and *stop* have consonant clusters at the start of the word. Some words have clusters at the end of them.
Directions: In the words below, circle the consonant cluster at the end of each word.

| rust | kept | vent | list | clasp |
| bend | lift | act | quilt | husk |

Practice: Look at the word list below. Then sort them into the correct group. Some words go in both groups.

| spray | bent | swift | spring |
| spent | stripe | lent | desk |

Beginning Cluster — Ending Cluster

Write 3 words fall into both groups? Write those on the line below.

For students who need more word work, assign page 223 from the *Applications Book and Word Work* on ending consonant clusters.

Independent Practice

Ask students who have demonstrated a strong understanding of the reading process and reading strategy to use what they've learned with a short biography from the library.

After they've chosen the selection they'd like to use, ask students to

■ write reading purpose questions they can use with the text

■ make a set of Key Word Notes that show their understanding of what they've read

If there is time, have students make a poster of their person. Have them cut out a hole for their face to stick through. Ask the students to prepare a short speech in first person that summarizes the Key Word Notes. They can give the speech while holding up the poster with their head in the opening.

Class Review

Divide the class into pairs. Ask students to work together to write three or more questions on the topic of reading a biography. Then have one pair "interview" another pair using the questions they've prepared beforehand. Questions that will work well with the activity include the following.

■ What is a biography?

■ What are some key topics you'd expect to see in a biography?

■ What reading tools work well with this type of text?

Test Book

Use the short-answer and multiple-choice tests on pages 46–47 to assess students' understanding of reading a biography.

Information Books and Encyclopedias

Goals

Here students learn how to read and respond to information texts. This week's lessons will teach them to

- ☑ understand their purpose for reading an informational text
- ☑ read an information book for key details
- ☑ take notes on what they learn
- ☑ find information in an encyclopedia

Background

Help students connect this week's lessons to their prior knowledge by asking them to

- ■ list the types of information books they've used in the past
- ■ discuss challenging aspects of reading for information
- ■ discuss how to choose good information books
- ■ tell when they've used an encyclopedia

Opening Activity

Arrange with your school librarian to give students a tour of the library. Ask students to bring their Reading Notebooks with them so they can take notes on what they learn. Have them note in particular the location of the following.

- ■ encyclopedias
- ■ dictionaries
- ■ thesauruses
- ■ books about their state
- ■ books about history
- ■ books about science

Weekly Plan

Lessons	Summary
1. **Before Reading: Information Books**	Work with students as they apply the Before Reading stage of the reading process to an informational text.
2. **During Reading: Information Books**	Help students read an information book for key details.
3. **After Reading: Information Books**	Discuss various note-taking tools students can use with informational texts.
4. **Using an Encyclopedia**	Focus students' attention on the features of encyclopedias.
5. **Review and Assess**	Informally assess students to decide if more guided practice is needed. Then give an assessment.

Lesson Materials

	Components	Pages
Plan	*Teacher's Guide and Lesson Plans*	266–277
Teach	*Reader's Handbook* *Overhead Transparencies*	166–173, 194 18
Practice	*Applications Book and Word Work*	83–87, 224
Assess	*Test Book*	48–49

Lesson 1 Before Reading: Information Books

For use with *Reader's Handbook* pages 166–167

Focus

In this lesson, students focus on applying the Before Reading stage of the reading process to information books.

Getting Started

Have students imagine they've been assigned to make a presentation on the water cycle. Where would they go for information on the subject? Write their ideas on the board. Electronic sources may come up, but explain that later students will learn about reading a website. Here they'll learn about reading information books.

Teaching Approach

Repeated exposure to the steps in the reading process will help students internalize and apply it to their own reading practice. The *Reader's Handbook* shows students how to adapt the process to fit the needs of particular genres, including information books.

Understand Your Purpose

Point out to students the importance of knowing their purpose before they begin reading an information text. Hold up an information book. Show students how much information is contained between its covers. Ask them to imagine how lost they might be if they opened the book without really knowing what they were looking for.

Next, direct students to page 166 in the handbook. Tell the class that the best all-purpose strategy for reading an information book is usually note-taking. On the board write a sample research assignment or copy the assignment from page 167 of the handbook.

Animal Report Assignment

1. Describe what pandas look like.

2. Explain what pandas eat.

3. Tell where pandas live.

Choose Information Books

Think aloud the steps of the assignment and then explain how students might go about completing it. Ask, "What books would you look in for information on this topic?"

Next, show students the reading purpose questions listed in the middle of the page. Guide students to understand the types of reference books they would consult for facts and details about the topic. Point out the elements students should look at when previewing an information book.

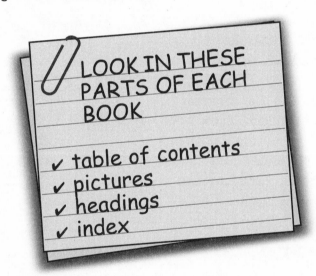

LOOK IN THESE
PARTS OF EACH
BOOK

✔ table of contents
✔ pictures
✔ headings
✔ index

Finish the lesson with a discussion of the strategy of note-taking. Direct students to the information on note-taking in the Strategy Handbook (pages 394–395). Remind the class that taking notes can help them understand and remember what they've read. Also point out that good readers take notes before, during, and after reading.

Wrap-up

Give each student a card with a general topic written on it (tigers, Egypt, snakes, states, and so on). Take the class to the library and ask them to write down five books (title and author) that will give information on the topic. List the titles on the back of the card.

Lesson 2 During Reading: Information Books

For use with *Reader's Handbook* pages 168–171

Focus

Work with students as they learn to read an information book for key details.

Getting Started

Have each student take an easy informational book on a topic they are interested in. Tell them to do a quick preview of it. Then have students make a poster showing what they learned about the topic in the preview. Allow students to share any new information they learned.

Show Overhead Transparency 18. Discuss what students should do as they look at an information piece. Lead a discussion on the process of extracting information from a reference book. Ask students, "What do you find most challenging about this type of reading? How can the strategy of note-taking help you?"

Teaching Approach

Tell students that note-taking is a skill they learn, like swimming or playing soccer. In this lesson, they will start learning more about the strategy of note-taking.

Look for Key Details

Remind students to keep their purpose in mind when reading an information book. Explain that their purpose questions will help them decide how much of the book to read.

Read the information under "Look for Key Details." Discuss the information students learn from the paragraph on pandas. Ask volunteers to name the most important details in the paragraph. Have the class look back at the questions on page 167 to see which of the details relates to their purpose for reading.

Take Notes

Discuss organizers students can use to keep track of their notes. Present several options and explain how they would work with information books. Begin with Summary Notes, which is shown on page 171.

Summary Notes

PANDAS

What They Look Like
   1. They weigh between 200 and
      300 pounds.
   2. When they stand on all four
      legs, they come up to my waist.

Explain that Summary Notes work well with information texts because students can use them to keep a running list of key details. Suggest that students use Summary Notes for their first set of notes on an information text. If they decide they need to find more information to meet their purpose, they can choose another tool such as a web. Tell students how well this organizer works with history, biography, and autobiography texts.

Wrap-up

Have students get together with a partner to read and take notes on pages 170–171. Ask, "Why is it important to remember your purpose when reading an information text? What should you do if you finish a reading but find that you still need more information about your topic?"

Lesson 3 After Reading: Information Books

For use with *Reader's Handbook* pages 172–173

Focus

Here students will review the steps of the After Reading stage of the reading process and consider how to apply them to an information book.

Getting Started

Read aloud a short nonfiction book on a basic topic they are familiar with. Tell students to sit and listen while you read. Then ask students to turn to a student next to them and have one talk for one minute about everything he or she can remember. When the student finishes, ask the student to talk about how he or she felt. Was it easy or hard for the student to keep talking? Then read the book a second time. Have the partners switch places and ask the new person to talk for 30 seconds. Again, discuss what was hard and what was easy. Now ask if the student thinks he or she knows more about the topic now then he or she did before. Guide them to understand that doing something with the material after they read it is important to understanding it.

Teaching Approach

Direct students to page 172. Explain that these four types of questions students should ask themselves when they finish reading an information text. Once again, have students return to the purpose questions on page 167. Ask, "How do the questions on page 172 relate to the questions on page 167?" Show students that one way of reflecting on a reading is to rephrase their original purpose questions.

Remind students of the value of the Reread stage of the reading process. Help them understand how to decide if they need to merely spot-reread (using the strategy of skimming) or if they need to reread a text in its entirety. Be sure students know that, in either case, they need to make additional notes about the topic. Present other reading tools that they might use for their notes. One reading tool that might also work well is a Key Word Notes organizer.

Key Word Notes

KEY WORDS	NOTES

Next, read aloud the information on how to keep track of different books while researching (page 172). Show students how to set up their note cards by drawing a blank note card on the board. Then direct them to look at the card at the bottom of page 172.

Title and Author List

Giant Pandas by Patricia A. Fink Martin
Giant Pandas: Gifts from China by Allan Fowler

Wrap-up

Ask students to read the "Summing Up" information on page 173. Have them copy in their Reading Notebooks the strategy and tools they should use with information books.

Then discuss what they found from their tour of the library. Ask them to reflect on what they've learned and then tell which books in the library could help them with which school subjects. Ask, "What books would you look at for information on a science topic? Which books would you look at for information on a historical event? What about for information about an author?"

Lesson 4 ▸ Using an Encyclopedia

For use with *Reader's Handbook* page 194

Focus

In this lesson, students will explore the features of an encyclopedia.

Getting Started

Distribute copies of your classroom encyclopedia for students to examine, or take students to the school library so that they can look at a set from the reference area. Have students preview the volume they have, paying particular attention to the parts of the book, the organization, and a typical page layout. Ask students to keep their own list of characteristics of encyclopedias.

Ask students to share the characteristics of an encyclopedia they found. Help them understand that encyclopedias are reference works that offer comprehensive information in all areas of knowledge. (You also might want to explain that some encyclopedias, such as an encyclopedia of games and puzzles, offer information on *specialized* areas of knowledge.)

Teaching Approach

Ask students to read silently the example from an encyclopedia on page 194. Call students' attention to key details in the entry and to elements of organization that are common to encyclopedia articles. Show students the *guide word,* or words at the top of every page. Then point out that articles are organized by *entry word.*

Parts of Encyclopedias

Explain that almost all encyclopedias contain illustrations, photos, maps, and other graphics. Encourage students to use these features to strengthen their understanding of the information presented. Once again, stress the importance of knowing your purpose ahead of time to prevent confusion and aimless leafing through the pages of the encyclopedia.

Using a Strategy

Next, have students complete Summary Notes for the sample encyclopedia article on tepees (page 194). Have them work alone or with a partner to list key details about tepees.

> ### Summary Notes

SUBJECT	Tepees
1.	
2.	
3.	

Using Electronic Media

If you have time, discuss with students how to use an on-line or CD-ROM encyclopedia. Discuss how to search an on-line encyclopedia and explain how to make the search as specific as possible. Be sure to point out that electronic encyclopedias will give a lot of possible articles to consider. Remind students to stick to their reading purpose.

Wrap-up

Encyclopedias have articles about people. Read or show an entry of a person the class has studied. Then tell students to design an encyclopedia page with an entry on themselves. Remind the class of the key features they should include. Bind all of the pages to make a class encyclopedia.

Lesson 5 | Review and Assess

Check Point

Use the Quick Assess checklist to informally evaluate students' understanding of how to read an information text. Based on their answers, divide them into two groups. One group can do the Independent Practice on the next page while the other group does the guided practice in the *Applications Book and Word Work*.

Guided Practice

For students who need reinforcement in reading information books and encyclopedias, use pages 83–87 in the *Applications Book and Word Work*.

Quick Assess

Can students

- ☑ identify the characteristics of information books?

- ☑ explain how to set a purpose for reading an information book?

- ☑ preview key parts of information books?

- ☑ discuss the strategy of note-taking and how to use it with information books?

- ☑ tell about the features of an encyclopedia?

For students who need more word work, assign page 224 from the *Applications Book and Word Work* on syllables.

Independent Practice

Ask those students who have demonstrated a strong understanding of how to read an information book to read and respond to an encyclopedia article you've chosen. Find an article that you feel will be of general interest and that seems to be on level for students' abilities. Then ask students to do the following.

■ Set their purpose for reading.

■ Take notes on key details in the article.

■ Summarize what they learned from reading the article.

Class Review

Divide the class into two or four teams. Have teams work together to brainstorm words that begin with each of the letters in the word *information*. Explain that each word they think of will earn them one point. Words that have to do with reading, writing, and researching will earn five points each. Decide in advance how much time students will have to complete the activity. When they finish, ask groups to read their words aloud while the class keeps score.

Test Book

Use the short-answer and multiple-choice tests on pages 48–49 to assess students' understanding of the material presented in this week's lessons.

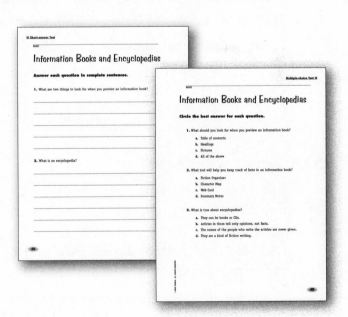

Websites and Graphics

Goals

Here students explore how to read a website, a bar graph, and a table. This week's lessons will help them learn to

☑ use the reading process with websites and graphics

☑ keep track of and evaluate the information they find on the Internet

☑ read bar graphs and tables

☑ draw conclusions about graphics

Background

Assess students' familiarity with the Internet and graphics as a source of information by asking them to

◼ define the terms *Internet* and *website*

◼ discuss the information available on the Internet

◼ think about the importance of evaluating the information they find on a website, graph, or table

◼ explain what a bar graph and a table are

Opening Activity

Open the lesson by asking students to reflect silently on the question, "What is the most interesting animal in the world?" Have them write the name of the animal at the top of a page in their Reading Notebooks. Take a poll of the class's answers and construct a rough bar graph of the data.

Then ask students to tell what they know about the animal's habits and habitats. Encourage them to list as many characteristics as they can think of, but explain that it is also okay to write "I don't know anything about this animal" in their notebooks. When students have finished, explain that one of their goals for this week is to find out what they can about their animal by using websites and then to present the information in some sort of graphic.

Weekly Plan

Lessons	Summary
1. **Reading a Website**	Work with students as they apply the Before Reading stage of the reading process to a website.
2. **Reading a Website** (continued)	Discuss with students methods for staying on track and writing notes while reading a website.
3. **Reading Bar Graphs**	Explore with students the importance of evaluating the information they find in bar graphs.
4. **Reading Tables**	Work with students as they learn to draw conclusions from tables.
5. **Review and Assess**	Informally assess students to decide if more guided practice is needed with a websites or graphics. Then give an assessment.

Lesson Materials

	Components	Pages
Plan	*Teacher's Guide and Lesson Plans*	278–289
Teach	*Reader's Handbook*	174–187
	Overhead Transparencies	19, 20
Practice	*Applications Book and Word Work*	88–95, 225
Assess	*Test Book*	50–51

Lesson 1 Reading a Website

For use with *Reader's Handbook* pages 174–176

Focus

In this lesson, you'll work with students as they apply the Before Reading stage of the reading process to a website.

Getting Started

Before students go on the computers, they need to have an understanding of the vocabulary. List the following terms on the board: *Internet, website, home page,* and *link.* Assign groups of students one term. Refer them to pages 204–205 in the handbook and help them come up with a definition for each term. Have students divide a blank paper into four sections. In each section they should illustrate the term and explain its meaning.

Teaching Approach

Begin by reviewing the three steps of the Before Reading stage of the reading process: Set a Purpose, Preview, and Plan.

Have a Clear Purpose

Explain to students that, when using the Internet for research, their general purpose will be to find information on a topic. Point out the diagram on page 175. Explain the importance of making your reading purpose as specific as possible. As a class, brainstorm some purpose questions for a variety of animals. Push the students to dig deep and to fine-tune their questions.

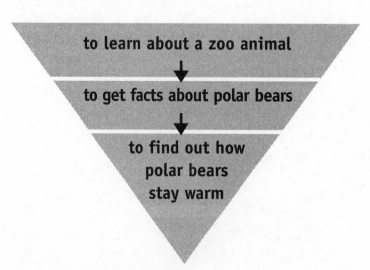

to learn about a zoo animal

↓

to get facts about polar bears

↓

to find out how
polar bears
stay warm

Preview the Website

Next, ask students to read the Preview text on page 176. Discuss the benefits of previewing a site before they begin reading, and then show students Overhead Transparency 19 to reinforce the teaching.

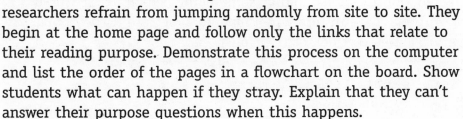

Follow the Links

Discuss the importance of planning ahead when doing research on the Internet. Point out that making a plan first can prevent students from "over-clicking" on a site. Remind students that good website researchers refrain from jumping randomly from site to site. They begin at the home page and follow only the links that relate to their reading purpose. Demonstrate this process on the computer and list the order of the pages in a flowchart on the board. Show students what can happen if they stray. Explain that they can't answer their purpose questions when this happens.

Stay on Track

Read aloud the text under the head "Stay on Track." Explain that students' first step should be to peruse the home page to find information that meets their purpose. Tell students to ignore any information that does not relate to their purpose. Students should decide which is the best link to follow from the home page and then go from there. Each time they reach a new Web page, students should stop and scan for information that meets their purpose.

Wrap-up

Ask students to return to the animal they chose in the opening activity. Then direct students to a zoo or wildlife website you've chosen beforehand. Have them set a purpose, preview, and plan how to read the site. Look at their purpose questions before they begin on the Internet. Remind students that they'll use their organizers for their during-reading notes.

Lesson 2 Reading a Website (continued)

For use with *Reader's Handbook* pages 177–180

Focus

Here students will learn how to stay on track and make notes while reading a website.

Getting Started

Distribute a copy of a maze for students to complete. (Check out www.clickmazes.com for simple mazes.) Hold a discussion about any problems they encountered. Most likely they will say they got distracted and hit a dead end at some point. Explain that this is a problem they may run into when reading a website if they don't pay attention and keep track of their purpose.

Teaching Approach

Begin the lesson by reading aloud page 177 in the handbook with students. Discuss the importance of paying attention to both a website's words and graphics.

Write Notes

After you finish your discussion on staying on track while reading a website, move on to the importance of noting key details.

Direct students' attention to page 178. Read aloud the text at the top of the page. Discuss. Then ask students to read carefully the Web page shown here and make their own set of Summary Notes on how polar bears stay warm.

Evaluate a Website

It's the user's responsibility to evaluate what he or she finds. Following is a list of questions to ask when evaluating a website. Modify the questions as needed to help your more reluctant readers and to find a site you will evaluate as a class.

Evaluating a Website

■ Is there a recognizable source named for the website?

■ Is the purpose of the site to sell something?

■ Is the information out-of-date?

Use the questions you ask as a class and make "warning flags" to hang near the classroom computers. These will serve as reminders when students use the Internet for future research.

Take Notes

Next, direct students' attention to page 179. Ask them to read silently the explanation at the top of the page. Then discuss the purpose of a Website Card and how it can help student evaluate various sites on the Internet.

After Reading

Request that students open their handbooks to page 180 and begin reading. Have them pause after reading the introduction in order to discuss what they've learned. Review the process of pausing to reflect on their original purpose for reading. Explain how important it is for students to decide if they've found all the information they need *before* they begin linking to other sites.

Wrap-up

This is an opportunity for students to finish their research on their own animal. Ask them to find where the animal lives, what it likes to eat, its color, and whether it is dangerous to human beings. Tell them the class will be putting this information together in a large table in Lesson 4.

⬬ Lesson 3 ⬭ Reading Bar Graphs

For use with *Reader's Handbook* pages 181–183

Focus

In this lesson, students will learn how to read bar graphs using a four-step plan.

Getting Started

Give each student a multiple-choice question or a question that has a set number of possible answers that they can ask everyone in the class. Examples include "Which of the following is your favorite vegetable: lettuce, cucumber, carrot, or pepper?" or "What is your favorite day of the week?" Have students answer the question for each student in the class. Tell students to hold on to their data.

Teaching Approach

Explain to students that graphics are often made of up numbers, pictures, and words. All of these elements are equally important for understanding the information in the graphic.

Read aloud the top of page 182. Make sure students understand what the word *compare* means. Tell them that bar graphs compare solid data that two of more things have in common. In the mammal graph their average weight is the solid data being compared. You cannot compare the color of jackets and present it in a bar graph, but you can compare the prices of the jackets and put the information in the bar graph.

Ask students to preview the bar graph. Use Overhead Transparency 20. Ask what they think are the most important pieces of the bar graph.

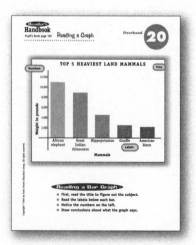

How to Read a Bar Graph

Follow these steps when reading a bar graph.

1. Read the title. What is the subject of the graph?

2. Read the labels below each bar.

3. Notice the numbers on the left.

4. Draw conclusions about what the graph says.

Tell students that the steps on page 183 are extremely important to follow when reading a bar graph. If they skip over a part, it is possible that they will miss key information that will help them draw a conclusion about it later.

Ask a few questions that can be answered by looking at the bar graph.

◼ Which animal weighs the least?

◼ About how much does a giraffe weigh?

Then allow students to come up with their own questions about the graph. Have them trade questions with a partner to see if they can answer the other's questions.

Wrap-up

Have students take their data from the Getting Started activity and make their own bar graph to present the data. Have them make up five questions that can be answered by looking at the graph. Attach these to the bottom and let students practice with bar graphs by answering the questions.

Lesson 4 Reading Tables

For use with *Reader's Handbook* pages 184–187

Focus

In this lesson, students will further their understanding of reading graphics. Their focus will be on reading a table.

Getting Started

Take a table from another source, such as a social studies or science textbook. Make sure the subject is something that they are familiar with. Cut it up into individual squares. Have students try to put it into some order that makes sense. Explain that in this lesson they will learn about a graphic that organizes information in an easy-to-read manner.

Teaching Approach

Explain that a table contains information in a format with columns and rows. It is able to show a number of facts about two or more subjects.

Read a Table

Point out the table of page 184 of the handbook. Allow students some time to look at it and try to come up with some thoughts about it. Hold a brief discussion on how they would preview the table.

Explain that there are steps to follow when reading a table. It may look overwhelming, but it can be broken down into bits of information so that it is more manageable to read. Ask students a variety of questions that can be answered by using the graph. Have students put their finger on the square with the answer. This will give them practice looking for information on a table.

Draw Conclusions

Explain that once you understand the information in a graphic and how it is organized, you can come up with conclusions about the information. Read aloud the top of page 186. Pull down a United States map so they can see where the five largest states are located.

Discuss questions that can help students draw conclusions and then point out the conclusion that one student came up with about Alaska. Direct students back to the bar graph on page 182. Ask students to discuss in pairs the questions located below and have them come up with their own conclusion about the bar graph.

◀ **How to Draw Conclusions** ▶

These questions can help you draw conclusions about a graphic. Make some notes in your notebook.

What similarities and differences do you see?

What is being compared?

Are there any unusual or surprising facts?

Have students share their conclusions of the bar graph. Point out that many students may have different thoughts. This is okay. Reinforce this by reading the top of page 187.

At the end of the lesson, have volunteers read aloud the Summing Up text at the bottom of page 187. Reiterate the importance of knowing what information is being presented in a graphic and understanding how it is organized. The words, numbers, and pictures in graphics are all equally important.

Wrap-up

In lesson 2, students were asked to come up with information on topics about their animal by researching on a website. Divide students into groups of four or five and have them compile all of their information into one table.

Lesson 5 Review and Assess

Check Point

Use the Quick Assess checklist to informally evaluate students' understanding of how to read a website and graphics. Based on their answers, divide them into two groups. One group can do the Independent Practice with new websites and graphics of their choosing and the other group can do the guided practice in the *Applications Book and Word Work*.

Guided Practice

For students who need reinforcement in reading a website, bar graph, and table, use pages 88–95 in the *Applications Book and Word Work*.

Quick Assess

Can students

☑ use the reading process with websites and graphics?

☑ explain why they should have a clear purpose in mind when reading a website?

☑ discuss why it is important to evaluate a website?

☑ describe the steps to read a bar graph and a table?

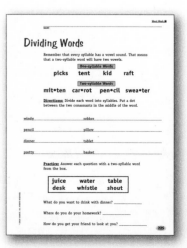

For students who need more word work, assign page 225 from the *Applications Book and Word Work* on dividing words.

Independent Practice

Ask students who seem comfortable using the reading process with a website and graphics to visit an educational website on their own and apply what they've learned. Direct students to a local or state government website and graphics or the website "for your school district. Work with students to establish a purpose for their reading and then have them begin researching.

Check that students are able to:

■ Write Summary Notes that reflect the information on the site.

■ Evaluate what they've seen by filling out a Website Card that they've created on their own.

Class Review

Ask those students who have trouble reading a website to join you at the computer. Go to the San Diego Zoo website or another zoo site of your choice. Then walk students through the site, pointing out which items would meet their original reading purpose. Continue discussing the site until students are familiar with its contents. Then work together to complete Summary Notes that reflect the information presented.

Test Book

Use the short-answer and multiple-choice tests on pages 50–51 to assess students' understanding of the material presented in this week's lessons.

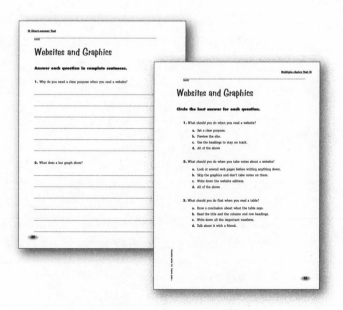

Elements of Nonfiction and Textbooks

Goals

There are many elements in these two sections. These lessons focus on just a few elements of nonfiction texts and school textbooks. During the week, you'll work with students to

☑ read and understand line graphs and circle graphs

☑ get meaning from diagrams and maps

☑ distinguish between fact and opinion

☑ use a glossary and index

Background

Help students connect to their prior knowledge by asking them to categorize the following terms into three groups: what they know well, what they are slightly familiar with, and what's brand new.

- circle graph
- line graph
- bar graph
- map
- diagram
- index
- opinion
- fact
- glossary

Opening Activity

Collect as many examples of real-world writing as you can find—magazines, newspapers, applications, schedules, directions, and recipes. Then divide the class into groups and assign one or two of the elements below to each group. Challenge group members to find as many examples of their element as they can in a set amount of time.

- bar graph
- map
- diagram
- circle graph
- glossary
- index

Next, direct their attention to the Elements of Nonfiction section (pages 188–205). Read aloud the introduction at the top of page 188. Then have students turn to Elements of Textbooks (pages 260–267). Finish by reading aloud the introduction to this section (see page 260).

Weekly Plan

Lessons	Summary
1. **Line Graphs and Circle Graphs**	Explore with students the characteristics of line and circle graphs.
2. **Diagrams and Maps**	Explain the purpose of diagrams and maps and discuss how they can shed light on a text.
3. **Fact and Opinion**	Help students distinguish between fact and opinion in a nonfiction selection.
4. **Glossary and Index**	Explain the purpose of a textbook glossary and index.
5. **Review and Assess**	Informally assess students to decide if more guided practice is needed. Then give an assessment.

Lesson Materials

	Components	Pages
Plan	*Teacher's Guide and Lesson Plans*	290–301
Teach	*Reader's Handbook*	188–190, 192, 195, 196, 198, 261, 264
Practice	*Applications Book and Word Work*	96–101, 226
Assess	*Test Book*	52–53

Lesson 1 · Line Graphs and Circle Graphs

For use with *Reader's Handbook* pages 190 and 196

Focus

In this lesson, students will explore the characteristics of and difference between line graphs and circle graphs.

Getting Started

Take a quick poll on your students' favorite school subject. Create a rough circle graph with the data on the board or a blank overhead. Then ask students to raise their hand when their birth month is called. Gather this data in a line graph for students to see. Next, create a Venn Diagram that helps the class sort characteristics of the two. Highlight that all graphs have titles.

◄ **Venn Diagram** ►

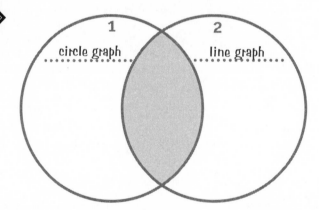

Give the students some time to come up with their own survey question to ask the students in the class and collect the data. Tell students they will make their own graphs at the end of the lesson.

Teaching Approach

Read aloud a paragraph that has a lot of numerical data in it. Then show your students a graph of that information. Ask which seems easier to understand.

Line Graphs

Direct students' attention to the information on page 196. Ask them to read to themselves the text at the top of the page and then take a few minutes to study this line graph.

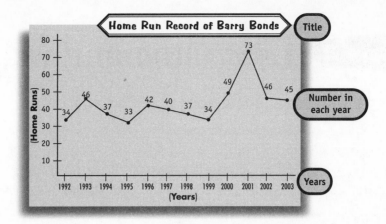

After they finish reading, ask students to retell the information in the graph. Discuss what it tells them about Barry Bonds. Have students make a list of three questions on their own that can be answered by using the graph. For example, "How many home runs did Barry Bonds hit in 1993?"

Circle Graphs

As a group, read the definition for circle graphs that appears at the bottom of page 190. Ask a volunteer to use the information to explain how a circle graph is different from a line graph.

Next, have students study the graph in the center of the page 190. Remind the class that the text and picture are equally important in a graphic. Ask questions about the graph, such as, "How much energy is used by cooking in a household?" Have students add three more questions about the circle graph to their list of questions. Then have students switch papers and answer each other's questions.

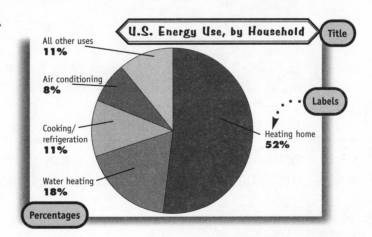

Wrap-up

Now that students understand graphs, have them transfer their data they collected earlier into one of two graphs—a line graph or a circle graph. Display their graphs in the hall.

Lesson 2 — Diagrams and Maps

For use with *Reader's Handbook* pages 192 and 198

Focus

Here students will activate prior knowledge of diagrams and maps and discuss how these elements can support key ideas in a text.

Getting Started

Write the following sentence on the board: "A picture is worth a thousand words." Ask students to discuss what they think it means. Use the discussion as a way to introduce the concept of diagrams and maps as "word pictures."

Teaching Approach

Begin by reading aloud the explanation at the top of page 192.

Diagrams

Have students study the river diagram. Ask, "What is the subject of this diagram? What does it tell you? What does it remind you of?"

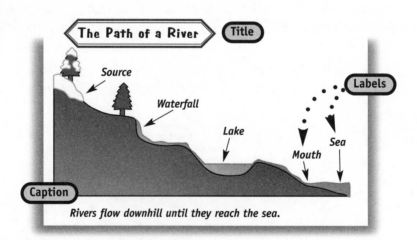

Diagram

The Path of a River — **Title**

Source

Waterfall

Lake

Labels

Mouth

Sea

Caption

Rivers flow downhill until they reach the sea.

Point out key components of the diagram: *title, labels,* and *caption.* Then post the steps students should follow when reading a diagram.

Steps for Reading a Diagram

Step 1: Look at the title. It can tell you the subject.
Step 2: Read the labels and caption.
Step 3: Draw conclusions about what the diagram means.

Maps

Ask students to tell the purpose of a map: "How do people use them? Why do writers include them with their writing?" Then have students thumb through their social studies books in search of maps. Ask students to list elements two or more maps have in common. These may include the maps' titles, compasses, keys, and scales. Many textbook maps have a caption as well. Explain that maps usually show the basic shape of an area of land or the heavens. Write the map characteristics on the board and define each. Then have students examine the map on page 198.

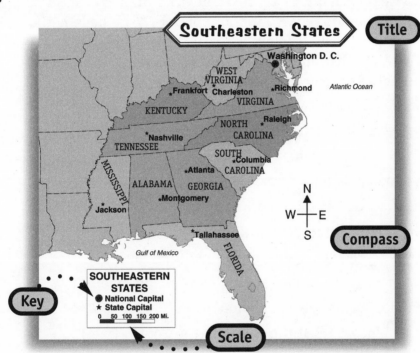

After they study the map, explain that this is an example of a political map—one that shows states, countries, and locations of cities. Have students compare this map to a physical map from their social studies texts. Help students understand that physical maps show mountains, rivers, and geographical features.

Wrap-up

Divide the class into small groups and give each group a piece of posterboard. Tell the class they will be preparing to teach these concepts to younger children. Have some groups write and then illustrate a "Plan for Reading a Diagram." Have the other groups come up with a "Plan for Reading a Map." Have one student from each group explain their work.

Lesson 3 Fact and Opinion

For use with *Reader's Handbook* page 195

Focus

Here students learn to distinguish between fact and opinion in a nonfiction selection.

Getting Started

 Give each student two squares of colored paper—one with an "O" on it and the other with an "F" on it. Then write on the board a fact, "You are all in the 3rd grade," and an opinion, "3rd grade is the greatest year in school!" Explain why each one is a fact or an opinion. Read this list and have students hold up the correct card. Keep a tally of the students' answers.

■ George Washington was a president. (fact)

■ This book has 448 pages in it. (fact)

■ Ben Franklin was the greatest inventor. (opinion)

■ Green looks good on our principal. (opinion)

■ Summer vacation is too long. (opinion)

■ We live in the United States. (fact)

■ Blue eyes see better than brown eyes. (opinion)

■ The colors of the U.S. flag are red, white, and blue. (fact)

■ Baseball is a great game. (opinion)

■ Abraham Lincoln freed the slaves in the South. (fact)

Tell students they will repeat this activity at the end of the lesson.

Teaching Approach

Tell students that in this lesson they will refresh their understanding of terms they may already know: *fact* and *opinion*.

Fact and Opinion

Ask students to define *fact* and *opinion*. Then have them read the definitions on page 195. Reiterate that a fact is something that can be proved true. An opinion is a belief or feeling about something.

Where to Find Facts and Opinions

Explain that nonfiction works such as textbooks and reference books are filled with facts. Ask, "In what type of nonfiction writing would you expect to see the author's opinion?" Students might suggest persuasive writing, editorials, letters to the editor, and so on.

Turn to page 195. Emphasize how important it is to be able to distinguish fact from opinion. Have students read silently the excerpt from *Amazing Flying Machines*. Ask, "What facts did you find?" Students might point to the second and third sentences. List these facts on the board.

Facts

■ flies forward

■ flies sideways and backward

■ can hover like a hawk

■ takes off and lands straight up and down

Wrap-up

Have students work in pairs to peruse magazine or newspaper articles for examples of facts and opinions. Then have volunteers read aloud one fact and one opinion and explain how they can tell the difference between the two.

If there is time give pairs a theme or topic, such as cookies or pizza. Have students come up with two facts and two opinions about it. Allow students to share their work. Ask them to give reasons to back up their opinions.

⬭ Lesson 4 ⬭ Glossary and Index

For use with *Reader's Handbook* pages 261 and 264

Focus

In this lesson, students will learn how to use a textbook's glossary and index.

Getting Started

Choose ten key terms from the students' math book. Make sure they appear in a chapter, the glossary, and index. Tell them they are going on a "scavenger hunt" to find the three pages where the terms show up.

Teaching Approach

The easiest place to find terms in a textbook is in the glossary. Have students turn to the glossary of their math textbooks. Give them a few minutes to look it over.

Glossary

Begin the lesson by defining *glossary*—an alphabetical listing of a book's key terms and their meanings. Ask students, "What is the difference between a glossary and a dictionary?" If students have trouble coming up with an answer, ask them to find science or social terms in the glossary of their math book. This should highlight that the glossary only includes words from that particular book. Then discuss how to use a glossary. Explain that in most textbooks, the glossary terms appear in boldface in the running text. Each time students come to a boldface word, they can check its meaning in the glossary if it is not clear in the text.

Use the information in the "Elements of Textbooks" on page 261 to reinforce your teaching. Read aloud the explanatory sentence at the top of the page and have students examine the sample glossary page provided.

Index

Ask students, "What is the difference between a glossary and an index?" Students should know that an index, like a glossary, appears at the back of a textbook. It lists the ideas, people, places, and topics in a textbook along with their page numbers. Explain that the purpose of an index, like a table of contents, is to help them find topics in the book. However, the index is more specific than the table of contents.

Have students turn to page 264. Ask them to read the explanatory text at the top of the page and then examine the sample index.

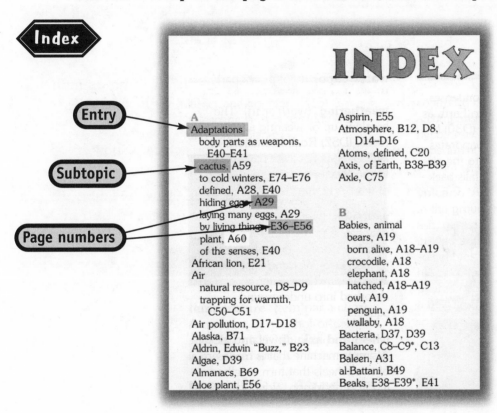

Ask students to practice using the index. Call out a term listed in the *Reader's Handbook* index. Their task is to write the page number where the term is found in the handbook. Have students hold up their paper when they find each term you call out.

Wrap-up

Review with students the purpose of a glossary and of an index. Then have students turn to their science or social studies textbooks. Give each student a list of five terms to find in the glossary and index. Later, discuss any problems students had as they researched.

Lesson 5 Review and Assess

Check Point

Use the Quick Assess checklist to informally evaluate students' understanding of various elements of nonfiction and textbooks. Based on their answers, divide them into two groups. One group can do the Independent Practice on the next page and the other group can do the guided practice in the *Applications Book and Word Work*.

Guided Practice

For students who need reinforcement in the elements of nonfiction and textbooks, use pages 96–101 in the *Applications Book and Word Work*.

Quick Assess

Can students

- ☑ tell how a circle graph is different from a line graph?

- ☑ explain what a diagram is and how to read it?

- ☑ identify key elements on a map?

- ☑ define fact and opinion and provide examples?

- ☑ describe what an index is and how it is organized?

- ☑ explain what you can expect to find in a glossary?

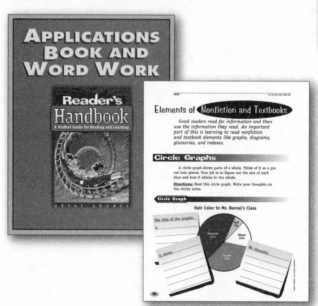

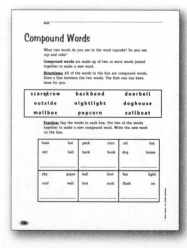

For students who need more word work, assign page 226 from the *Applications Book and Word Work* on compound words.

Independent Practice

Direct students who have demonstrated a strong understanding of the elements discussed to choose one or more additional nonfiction or textbook elements to explore. In their Reading Notebooks, and using their own words, students should define the element, explain how it is used, and provide an example that is different from the ones shown in the *Reader's Handbook*.

Then ask students to do the following:

- ■ present their assigned element to the rest of the class.
- ■ explain how the element works and where readers might expect to find it.

Class Review

Have students thumb through the *Reader's Handbook* in search of the elements discussed in this lesson. Have them create in their Reading Notebooks a chart similar to the following so that they can record what they find and perhaps refer to it as needed later in the year.

Elements of Nonfiction/Textbooks

Element	Handbook Page Number	Comments
Line graph		
Circle graph		
Map		
Diagram		
Glossary		
Index		

Test Book

Use the short-answer and multiple-choice tests on pages 52–53 to assess students' knowledge of line and circle graphs, diagrams, maps, facts and opinions, glossaries, and indexes.

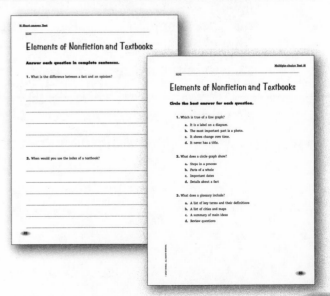

WEEK 24

Reading Social Studies

Goals

Here students read a chapter from a social studies textbook. This week's lessons will help them to

☑ read and understand social studies textbooks
☑ develop their ability to use graphic organizers

Background

Help students connect this lesson to their prior knowledge by asking them to

■ talk about what readers can learn from a social studies text

■ consider the difficulties of reading textbooks

■ think about the elements they'd expect to find in a social studies book

Opening Activity

 Activate students' interest in the reading to come by displaying current pictures of Washington, D.C. Under each picture, write a short, easy-to-read caption. Have students take turns viewing the art in your gallery. If you like, divide the gallery into "Past" and "Present." Include historical photos in the "Past" section. You might download materials from the following websites.

■ www.citymuseumdc.org/Learn_About_DC/ Publications/Washington_History.asp

■ www.cr.nps.gov/nr/travel/wash/learnmore.htm

■ www.whitehousehistory.org

Weekly Plan

Lessons	Summary
1. **Before Reading: Social Studies**	Here students apply the Before Reading stage of the reading process to a social studies textbook.
2. **During Reading: Social Studies**	Strengthen students' knowledge of the strategy of using graphic organizers.
3. **During Reading: Social Studies** (continued)	Explore with students the importance of reading for names, dates, events, and key topics in a social studies text.
4. **After Reading: Social Studies**	Reinforce students' understanding of the After Reading stage as they apply it to a social studies chapter.
5. **Review and Assess**	Informally assess students to decide if more guided practice is needed. Then give an assessment.

Lesson Materials

	Components	Pages
Plan	*Teacher's Guide and Lesson Plans*	302–313
Teach	*Reader's Handbook*	208–221
	Overhead Transparencies	21, 22
Practice	*Applications Book and Word Work*	102–111, 227
Assess	*Test Book*	54–55

Lesson 1 Before Reading: Social Studies

For use with *Reader's Handbook* pages 208–209, 214

Focus

Here students will review the Before Reading stage of the reading process and use it to prepare for reading a social studies chapter.

Getting Started

Divide the class into groups of three or four. Have them use their social studies textbooks to make a list of elements (maps, table of contents, charts, etc.) they find in the pages. Compare lists as a class and come up with one overall list of social studies book elements.

Teaching Approach

Begin by reading aloud the introduction to "Reading Social Studies." Discuss the goals listed there.

A Set a Purpose

Discuss the first step of the reading process and then work with the class as they set a purpose for reading the social studies chapter "A Capital for the U.S.A." Read page 209 and ask students to look at the purpose questions.

B Preview

When students are ready to move on, ask them to read the Preview text on page 209. Point out the Preview Checklist and discuss the importance of the items listed. Check to see which of the elements the class listed are in the Preview Checklist. Use Overhead Transparencies 21 and 22 to point out the items on the checklist. Then have students do their own previews of "A Capital for the U.S.A."

Preview Checklist

✔ title and headings

✔ pictures, maps, charts, and diagrams

✔ names, dates, and words in boldface

✔ previews, summaries, and questions

C Plan

As a group, read Plan on page 214. Point out that a few minutes spent thumbing through the pages in a textbook chapter can yield a wealth of valuable information.

Next, present the strategy of the using graphic organizers. Explain to students that graphic organizers are "word pictures." Readers create them as a way of organizing—and visualizing—important ideas in a text.

When you've finished your explanation, ask students to read the information about the strategy on page 214. Point out the K-W-L Chart, which your students may have seen before. Tell the class that you'd like them to get into the habit of creating their own organizers before they begin reading. A K-W-L Chart is one of many organizers that work well as Before Reading tools.

K-W-L Chart

WHAT I KNOW	WHAT I WANT TO KNOW	WHAT I LEARNED

Wrap-up

Ask students to draw a K-W-L Chart in their notebooks and then complete the K and W columns for a chapter in their social studies text, which you will be doing in class next. Point out that when they read this chapter, a part of their purpose will be to find answers to the questions they've written in the W column.

⬬ Lesson 2 ⬭ During Reading: Social Studies

For use with *Reader's Handbook* pages 210–215

Focus

Here students will activate prior knowledge of graphic organizers and discuss how to use this strategy with a social studies text.

Getting Started

Have students turn to page 210 and look carefully at the Preview box. Explain that most social studies chapters open with an element similar to this one and that students need to pay particular attention to the questions, statements, and vocabulary included there. Have students design their own preview box for a chapter in the book that could be about their life.

Teaching Approach

Remind students of their purpose for reading "A Capital for the U.S.A."

D ⬤ Read with a Purpose

Explain that there is always plenty to learn from a textbook chapter. Reading slowly and carefully is essential, as is taking good notes.

Direct students to turn to page 215. Read aloud the text at the top of the page and point out the Tools box on the right-hand side. Have students look at a sample Timeline and Web on pages 423 and 425 in the Reading Tools section of the handbook. After they finish reading, tell students that they will complete one of these organizers.

During the second half of the lesson, work with students as they do a slow and careful reading of the social studies chapter. You might choose to have them read in small groups or read silently on their own. Encourage students to look for answers to their K-W-L questions and to write what they find in the L column of the chart.

K-W-L Chart

WHAT I KNOW	WHAT I WANT TO KNOW	WHAT I LEARNED
• Washington, D.C., is not in any state. • The White House is there.	• Why was Washington, D.C., chosen? • Who decided what the city should be like?	• People wanted the new capital to be in the middle of the northern and southern states. • Pierre L'Enfant and Benjamin Banneker helped plan the city. • The <u>D.C.</u> stands for District of Columbia.

When students finish reading, discuss their reactions to the text. Ask which parts they found most difficult and which they thought were easiest. Then divide the class into small groups and ask students to share their organizers. Have group members note similarities in questions in the W column and answers in the L column. Then discuss the value of using an organizer like a K-W-L Chart while reading. Explain that in the next lesson, students will learn about two additional organizers that work well with this kind of reading.

Wrap-up

Invite students to return to the social studies chapter in their books and preview it. Direct them to do a slow and careful reading of the chapter. They should be looking for information to put in the L column of their K-W-L Chart.

Lesson 3 During Reading: Social Studies (continued)

For use with *Reader's Handbook* pages 216–218

Focus

In this lesson, students explore the importance of reading for names, dates, events, and key topics in a social studies textbook.

Getting Started

Draw a chart with the headings *Names, Dates,* and *Events* on the board and have students copy it into their Reading Notebooks. Then ask study groups to do a round-robin reading of the social studies chapter. Each time they come to an important name, date, or event, they should record it in their charts.

Teaching Approach

Explain to the class that in this lesson you'll discuss what students should look for when reading a social studies textbook.

D Read with a Purpose (continued)

Remind the class that good readers know how to spot key details and then use their critical thinking skills to create meaning from the details.

1. Read for Names, Dates, and Events

First, direct students' attention to the explanatory text on page 216. Reinforce that keeping track of names, dates, and events in a Web or Timeline can make it easier for students to figure out what's important in a chapter. To that end, students need to create the organizer they want to use *before* they begin reading.

1790 — Congress decided where the new capital should be.

1800 — President John Adams and his wife moved into the White House.

2. Keep Track of Different Topics

Next, direct students' attention to page 217. Once again, read aloud the information at the top of the page and walk students through the organizers that follow. Discuss why it's important to search for key topics in a social studies chapter and how chapter headings can help. Tell students explicitly that the headings can be used to create a Web in their Reading Notebooks.

Web

A CAPITAL IS NEEDED

Some leaders wanted the capital city to be in the South.

Some leaders wanted it in the North, like Boston or New York.

E Connect

After your discussion of key topics, help students consider the importance of making a personal connection to the information presented in a social studies chapter. Review what's involved in the Connect step. Explain that by connecting what they read to their lives they will remember more and be more interested in what they read.

I wonder why he left before everything was finished. People were probably mad at him.

Wrap-up

Give three or four sticky notes to students. Ask them to read through the chapter they have been reading throughout this unit and make three or more notes on their personal connections.

Lesson 4 After Reading: Social Studies

For use with *Reader's Handbook* pages 218–221

Focus

In this lesson, you'll reinforce students' understanding of the After Reading stage as they apply it to a social studies chapter.

Getting Started

Ask students to recall the last book they read. When they have trouble remembering, make the point that we often need to refresh our memories by going back and rereading.

Teaching Approach

Remind students of the purpose of the Pause and Reflect step of the reading process. Explain that this is the point at which readers need to look back at their original purpose to see if they've found out what they need to know.

 ## Pause and Reflect

Ask students to reflect on their own purpose questions. Then ask

■ Have you met your reading purpose?

■ What else do you need to find out?

Point out the three questions listed in the handbook. Explain that if students are unsure of their answers—or if they've decided they want to find out more about the subject—they will need to do some rereading. Students should know that most textbook chapters will require a second reading, and perhaps even a third. There's simply too much information to absorb with a single reading.

G Reread

Read aloud the text under Reread on page 219. Help students understand that most readers feel that *rereading* a social studies chapter is easier than reading it the first time. In some cases, students will need to reread word for word. Other times, they'll need to reread only parts of a selection. If they're left with only one or two simple questions after reading the chapter for the first time, then skimming should be adequate. If, on the other hand, they found the chapter difficult to navigate or challenging, they should plan to reread all of it.

H Remember

Explain that the information students read loses meaning unless they find a way to remember it. In the case of social studies, students should return to the K-W-L Chart they started before reading in order to make additional notes in the L column.

Another option is to have students make notes on a whole new organizer. "Reworking" their notes on a different organizer can help them further process key information from the text. A Main Idea Organizer will work for any section of a social studies chapter.

◀ **Main Idea Organizer** ▶

SUBJECT		
MAIN IDEA		
DETAIL	DETAIL	DETAIL

Wrap-up

Review with students the three steps of the After Reading stage (Pause and Reflect, Reread, and Remember) of the reading process. Ask three volunteers to summarize each step and explain how they used it with the social studies chapter.

Lesson 5 Review and Assess

Check Point

Use the Quick Assess checklist to informally evaluate students' understanding of how to read a social studies textbook. Based on their answers, divide them into two groups. One group can do the Independent Practice on the next page and the other group can do the guided practice in the *Applications Book and Word Work.*

Guided Practice

For students who need reinforcement in reading their social studies textbooks, use pages 102–111 in the *Applications Book and Word Work.*

Quick Assess

Can students

☑ apply the reading process to social studies texts?

☑ explain what to look for when previewing a social studies textbook?

☑ say why graphic organizers are helpful when reading social studies?

☑ describe and use two graphic organizers that work well with social studies textbooks?

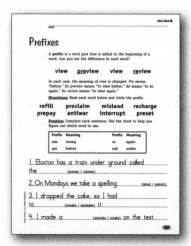

For students who need more word work, assign page 227 from the *Applications Book and Word Work* on prefixes.

Independent Practice

Students who demonstrate a strong understanding of how to read social studies textbooks can apply their knowledge to another chapter from a social studies textbook. Assign a chapter from students' own social studies text. Ask students to do the following:

■ Write reading purpose questions for the chapter.

■ Employ the strategy of using graphic organizers as they read. Suggest that they fill out a K-W-L Chart as they go.

Class Review

Divide students into small groups. Ask group members to work together on a preview of a chapter in your class social studies text. Then come together as a group and discuss what they learned from their previews. Ask students:

■ Why is it important to preview a social studies text before you begin reading?

■ How can you find out what the chapter is about?

■ What kinds of notes should you take when reading this type of textbook chapter?

■ What are three reading tools you might use?

Test Book

Use the short-answer and multiple-choice tests on pages 54–55 to assess students' understanding of the material in this week's lessons.

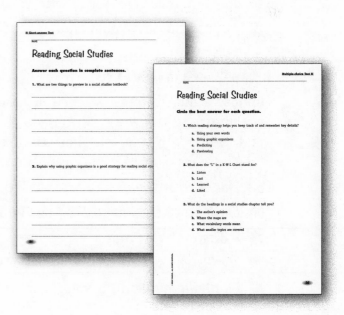

WEEK 25

Reading Science

Goals

Here students read a science chapter called "How Plants Make Food." This week's lessons will help them learn to

- ☑ read and understand science textbooks
- ☑ use the strategy of note-taking when reading science writing

Background

Help students connect this week's lessons to their prior knowledge by asking them to

- ■ discuss what they would expect to find in a science textbook chapter
- ■ think about how most science textbooks are organized
- ■ compare reading science with reading in other subject areas
- ■ explore the more challenging aspects of reading science

Opening Activity

Choose a high-interest science novel or short story to read aloud over the course of the week. Encourage students to visualize the characters and events in the novel. Then ask them to draw pictures of what they "see." Books that will work well for this lesson include the following

- ■ *The Case of the Stinky Science Project* by James Preller
- ■ *Elaine and the Flying Frog* by Heidi Chang
- ■ *I Was a Third Grade Science Project* by Mary Jane Auch
- ■ *My Sister, My Science Report* by Margaret Bechard
- ■ *Plantzilla* by Jerdine Nolen

Weekly Plan

Lessons	Summary
1. **Before Reading: Science**	Work with students as they apply the Before Reading stage of the reading process to a science textbook chapter.
2. **During Reading: Science**	Teach students to apply the reading strategy of note-taking as they read a science textbook chapter.
3. **During Reading: Science** (continued)	Help students practice taking notes and making connections as they read a science text.
4. **After Reading: Science**	Work with students as they apply the After Reading stage of the reading process to science.
5. **Review and Assess**	Informally assess students to decide if more guided practice is needed. Then give an assessment.

Lesson Materials

	Components	Pages
Plan	*Teacher's Guide and Lesson Plans*	314–325
Teach	*Reader's Handbook*	222–233
	Overhead Transparencies	23, 24
Practice	*Applications Book and Word Work*	112–120, 228
Assess	*Test Book*	56–57

Lesson 1 Before Reading: Science

For use with *Reader's Handbook* pages 222–223, 228

Focus

Here students review the steps of the Before Reading stage and discuss how to apply each step when reading a science textbook.

Getting Started

Ask students what they usually do to prepare for reading a science textbook chapter. What do they do when they hear the assignment? What do they do before they start reading? Then talk about which techniques that students currently use seem to work well.

Teaching Approach

Ask a volunteer to name the three Before Reading steps and explain how using them might improve their ability to read and respond to a science textbook.

A Set a Purpose

Before they read a science text, students should set a meaningful purpose for reading. Explain that setting a purpose for reading science can be as easy as asking a *what, how,* or *why* question about the chapter title. Read with the class pages 222 and 223. Tell them that they will be reading a chapter called "How Plants Make Food." What other purpose questions can they suggest? List these on the board and encourage them to come up with an exhaustive list. Make sure they understand to keep going after the first question.

B Preview

Read aloud the Preview text on page 223 and walk students through the checklist at the bottom of the page. Have students watch you preview of "How Plants Make Food" (pages 224–227). Use Overhead Transparencies 23 and 24 as support.

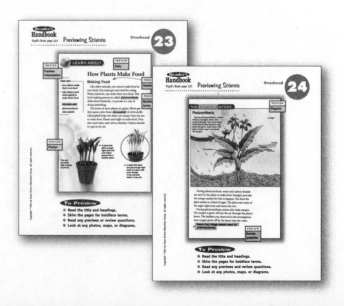

 **Plan**

As a group, read the introduction to the Plan section on page 228. Ask students, "Which of the items listed did you notice in your previews?" Remind the class that every reader previews in a slightly different way.

Review with students the strategy of note-taking. Remind them what they've learned thus far about taking notes. Then ask them to read to themselves the explanation of how note-taking works with science on page 228.

Remind the class that many different reading tools work well with note-taking. However, because science is very much the study of processes, many readers find Process Notes work the best.

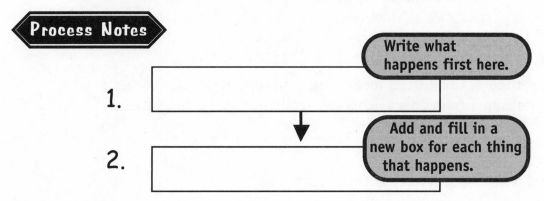

Wrap-up

 At the end of the lesson, have students draw a Process Notes organizer in their Reading Notebooks. Have them practice using Process Notes by filling in the organizer with details on a process they do every day, such as making the bed in the morning.

Lesson 2 During Reading: Science

For use with *Reader's Handbook* pages 229–230

Focus

In this lesson, students will use the strategy of note-taking to help them read and respond to a science text.

Getting Started

Ask students to discuss what they find particularly challenging about reading science. Have them support their comments with specific experiences they've had with their own science textbooks. Then explain that the reading process can make even the most challenging science chapter easier to read and understand.

Teaching Approach

Even though this lesson focuses on reading science textbooks, it applies almost equally well to any science reading. Help students understand that what applies to science textbooks applies to all science reading.

D Read with a Purpose

Ask a volunteer to remind the class of their purpose for reading "How Plants Make Food." Then post on the board the following two purpose questions and leave them up for the duration of the unit.

■ How do plants make food?

■ What do they do with the food they make?

Encourage students to make Process Notes that relate to each question.

Understand a Process

Discuss the notion of a "process" in science. Explain that a scientific process is a series of events that occur in nature. For an example, draw on the board a flower seed planted in soil, a sprouted seed, and a blooming flower. Tell the class that a flower growing from a seed is a process that occurs naturally.

Then ask students to look at the Process Notes at the bottom of the page. Ask them to think about these notes as they read.

Understand Cause and Effect

Once you're sure students understand the idea of a scientific process and how Process Notes can help them explore it, have them turn to page 230. Ask students to summarize what cause and effect means. Then tell the class that a Cause-Effect Organizer can help them consider why something happens. Walk students through the first organizer, explaining individual items as you go.

Cause-Effect Organizer

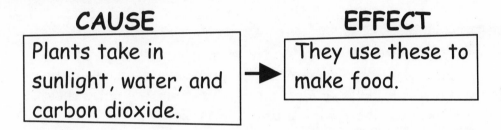

CAUSE

| Plants take in sunlight, water, and carbon dioxide. |

→

EFFECT

| They use these to make food. |

Next, discuss variations on the cause-effect pattern. Point out to students that many times, a single effect will have a number of causes, or a single cause will lead to a number of effects. Provide examples from the natural world. Then discuss the organizer shown at the bottom of page 230.

Wrap-up

Ask volunteers to summarize the purpose of Process Notes and how students can use them when reading science. Then do the same for a Cause-Effect Organizer. Finish by having students draw a Process Notes organizer and Cause-Effect Organizer in their notebooks. Explain that you'd like them to take notes on the organizers as they read "How Plants Make Food."

Lesson 3 During Reading: Science (continued)

For use with *Reader's Handbook* pages 224–227, 231

Focus

In this lesson, students will practice taking notes on and making connections to science writing.

Getting Started

List on the board what students have learned up to this point about how plants make food. Explain that the purpose of reading slowly and carefully is to find key ideas and information. The notes they take are "permanent records" of that information.

Teaching Approach

Explain to students that, as they read, they have to find the most important information and take notes on it.

D Read with a Purpose (continued)

Have students begin reading "How Plants Make Food." Use your voice to draw attention to key details that students should record in their notes.

In your guided reading, stop at the end of each page to ask such comprehension questions as

■ What is chlorophyll? What does it do? (page 224)

■ What are four things a plant needs for photosynthesis? (page 225)

■ What compound does a plant give off during photosynthesis? (page 225)

■ How do plants use the food they make? How do animals and humans use it? (page 226)

When students finish reading, have them use their notes to help them complete the Review questions on page 227.

E **Connect**

Help students understand that, as they read science, they need to make personal connections to the material. These connections, which may come in the form of questions or observations, can make the text easier to read and understand.

Ask the class to turn to page 231. Read aloud the Connect text at the top of the page and remind students of the connections they've made to other texts. Then point out the sticky note in the middle of the page. Discuss.

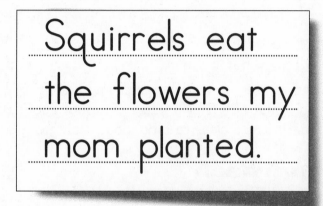

Squirrels eat the flowers my mom planted.

Ask students to return to "How Plants Make Food" with sticky notes in hand. Encourage them to make their own connections to the text by either relating it to their own lives or considering how the material relates to something else they've seen or studied.

Wrap-up

Invite students to share the connection comments they made. Then ask them to write a short entry in their Reading Notebooks where they further explore their ideas about "How Plants Make Food." Have students choose one of the following prompts and use it in the first sentence of their entries.

■ I wonder why . . .

■ This reminds me of . . .

■ Recently, I . . .

■ Something I don't understand is . . .

Lesson 4 After Reading: Science

For use with *Reader's Handbook* pages 231–233

Focus

In this lesson, you'll work with students as they consider how to apply the After Reading stage of the reading process to a science textbook chapter.

Getting Started

 Ask students to discuss in small groups the science chapter they just read. Have them explore as a group their impressions of the reading and then decide what else they'd like to find out about the topic. Then come together as a class to talk about each group's work.

Teaching Approach

Help students understand that taking the time to pause and reflect is an absolutely essential part of reading science. All students, no matter how knowledgeable about the content area, need to be encouraged to spend a moment processing what they've read.

F Pause and Reflect

Read aloud the explanation of how to pause and reflect upon science. Then invite the class to answer each of the three questions at the bottom of page 231. When they've finished, have students tell how rereading might help them better understand the subject.

G Reread

There are two ways to complete the Reread step of the reading process. The first involves rereading the entire chapter, word for word. Encourage students who found the material particularly challenging to do a second careful reading of the material or at least parts of it. If you feel they would benefit, show them a Web or Summary Notes that they might use as they're rereading. Sometimes taking notes in a slightly different way can make the material easier to process.

Main Idea Organizer

SUBJECT		
MAIN IDEA		
DETAIL	DETAIL	DETAIL

Some students may need to reread only parts of the chapter. Readers who are comfortable with the material might choose to read again only the parts that struck them as particularly important or interesting. Be prepared to model how to skim for key elements in a reading.

H Remember

The best way to remember material from a science textbook is to somehow take ownership of it. Readers can do this in various ways, including performing an experiment that relates to the reading or orally retelling what they've learned.

Have volunteers read aloud the explanatory text at the top of page 233. Then discuss the suggestions for how to remember information in the chapter. Ask the class to complete one of the activities described. Provide them with flashcards or have students make their fact lists in their Reading Notebooks.

Wrap-up

Have students look at the Summing Up box at the bottom of page 233. Read aloud the information on note-taking and then discuss the two reading tools listed. Finish by making suggestions of other reading tools that would work well with science.

Lesson 5 Review and Assess

Check Point

Use the Quick Assess checklist to informally evaluate students' understanding of how to read a science text. Based on their answers, divide them into two groups. Ask one group to complete the Independent Practice on the next page and the other group to do the guided practice in the *Applications Book and Word Work*.

Guided Practice

For students who need reinforcement in reading their science textbooks, use pages 112–120 in the *Applications Book and Word Work*.

Quick Assess

Can students

- ☑ apply the reading process to science writing?

- ☑ describe what to do when previewing science textbooks?

- ☑ take a variety of notes that might be useful when reading science textbooks?

- ☑ explain how to make a personal connection to a science textbook?

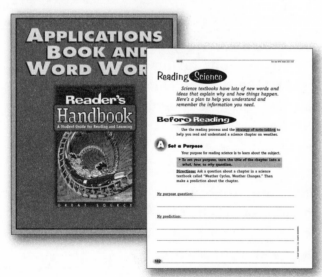

For students who need more word work, assign page 228 from the *Applications Book and Word Work* on prefixes that mean *not*.

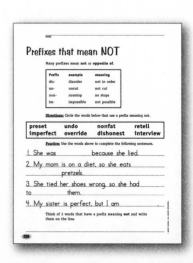

Independent Practice

Students with a strong understanding of the reading process and the strategy of note-taking might apply their knowledge to another science textbook chapter.

After students choose a chapter of interest, have them do the following.

▮ Write a reading purpose question for the chapter.

▮ Make Process Notes about the reading and then create a Cause-Effect Organizer that reflects their understanding of the subject matter.

Class Review

Divide the class into three small groups. Assign each group a different stage of the reading process: Before Reading Science, During Reading Science, and After Reading Science. Have groups work together to come up with a list of five to eight quiz questions that explore their stage in the process. (Examples: *What are two purpose questions that work well with science? Why is note-taking a helpful strategy to use with science?*) After groups finish their lists, work as a class to create a Reading Science quiz show. Ask one student from each group to act as a panelist. Then have a quiz show "host" ask science questions of the panel.

Test Book

Use the short-answer and multiple-choice tests on pages 56–57 to assess students' understanding of the material presented in this week's lessons.

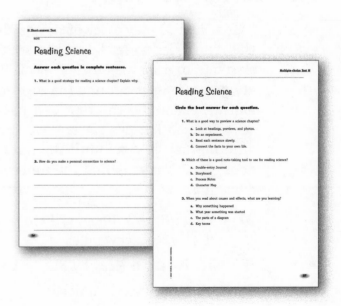

Reading Math B

WEEK 26
Reading Math

Goals

Here students learn how to use the reading process with a math textbook. This week's lessons will teach them to:

- ☑ read a math book for key information
- ☑ use the strategy of visualizing and thinking aloud

Background

Help students connect this week's lessons to their prior knowledge by asking them to:

- ■ discuss their experiences with reading a math text
- ■ recall elements common to math textbooks
- ■ express difficulties they have reading math
- ■ discuss strategies they use currently when reading math

Opening Activity

Gather and display a set of novels that relate to math. Choose one that you'd like to read aloud to students, and leave others for students to examine on their own. Begin by explaining that you are going to read a funny (or scary or suspenseful) story about math. Read aloud the first few pages. Ask students to visualize a scene the author describes. Have them draw a picture of the scene and then put it away until the next time you read aloud from the book. Most students find the following "math novels" particularly engaging.

- ■ *Amanda Bean's Amazing Dream: A Math Story* by Cindy Neuschwander
- ■ *More or Less a Mess* by Sheila Keenan
- ■ *Math Man* by Teri Daniels
- ■ *Arthur and the No-Brainer* by Marc Brown
- ■ *The Case of the Shrunken Allowance* by Joanne Rocklin

Weekly Plan

Lessons	Summary
1. **Before Reading: Math**	Work with students as they apply the Before Reading stage of the reading process to reading math.
2. **During Reading: Math**	Teach students how to use the reading strategy of visualizing and thinking aloud with a math text.
3. **During Reading: Math** (continued)	Continue the discussion of visualizing and thinking aloud and show students how to connect to a math text.
4. **After Reading: Math**	Review the After Reading stage of the reading process and work with students as they apply it to math.
5. **Review and Assess**	Informally assess students to decide if more guided practice is needed. Then give an assessment.

Lesson Materials

	Components	Pages
Plan	*Teacher's Guide and Lesson Plans*	326–337
Teach	*Reader's Handbook*	234–245
	Overhead Transparencies	25, 26
Practice	*Applications Book and Word Work*	121–130, 229
Assess	*Test Book*	58–59

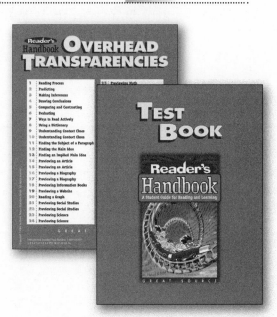

Lesson 1 ▸ Before Reading: Math

For use with *Reader's Handbook* pages 234–235, 238

Focus

In this lesson, students focus on the Before Reading stage of the reading process as they prepare to read math.

Getting Started

Return to the math novel you read from as an opening activity. Ask students to examine the drawings they made as they listened. Then read another excerpt and have them either add to their pictures or visualize a new scene in the book. Help students understand that visualizing can help them "see" abstract ideas like the ones the author describes.

Teaching Approach

Begin the lesson by explaining that students will spend the week learning how to use the reading process with a math text. Ask students to turn to page 234 and read silently the introductory paragraphs and Goals box. Discuss each of the two goals and invite students to add their own goals to the list.

A Set a Purpose

Ask the class to turn to page 235 and read the information at the top of the page. Explain that in this lesson, students will read a math chapter called "Multiply with 2." Invite students to write their own purposes for reading the chapter and then compare what they wrote with the two purpose questions on page 235.

B Preview

After students have established their purpose for reading, they are ready to begin previewing. Explain to the class that Preview is one of the most important steps of the reading process because it helps readers activate prior knowledge of a topic. Students should preview for a sense of what the chapter is about and then reflect upon what they already know about the subject. Direct students' attention to the Preview Checklist.

Preview Checklist

✔ lesson title and headings
✔ sample problems and their solutions
✔ practice problems
✔ boxed items and questions

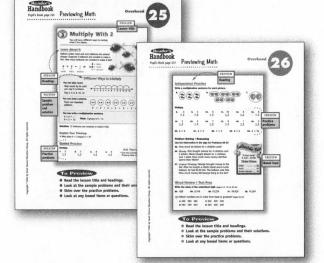

Have students use this checklist to help them preview "Multiply With 2." Model this process with Overhead Transparencies 25 and 26. Point to each item from the checklist.

C Plan

After students preview the chapter, review the purposes they wrote. Then, as a group, turn to the Plan section on page 238. Ask the class, "What grabbed your attention during your preview?" Have students compare what they noticed with the three ideas listed at the top of the page.

Then explain to students that visualizing and thinking aloud is often the best all-purpose strategy to use with a math text. Ask students: "What does it mean to visualize? How do you think aloud? How can these two strategies help you read math?" In the next lesson, you'll ask students to apply the strategy to "Multiply With 2."

Wrap-up

Bring students together to discuss what they've learned thus far. Have students practice using the strategy of visualizing and thinking aloud with simple addition problems. Assign each student a problem such as $3 + 5$ and have them show how to solve the problem using the strategy. You can put their pages into a book and share it with a younger grade.

Lesson 2 During Reading: Math

For use with *Reader's Handbook* pages 236–241

Focus

In this lesson, students will learn to use the strategy of visualizing and thinking aloud with a math text. In addition, they'll explore the importance of understanding and solving the sample problems in a math chapter.

Getting Started

Read a word problem to students. Ask them to draw the problem. Then compare students' drawings. Try doing this process backward— show students an example of a drawing and Think Aloud you did for a problem. Ask students to write what they think the problem was. Share the actual problem when they finish.

Teaching Approach

Ask students to review the purpose questions they wrote in a previous lesson.

D Read with a Purpose

Return to your discussion of visualizing and thinking aloud. Ask a volunteer to explain how the strategy works with math. Model the strategy for students if you think they will benefit. Then read aloud the information at the top of page 239 and ask students to do their own careful readings of "Multiply With 2." Distribute sticky notes that students can use while reading.

When the class has finished, ask, "What is the chapter mostly about? What did you learn from it?"

1. Understand Sample Problems

Have students look at the sample problems in "Multiply With 2." Then explain that the problems are there to help them understand the concept and that it's a mistake to skim or skip this part of a math chapter. It is best to try and work through them. Point out the technique of drawing a picture in the sample problem.

2. Look for Key Terms

Next, read aloud the relevant text on page 239. Have students look at the sample problem in the middle of the page. Explain its purpose. Point out that sample problems usually make use of a lesson's key terms—in this case, *factor* and *product*.

Balloon artists twist and turn balloons into animal shapes. Suppose 2 balloons are needed to make a fish. How many balloons are needed to make 6 fish?

$$6 \times 2 = \blacksquare \quad \text{or} \quad \begin{array}{r} 2 \\ \times\, 6 \\ \hline \blacksquare \end{array}$$

6 ↑ factor   2 ↑ factor   ■ ↑ product

2 ←factor
× 6 ←factor
■ ←product

Sample problem

3. Solve Practice Problems

Point out to students that, in addition to sample problems, most math chapters contain a set of practice problems. If students find that they can't solve the practice problems, they need to return to the explanation of the skill and begin rereading. Remind students that reading slowly and carefully is key to understanding what each problem is asking.

Read aloud the text that accompanies the practice problems, and then model how you would use the strategy of visualizing and thinking aloud to solve problem number 8. Have volunteers do the same for numbers 9 and 10. Then direct students to solve the remainder of the practice problems, drawing pictures and writing Think Alouds as they go.

Practice Problems

14.	15.	16.	17.	18.	19.
2 × 4	2 × 3	7 × 2	9 × 2	1 × 2	2 × 2

Wrap-up

Ask students to work with a study partner and explain to each other the strategy of visualizing and thinking aloud. Have them write what the strategy is and how to use it, and then comment on how it might help them.

Lesson 3 During Reading: Math (continued)

For use with *Reader's Handbook* pages 242–243

Focus

In this lesson, students will continue their exploration of the strategy of visualizing and thinking aloud and practice connecting to a math text.

Getting Started

Before you return to the Read Aloud, ask volunteers to make predictions about what will happen in the story you are reading to the class. Discuss how making a prediction about a story can be similar to estimating the answer to a math problem. Then have students write a sentence or two about the math difficulty that the novel's main character experiences. Ask students to explain a personal connection they've been able to make to the main character, plot, or conflict.

Teaching Approach

This lesson is intended to give students a chance to deepen their understanding of the strategy of visualizing and thinking aloud.

D Read with a Purpose (continued)

Begin the lesson by asking students to read the bottom of page 242. Discuss the importance of practicing math skills. Remind the class that they should treat any math homework they receive as yet another opportunity to practice what they've learned.

Work with students as they continue doing practice problems. Point out the Guided Practice section on page 236 and discuss ways students can use a textbook element such as this. Also, be sure students take note of the boxed items on the page. Discuss how these can shed light on what they're learning.

E Connect

Students should know that their final step at the During Reading stage is to make personal connections to the material. Making connections is particularly important with math since many students have a difficult time seeing the relevance of the mathematical concepts they've learned.

Direct students to read silently page 243, including the comment one student made while reading "Multiply With 2." Ask students, "How can a comment such as this help you better understand the material?"

> My family has 6 people. If we each want 2 slices of pizza, we need to have 12 slices!

Help students understand that one way to make math easier to read and understand is to think about how the skill can be used in real life. The pizza comment is an example of how a reader has applied the subject (multiplying by two) to a real-life situation.

Wrap-up

Divide the class into groups of three or four. Ask groups to discuss what it means to "connect" with a math text and how they can go about doing it. Then ask each group to make their own connections to "Multiply With 2." Have them make a list of times in real life it would be helpful to multiply with two. Challenge the class as a whole to come up with 50 examples.

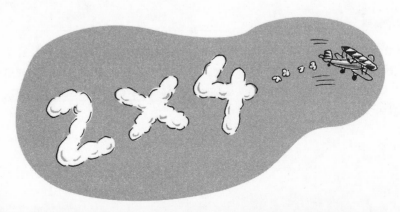

Lesson 4 After Reading: Math

For use with *Reader's Handbook* pages 244–245

Focus

In this lesson, students will consider how they can apply the After Reading stage of the reading process to a math text.

Getting Started

Help students understand how to go back to the practice problems on page 241 and review them. The best way to see if they grasped the concept is to have them think aloud. Pair up students and have them talk through each problem—a true Think Aloud.

Teaching Approach

Guide students to see the value of reflecting after they read. Checking their work after reading or even rereading when necessary is a valuable skill to learn.

F Pause and Reflect

Remind students of the purpose of the Pause and Reflect step. Help them understand that it involves self-assessment—no one will be standing over their shoulders deciding whether or not they've understood what they read.

Next, ask students to turn to page 244. Read aloud the introductory paragraph and the information under Pause and Reflect. Have students read the three bulleted questions and decide their own answers to each question. Discuss their responses. Then ask

■ Have you met your reading purpose?

■ Did you learn what you set out to learn from the reading?

G Reread

Remind students that most math chapters will require at least two careful readings. Because text is kept to a minimum in a math book, students should do a word-for-word rereading of any math material they've been assigned.

G Reread (continued)

Encourage students to use a different tool to help them reread a math chapter. For example, you might have them create a Summary Notes organizer before they begin their second reading and then use the organizer to record key concepts and definitions.

Encourage students to use their own words when writing notes on the organizer. This will make it easier for them to process and remember what they've read.

Summary Notes

> # MULTIPLY WITH 2
> There are many different ways to multiply with 2.
> 1. Use a number line.
> 2. Draw a picture.
> 3. Write a multiplication sentence.

H Remember

If students have read the math chapter correctly, completed the practice problems, and made personal connections to the text, remembering what they've learned shouldn't be a problem. Explain to the class that the best way to remember math is to use it—over and over again. Also point out that in a math text, most chapters build upon information taught in a previous chapter.

Wrap-up

Write three practice problems on the board. Tell the class you'd like them to use what they've learned to solve the problems. Pass out three sheets of paper to each student. Have them put one problem at the top of each page and use the rest of the page for visualizing and thinking aloud. At the bottom of the page, students should write their answers and explain how they can check to see if their answers are correct.

Lesson 5 · Review and Assess

Check Point

Use the Quick Assess checklist to informally evaluate students' understanding of how to read math. Based on their answers, divide them into two groups. Have one group do the Independent Practice on the next page and the other group do the guided practice in the *Applications Book and Word Work*.

Guided Practice

For students who need reinforcement in reading math texts, use pages 121–130 in the *Applications Book and Word Work*.

Quick Assess

Can students

☑ apply the reading process to math textbooks?

☑ tell what to do when previewing math textbooks?

☑ explain why visualizing and thinking aloud is helpful for math problems?

☑ use visualizing and thinking aloud with math problems?

For students who need more word work, assign page 229 from the *Applications Book and Word Work* on plurals.

Independent Practice

Have students who demonstrate a strong understanding of the reading process and strategy apply their knowledge to another math chapter. Invite students to choose a chapter they have already learned in math class. Then ask them to do the following.

■ Write a reading purpose question for the chapter.

■ Use the strategy of visualizing and thinking aloud to help them "see" the answers to the practice problems.

■ Report on the personal connections they were able to make to the reading.

Class Review

Create a list and post it on the board. Title it *What I've Learned About Reading Math*. Then work with students to complete the two columns. As students generate text for the chart, discuss the importance of the following.

■ previewing a math text

■ making connections to math

■ remembering what you've learned from a math chapter

Test Book

Use the short-answer and multiple-choice tests on pages 58–59 to assess students' understanding of the material presented in this week's lessons.

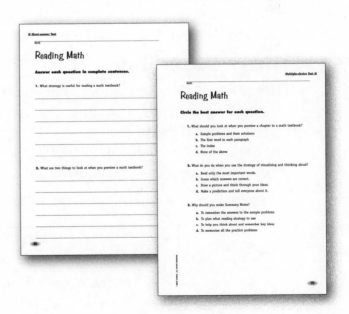

WEEK 27

Word Problems and Questions

Goals

Here students will learn how to use the reading process with word problems and textbook questions. This week's lessons will teach them to

- ☑ preview a word problem
- ☑ use a four-step plan to solve word problems
- ☑ use a four-step plan to read and answer questions in textbooks
- ☑ understand the difference between fact and critical thinking questions

Background

Help students connect this week's lessons to their prior knowledge by asking them to

- ■ find examples of word problems in their math textbooks
- ■ talk about the challenges they often present
- ■ discuss the kinds of questions they expect to see in math, social studies, and science textbooks

Opening Activity

Use the first five minutes or so of every lesson to present an interesting word problem for students to solve or a critical thinking question for them to puzzle over. Help students use strategies described in the *Reader's Handbook* to find the correct answers. You might begin with the following word problem.

> One dit and one dat together cost 3 cents. One dit and one dot together cost 4 cents. One dot and one dat together cost 5 cents. How much does a dit cost by itself?

(Answer: A dit costs one cent.)

338

Weekly Plan

Lessons	Summary
1. **Word Problems**	Work with students as they preview a word problem and learn a four-step plan they can use to solve it.
2. **Word Problems** (continued)	Support students as they apply the four-step plan and the strategy of visualizing and thinking aloud to a word problem.
3. **Questions**	Discuss a four-step plan students can use to read and answer textbook questions.
4. **Questions** (continued)	Enhance students' understanding of the difference between fact and critical thinking questions.
5. **Review and Assess**	Informally assess students to decide if more guided practice is needed. Then give an assessment.

Lesson Materials

	Components	Pages
Plan	*Teacher's Guide and Lesson Plans*	338–349
Teach	*Reader's Handbook* *Overhead Transparencies*	246–259 33, 34
Practice	*Applications Book and Word Work*	131–136, 230
Assess	*Test Book*	60–61

⬭ Lesson 1 ⬭ Word Problems

For use with *Reader's Handbook* pages 246–248

Focus

In this lesson, students learn how to preview a word problem and activate a four-step plan they can use to solve it.

Getting Started

Work with students as they read and begin the process of solving the dit and dat word problem of the Opening Activity on page 338. Model for the class the words in the problem that should be highlighted, and then discuss what they think a "dit" and "dat" might look like.

Teaching Approach

Explain to students that the reading process can help them solve the word problems in their math textbooks and on exams. Begin by reading aloud page 246 of the *Reader's Handbook*. Point out the Goals box and discuss each goal listed. Then have the class turn to page 247 and read the Before Reading section of the lesson on their own. Preview the problem that appears at the bottom of the page.

Preview a Word Problem

Help students understand that every word problem has two essential parts: the *given* and the *unknown*. In the given, students will find the key facts they need to solve the problem.

Sample Word Problem

PREVIEW
Key facts

Rachel started playing the drums in second grade. She has been practicing 20 minutes each week. Her teacher wants her to practice more!

If she begins practicing 5 extra minutes each week, how many weeks will it take until she is practicing 45 minutes each week?

PREVIEW
Main question

Use a Four-step Plan

Ask students to preview the music lesson problem (page 247) and then discuss key details they noticed in their previews. Point out that many word problems will contain a combination of essential and nonessential information. Remind students to be aware of details that have nothing to do with solving a problem, such as when Rachel started playing the drums.

Next, have students turn to page 248. Ask them to read silently the four-step plan described on the page, and then walk them through each step. Ask questions that help them understand the purpose of each step, including

■ Why is it important for you to read a word problem several times before you try to solve it?

■ What should you look for in word problems?

■ At what step do you decide the operation you need to use to solve the problem? What words in a problem can give you clues about the correct operation?

■ How do you figure out what information you need to solve a problem?

■ How do you check your math work? Why do you need to do this? Should you check every answer or just a few of them?

After your discussion, have students record the four steps for solving word problems in their Reading Notebooks. Explain that in the next lesson you'll practice using the plan with sample word problems.

Wrap-up

As a class, review what students have learned about word problems. Have a student summarize the purpose of the four-step plan. Then discuss which of the steps students currently use when solving word problems. Find out which steps they skip and why. Use the information to help you plan the second part of your "Word Problems" lesson.

Lesson 2 Word Problems (continued)

For use with *Reader's Handbook* pages 249–252

Focus

Here students will apply the four-step plan for solving a word problem and recall how the strategy of visualizing and thinking aloud can help them arrive at the correct answer.

Getting Started

Ask students to use the strategy of visualizing and thinking aloud to solve the dit and dat problem. Have a volunteer draw on the board a picture that represents the problem. Then work with students as they think aloud the solution.

Teaching Approach

Begin by explaining to the class that one of the hardest parts in solving word problems is getting a handle on the language. Students will need to "translate" a problem into mathematical terms and choose the operation they need to use to solve the problem. The four-step plan described on page 248 can help.

Step 1: Read

Tell the class that you'd like them to begin applying the plan to the music lesson problem shown on page 247. Point out to students that the Think Aloud at the bottom of the page is a model for the kind of thinking they'll do as they translate the words in a problem into mathematical terms.

Step 2: Plan

After students have read the problem and know the key facts, they need to decide how they will arrive at a solution. Explain that the strategy of visualizing, which they learned about in "Reading Math" (pages 238–242), can help. Then have students read the top of page 250 and examine the sample table. Help the class understand that graphics such as tables, diagrams, and even graphs can help them "see" their way to the problem's solution. Choosing a table, graph, or diagram can be part of the plan that helps them solve the problem.

Visualizing

WEEK	1					
MINUTES	20					

Step 3: Solve

Next, have students solve the music lesson problem using a table similar to the one shown on page 250. Ask them to subvocalize as they work their way through the operations. When they finish, have students make notes on what they did to solve the problem.

Think Aloud

WEEK	1	2	3	4	5	6
MINUTES	20	25	30	35	40	45

Wrap-up

Finish the lesson by asking students to complete Step 4 of the plan. Have students follow along as you read aloud the explanation on page 251. Help the class understand how they can check their work by solving the problem in a different way. Finish by asking students to sum up what they learned about solving word problems. Then assign groups of students to work through a few word problems from their math text. Have them demonstrate how to use the four-step plan.

Lesson 3 Questions

For use with *Reader's Handbook* pages 253–255

Focus

In this lesson, students will explore the differences between fact and critical thinking questions and learn strategies to help answer both kinds.

Getting Started

Ask students to take a section of their Reading Notebooks and make them into a small "strategy handbook" of their own. Explain that first, you'd like them to make notes about the steps to solve word problems. Then ask them to illustrate the pages of their handbooks and share their work with a partner.

Teaching Approach

Begin the lesson by explaining to students that the textbooks they use in school contain two basic types of questions: fact and critical thinking. Ask students, "What is a fact question? How do you answer it? What is a critical thinking question? How do you answer *those* types of questions?"

Next, have students turn to page 253. Point out the Goals box and discuss the two goals listed. Explain that the key to answering questions is reading carefully and that the reading process can help.

Questions

As students preview, they should watch for the question's key words—that is, those that tell them what the question is about and how to answer it. Model a preview for each question on Overhead Transparencies 33 and 34.

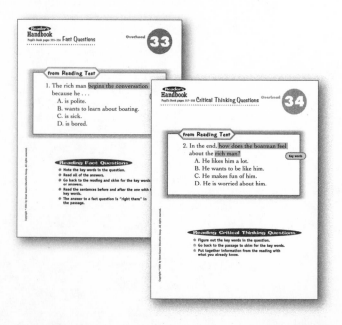

Use a Four-step Plan

After students conduct their own previews of the science questions on page 254, have them read the four-step plan shown on page 255.

Plan for Answering Questions

1. Read the question slowly and carefully.

2. Ask yourself, "What is this question asking me to do?"

3. Decide what information you need to answer the question.

4. Find the key words in the question. Then look over the material to find these same key words. Read one sentence before and one sentence after each key word.

Discuss with students the importance of individual steps in the plan. Ask these questions to gauge their understanding.

■ Why might you need to read a question more than once before answering it?

■ What is the purpose of Step 2 of the four-step plan?

■ How do you figure out what information you need to answer a question?

■ Why should you look at one sentence before and one sentence after a key word sentence?

Wrap-up

Ask students to work with a partner and explain what they've learned thus far about answering textbook questions. Then discuss as a class their explanations.

Lesson 4 Questions (continued)

For use with *Reader's Handbook* pages 256–259

Focus

Here students will continue to learn about how to answer both fact and critical thinking questions.

Getting Started

Have students make notes about ideas they can use when answering fact questions and strategies they can use when answering critical thinking questions. Again, generate interest in the project by asking students to illustrate their work.

Teaching Approach

Students focus here on learning how to identify and respond to two different kinds of questions: fact questions and critical thinking questions.

Answer Fact Questions

Begin by reminding students that fact questions in a textbook require them to recall details from the reading. This means that the answer to every fact question can be found somewhere "right there" in the text.

Next, direct students to turn to page 256. Read the explanation at the top of the page and the sample question about the moon.

Sample Question

> INVESTIGATION 1 WRAP-UP
>
> **REVIEW** **1.** Describe two ways in which the Moon differs from Earth.

Help students apply the four-step plan to this question. Ask students to identify key words in the question and then skim the passage at the bottom of the page for these same key words. Once they find their key words, they need to read one sentence before and one sentence after the key word sentence.

Answer Critical Thinking Questions

Once students understand how to use the four-step plan with fact questions, discuss how the plan can help them with questions that require critical thinking. Begin by reminding students that to answer critical thinking questions, they need to draw their own conclusions about a fact or idea. Show students the formula they can use for finding the answer to a critical thinking question.

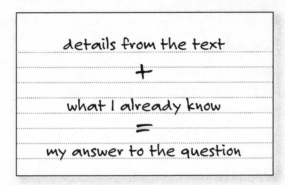

details from the text

+

what I already know

=

my answer to the question

Direct students to page 257. Have them follow along as you read the explanation at the top of the page. Then have them examine the sample question, taking note of the key words. Walk students through the "Steps for Critical Thinking Questions."

Point out that the strategy of thinking aloud works well with critical thinking questions because it encourages students to talk their way through to an answer. Ask students to read the sample Think Aloud on page 258, and then discuss.

Finish the lesson by having students read the After Reading discussion on page 259. Point out the questions students can ask themselves when checking their work. Ask them to keep in mind that the best possible question they can ask themselves when checking their answer is the all-purpose, "Does my answer make sense?" Students should know that if the answer doesn't make sense, it is likely to be wrong.

Wrap-up

Ask students to read Summing Up on page 259. Ask students, "What is a four-step plan you can follow to help you answer fact and critical thinking questions?" Then write on the board a critical thinking question from students' science or social studies textbooks. Work through it together as a class and apply the four steps to the question and then think aloud the answer.

Lesson 5 Review and Assess

Check Point

Use the Quick Assess checklist to informally evaluate students' understanding of how to read and respond to word problems and textbook questions. Based on their answers, divide them into two groups. Have one group do the Independent Practice on the next page and the other group do the guided practice in the *Applications Book and Word Work*.

Guided Practice

For students who need reinforcement in reading word problems and questions, use pages 131–136 in the *Applications Book and Word Work*.

Quick Assess

Can students

☑ highlight the main question and key facts in a word problem?

☑ describe a four-step plan to solve word problems?

☑ explain how to find the answer to fact questions?

☑ tell what is needed to answer a critical thinking question?

For students who need more word work, assign page 230 from the *Applications Book and Word Work* on y endings.

Independent Practice

Students who have demonstrated a strong understanding of the reading process and the thinking process they can use with word problems and fact and critical thinking questions can apply their knowledge to practice problems and questions in their textbooks.

Then, ask students to do the following:

▪ Write directions for how to preview a word problem or a textbook question.

▪ Discuss their answers with a partner.

▪ Explain the four-step plan they used to solve the word problems or answer the fact and critical thinking questions.

Class Review

Have students create word problems of their own. Encourage them to use funny words and imaginative situations. When they've finished, ask them to switch papers with a partner and solve. Then ask the following:

▪ What did you notice on your preview of the word problem?

▪ How did visualizing and thinking aloud help you find the answer?

Test Book

Use the short-answer and multiple-choice tests on pages 60–61 to assess students' understanding of the material presented in this week's lessons.

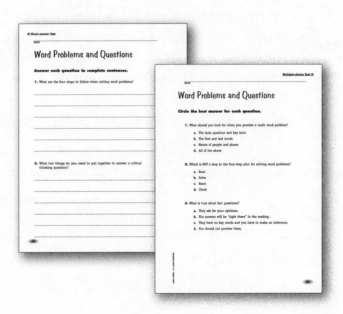

Reading a Folktale

Goals

Here students will read a folktale called "The Lion and the Mouse." This week's lessons will help them learn to

> ☑ read and understand folktales
>
> ☑ use the reading strategy of summarizing

Background

Help students connect this week's lessons to their prior knowledge by asking them to

- share folktales with which they are familiar

- talk about what they know about folktales

- list questions they have about reading folktales

Opening Activity

To reinforce students' understanding of the universal appeal of folktales, read aloud tales from around the world as students work through this unit. Encourage students to look for similarities among the tales, including their brevity, use of humor, talking animals, happy endings, and stated or unstated lessons. Books that will work well for this lesson include

- *Mightier Than the Sword: World Folktales for Strong Boys* by Jane Yolen

- *Nelson Mandela's Favorite African Folktales* selected by Nelson Mandela

- *Can You Guess My Name: Traditional Tales from Around the World* selected and retold by Judy Sierra

- *Fiesta Femenina: Celebrating Women in Mexican Folktales* retold by Mary-Joan Gerson

Weekly Plan

Lessons	Summary
1. **Before Reading: Folktale**	Work with students as they apply the Before Reading stage of the reading process to prepare for reading a folktale.
2. **During Reading: Folktale**	Teach students how to use a Story String to help them keep track of events as they read a folktale.
3. **During Reading: Folktale** (continued)	Help students use active reading strategies when reading a folktale.
4. **After Reading: Folktale**	Develop students' understanding of the After Reading stage of the reading process as they apply it to a folktale.
5. **Review and Assess**	Informally assess students to decide if more guided practice is needed. Then give an assessment.

Lesson Materials

	Components	Pages
Plan	*Teacher's Guide and Lesson Plans*	350–361
Teach	*Reader's Handbook* *Overhead Transparencies*	270–281 27, 28
Practice	*Applications Book and Word Work*	137–146, 231
Assess	*Test Book*	62–63

Lesson 1 Before Reading: Folktale

For use with *Reader's Handbook* pages 270–275

Focus

In this lesson, students focus on the Before Reading stage of the reading process as they prepare to read a folktale.

Getting Started

Put the phrase "You learn from your mistakes" on the board. Ask students what they think this means. Give some personal examples and allow students to share some of their experiences. Then ask students to design a Storyboard that tells the story of an event that ends with the character learning a lesson. This can be something that happened to them or it can be made up. Explain to students they are putting together a personal folktale.

Teaching Approach

As you begin, tell students they will learn about one genre of literature (folktales) and learn how to read it by using the reading process.

 Set a Purpose

Have students look at "Set a Purpose" on page 271 of the *Reader's Handbook*. Read aloud the two questions students should ask themselves to set their purposes for reading a folktale. Point out that these questions are general; students can use them for any folktale. Explain that students might have additional questions based on the particular folktale they are reading. Ask students to think up another question about "The Lion and the Mouse" based on its title, such as "Why would a mouse be around a lion?"

 Preview

Walk students through the Preview Checklist. Show students how to preview a folktale using Overhead Transparencies 27 and 28. Point to each item from the Preview Checklist on the overhead.

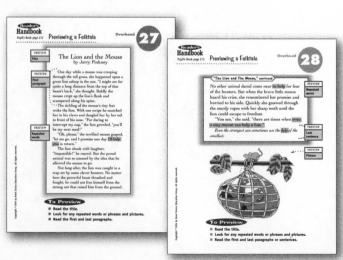

352

C Plan

As a group, read Plan on page 274. Have students add items they learned from the preview.

Talk about how students would plan to read a folktale. Remind them that their plan should match their purpose for reading; in this case, their purpose is to answer two key questions about the folktale. Point out that summarizing is an excellent strategy for helping students focus on the most important information in the folktale.

Introduce the Story String as a good reading tool to use. Explain that this tool helps readers remember important events and keep them in the right order. Point out how well a Story String works with the reading strategy of summarizing. It will focus students on the most important parts of the folktale. Explain that students will create their Story String after they read "The Lion and the Mouse." Then walk through the Story String on page 275.

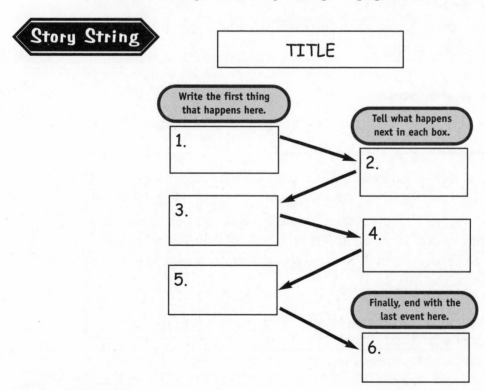

Story String

TITLE

Write the first thing that happens here.

1.

Tell what happens next in each box.

2.

3.

4.

5.

Finally, end with the last event here.

6.

Wrap-up

Ask students to find a partner and set up a Story String. Tell them to summarize the day in the Story String. Allow groups to switch papers and check each other's organizers to see that they have:

■ the title

■ two or three boxes filled in with only important events of the day

Lesson 2 During Reading: Folktale

For use with *Reader's Handbook* page 276

Focus

Here students learn how to keep track of events as they read a folktale.

Getting Started

Choose a folktale to read aloud to the class. Before you start reading, give students the title and ask them to predict what it will be about. Allow students to share their thoughts. Then take it a step further and ask them what the lesson of the folktale may be about. After students share their ideas, read the folktale to the class.

Teaching Approach

Focus students on the idea that they read to find something. That's their purpose for reading.

D Read with a Purpose

Review with students their purpose for reading a folktale.

■ to find out what happens in a folktale

■ to find out what the lesson is

Explain that in this lesson students will focus on their first purpose: finding out what happens in a folktale. Remind them to create their Story Strings to help them keep track of events and summarize the story.

Explain to students that because folktales tend to be brief, lots of activity happens in a short amount of text. Review what students learned about summarizing. Then have students read with a partner "The Lion and the Mouse" on pages 272–273. Encourage partners to fill in their Story Strings as they read. Remind students to focus on the most important ideas, not the smaller details, as they create their Story Strings.

Story String

"THE LION AND THE MOUSE"

1. A mouse creeps up a lion's back while he's sleeping.

2. The lion wakes up and is about to eat the mouse.

3. The lion lets the mouse go.

4. The mouse says she'll help him one day.

5. The lion gets caught in a trap.

6. The mouse helps the lion get free.

After students complete their organizers, have them compare their Story Strings to the one in the handbook. Tell them to discuss how and why the Story Strings are different.

Wrap-up

Invite student volunteers to share their summaries of "The Lion and the Mouse." Encourage volunteers to use their Story Strings as a basis for their summaries. Remind them that a summary includes only the most important information from the tale. Discuss how easy or difficult it was for students to use a Story String to help them summarize a folktale.

Lesson 3 During Reading: Folktale (continued)

For use with *Reader's Handbook* pages 277–278

Focus

In this lesson, students continue using active reading strategies as they read a folktale.

Getting Started

Make a list of fictional and nonfictional characters your class has read about or learned about this year. Assign students a character and explain they will act out the person in a game of charades. After the game, talk with the class about the differences between imaginary characters found in fiction, such as folktales, and real people who appear in nonfiction. Make clear that in fiction authors have much more freedom to do what they want with their characters.

Teaching Approach

Tell students that here they will learn more about what good readers do as they are reading a folktale.

D Read with a Purpose (continued)

Review with students their two purposes for reading.

1. To find out what happens
2. To find out what the lesson is

Point out that by creating their Story Strings students kept track of the events in the folktale. The next step is to find the lesson of the folktale. Ask students to return to the folktale and point to its lesson. Explain that when a folktale includes a stated lesson, it may be set aside from the rest of the tale by extra spacing and sometimes *italics*.

Make clear that not all folktales include a lesson. In these instances, students need to look for clues in the tale to come up with the lesson. Walk students through the excerpt. Have students look over the folktale for more information about the main characters. Explain that knowing what the main characters are all about can help readers begin to piece together the folktale's lesson.

E Connect

As a class, talk about the importance of connecting to what you read. Remind students that connecting is an important step in the During Reading stage of the reading process. Talk about the different ways to connect to a story or folktale. Then walk students through page 278. Give students time to reflect on their answers. Point out the sample connections. Encourage students to make their own connections to the text. Complete the activity by having students write two or three connections in their Reading Notebooks. If they are stuck, have them use the questions on page 278 as a guide.

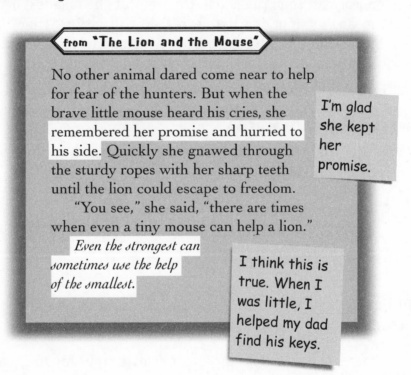

from "The Lion and the Mouse"

No other animal dared come near to help for fear of the hunters. But when the brave little mouse heard his cries, she remembered her promise and hurried to his side. Quickly she gnawed through the sturdy ropes with her sharp teeth until the lion could escape to freedom.

"You see," she said, "there are times when even a tiny mouse can help a lion."

Even the strongest can sometimes use the help of the smallest.

I'm glad she kept her promise.

I think this is true. When I was little, I helped my dad find his keys.

Wrap-up

Invite students to share their connections with the class. Then have them write a short journal entry in which they further explore their ideas about the folktale's lesson. Ask students to reflect on the lesson in their Reading Notebooks. Encourage students to think of times in their own lives where this lesson proved true or false.

Lesson 4 After Reading: Folktale

For use with *Reader's Handbook* pages 279–281

Focus

In this lesson, students will learn to apply the After Reading stage of the reading process when reading a folktale.

Getting Started

Refer students to the lesson in "The Lion and the Mouse." (Even the strongest can sometimes use the help of the smallest.) Clarify what it means by applying it to a real-life situation. Then have students work in pairs to come up with some of their own situations where the lesson can be used. Ask them to share their ideas with the class.

Teaching Approach

Tell students that after reading they need to return to their original purpose for reading. Then ask

■ Have you met your reading purpose?

■ Did you find out what you wanted to from the reading?

F Pause and Reflect

Point out the most important question to ask after reading.

■ Is there anything that confuses me?

Whether reading for a class assignment or simply for fun, clearing up any confusion is critical for understanding and enjoying what you read. It is important during this step to take the time to identify what is confusing and to take steps to remedy it.

G Reread

Remind students that readers don't always learn everything from a single reading. Good readers know that by going back and rereading parts of the selection again, they can "fix up" their understanding.

Reinforce students' understanding of effective rereading by working through the sample. Then have students reread to clarify what they found confusing about the tale.

Remember

Talk about ways readers can remember what they read, such as writing a summary in their Reading Notebook or sending an email about a story to a friend. List students' ideas on the board.

Explain that students can also rely on reading tools to help them remember what they read. One reading tool that can help students remember any type of fiction is a Fiction Organizer.

Point out the Fiction Organizer on page 281. It includes the basic story elements: characters, setting, and plot. Make clear that a Fiction Organizer can be modified to fit a particular story. For example, if a reader wanted to remember the lesson of "The Lion and the Mouse," he or she could add another box to the organizer labeled "Lesson."

Fiction Organizer

| **CHARACTERS** a mouse and a lion | **SETTING** a place with other animals and tall grass |

TITLE AND AUTHOR "The Lion and the Mouse" by Jerry Pinkney

PLOT A small mouse rescues a great lion.

Wrap-up

As a class, review the unit goals from page 350 in this book. Then invite students to gather in small groups to talk about how well they met these goals. Groups might use these prompts to jump-start their discussion.

■ What was the most important thing I learned about reading folktales?

■ How would I teach other students to summarize a folktale?

■ Do I think that summarizing is a good strategy for reading folktales? Why or why not? What other strategies could I use?

Lesson 5 Review and Assess

Check Point

Use the Quick Assess checklist to informally evaluate students' understanding of how to read a folktale. Based on their answers, divide the class into two groups. One group can do the Independent Practice on the next page and the other group can do the guided practice in the *Applications Book and Word Work.*

Guided Practice

For students who need reinforcement in reading folktales, use pages 137–146 in the *Applications Book and Word Work.*

Can students

☑ apply the reading process to a folktale?

☑ tell how to preview a folktale?

☑ describe an organizer to use with folktales?

☑ explain why summarizing will help them read folktales?

For students who need more word work, assign page 231 from the *Applications Book and Word Work* on adding *ed.*

Independent Practice

For students that demonstrate a strong understanding of the reading process and strategy, have them apply their knowledge to reading another folktale.

Then ask students to do the following:

■ Write reading purpose questions for the folktale.

■ Create a Story String and a Fiction Organizer for the folktale.

Class Review

Have students gather in groups of six. Explain that groups will make posters describing how to use the reading process when reading a folktale. Within each group, assign pairs of students the Before, During, or After Reading stages of the reading process. Encourage groups to be creative as they design their posters. For example, students might choose to sketch the important parts of their stage rather than write them. Have pairs design a rough copy of their portion of the poster on paper before adding it to the poster.

After groups complete their posters, hang them in the classroom as reminders for students as they continue to work through the fiction section of the *Reader's Handbook*. Encourage students to look over the posters when they apply the reading process to other types of fiction to see how the process compares to reading folktales.

Test Book

Use the short-answer and multiple-choice tests on pages 62–63 to assess students' understanding of the material presented in this week's lessons.

WEEK 29
Reading a Novel

Goals

Here students read an excerpt from the novel *Flat Stanley*. This week's lessons will help them learn to

- ☑ understand the characters, setting, and plot of a novel
- ☑ use the reading strategy of using graphic organizers

Background

Help students connect this week's lessons to their prior knowledge by asking them to

- ■ discuss what they know about novels
- ■ think about how to apply the reading process when reading a novel
- ■ compare reading novels with reading other types of fiction
- ■ explore the more challenging aspects of reading novels

Opening Activity

Write the following headings on the board: *Title, Interesting Characters, Exciting Plot,* and *Other Reasons*. Hold a class discussion about favorite novels. Begin by sharing your own favorite novels from childhood. Provide a brief summary, and explain why these are your favorites. List your titles on the board, and then place a tally mark under one of the three headings (provide specifics under *Other Reasons*). Invite volunteers to share their favorite novels. Add their reasons under the correct heading(s). After completing the activity, tally the marks to see which story element was mentioned most as a reason for considering a novel a favorite. Were students surprised by the results? What does this informal poll tell students about what they look for most when choosing novels?

Weekly Plan

Lessons	Summary
1. **Before Reading: Novel**	Review with students the steps of the Before Reading stage of the reading process and discuss how to apply each step to a novel.
2. **During Reading: Novel**	Explore how to apply the During Reading stage of the reading process to a novel, particularly the story elements of plot and characters.
3. **During Reading: Novel** (continued)	Apply the During Reading stage of the reading process to a novel. Reinforce their understanding of setting and making connections as they read.
4. **After Reading: Novel**	Apply the After Reading stage of the reading process to a novel.
5. **Review and Assess**	Informally assess students to decide if more guided practice is needed. Then give an assessment.

Lesson Materials

	Components	Pages
Plan	*Teacher's Guide and Lesson Plans*	362–373
Teach	*Reader's Handbook*	282–293
	Overhead Transparencies	29, 30
Practice	*Applications Book and Word Work*	147–155, 232
Assess	*Test Book*	64–65

Lesson 1 Before Reading: Novel

For use with *Reader's Handbook* pages 282–286

Focus

Here students review the steps of the Before Reading stage of the reading process and discuss how to apply each step to a novel.

Getting Started

Lay out five to ten novels on a table. Ask a few students to come up and choose one they would like to read. Have the rest of the class observe how the students made a decision of what book to read. Do they look at interesting book covers? Read book jackets or back covers? Skim a page or two? Point out that all of these are previewing strategies, just like the ones students have been using throughout their work in the *Reader's Handbook*.

Teaching Approach

Have students read page 282. Discuss students' thoughts about reading novels. Do the number of pages, characters, and events in a novel overwhelm them? Remind them that the reading process will help them enjoy the adventures and characters that novels bring to life.

A Set a Purpose

Explain that whether they are reading a novel for fun or for an assignment, setting a purpose will help them keep track of all the different parts of a novel. Reinforce your teaching by asking students to read the directions on how to set a purpose on page 283. Tell the class that they will be reading an excerpt from a novel called *Flat Stanley*. Remind students that the purpose questions in the *Reader's Handbook* are general and can be used for any novel. They might have additional questions to add for this specific novel, such as "Why is it called *Flat Stanley*?" Challenge students to come up with one more purpose question of their own.

B Preview

Read aloud the Preview text on page 283 and walk students through the Preview Checklist. Talk about why novels may be more difficult to preview than other types of text and how the items on the checklist might help them.

Then model how to preview a novel by thinking aloud as you work through pages 284–285. Use Overhead Transparencies 29 and 30 to point to each item. As you preview, make clear what clues you gather from each item on the checklist. After you finish, talk about the preview. What checklist items did students find most useful?

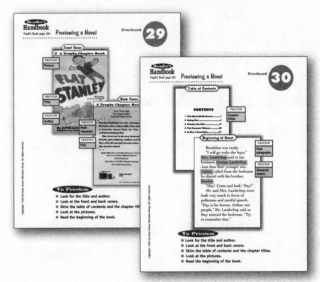

C Plan

Remind students that one of the reasons for setting a purpose and previewing is to develop an effective plan for reading. Then ask, "Where in the preview would readers find this piece of information?" Invite students to add more items to the list.

Next, review with students the strategy of using graphic organizers. Have them read the bottom of page 286 to see how using graphic organizers works with novels. Then discuss the Fiction Organizer. Have students look back over the three purpose questions on page 283 of the handbook. Lead students to see that each question corresponds to one of the three boxes in the Fiction Organizer.

Wrap-up

At the end of the lesson, have students draw a Fiction Organizer in their Reading Notebooks. Have them fill it in for a story that could be written about the classroom they are in now.

Lesson 2 During Reading: Novel

For use with *Reader's Handbook* pages 287–288

Focus

In this lesson, students will begin exploring how to apply the During Reading stage of the reading process to a novel. Here they will focus on plot and characters.

Getting Started

Review the Fiction Organizer on page 286. Talk about the three story elements in the organizer—plot, characters, and setting. Explain that in this lesson students will focus on understanding the plot and characters in novels.

Teaching Approach

Begin by talking about what students already know about plot and character.

D Read with a Purpose

1. Plot

Review with students their purpose for reading *Flat Stanley*. Remind them that they need to answer the first purpose question.

■ What happens in the novel?

Have students focus on the plot of the novel. Reinforce students' understanding of plot by reading aloud and discussing page 287. Make sure students understand two key points about plot.

1. Plot is the action and events of a novel.

2. Most plots revolve around a problem and how the characters try to solve it.

Assess students' understanding of plot by returning to the class list of favorite novels. Have student volunteers share the main problem of the characters in their favorite novels.

2. Characters

Once you're sure students understand the role of plot in a novel, move on to the second purpose question.

■ Who are the main characters in the novel?

Point out the key phrase in this question: main characters. Explain that some novels have lots of characters. Make clear that the main characters are those who play the biggest parts in the story's plot and who the author spends the most time describing.

Move on to discussing how readers can learn more about the main characters in a novel. Explain that active readers pay attention to what characters say, act, think, feel, and look like and what other characters think of them. Tell the class that a Character Map can help readers keep track of what a character is like. Explore the Character Map for Stanley on the bottom of page 288. Talk about the last box in particular. Explain that this space gives readers a chance to stop and think about how they feel about the character. Point out that by making connections to the characters, students will get more involved in the novel as a whole.

Character Map

WHAT HE SAYS AND DOES He goes under doors.	WHAT OTHERS THINK Parents are proud.
STANLEY	
HOW HE LOOKS AND FEELS He likes being flat.	HOW I FEEL I'm surprised that he is not upset.

Wrap-up

Ask volunteers to summarize the purpose of a Character Map and how students can use it when reading novels. Finish by having students draw a Character Map in their notebooks. Tell students to fill in a Character Map for a family member.

Lesson 3 During Reading: Novel (continued)

For use with *Reader's Handbook* pages 289–291

Focus

In this lesson, students continue exploring how to apply the During Reading stage of the reading process to a novel. Here they will focus on the setting and on making connections as they read.

Getting Started

Review what students learned about the character of Stanley and his problem. Ask students to use what they have learned to begin filling in a Fiction Organizer. Explain that in this lesson, students will focus on the last box in the organizer—a novel's setting.

Teaching Approach

Remind the class that in this lesson they will continue focusing on how to read a novel with a purpose.

D Read with a Purpose (continued)

Review the last purpose question from page 283.

■ Where and when does the story take place?

Explain that in order to answer this question students need to understand how to find out about the novel's setting (or settings). Talk about what students already know about setting. Then have students read page 289. Were students surprised to learn that setting is not just *where* a novel takes place, but also *when*? Then talk about why setting is important in some novels and not others.

Fiction Organizer

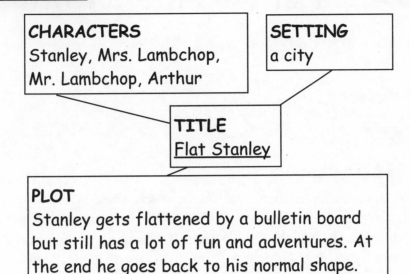

CHARACTERS
Stanley, Mrs. Lambchop,
Mr. Lambchop, Arthur

SETTING
a city

TITLE
Flat Stanley

PLOT
Stanley gets flattened by a bulletin board
but still has a lot of fun and adventures. At
the end he goes back to his normal shape.

Use the Fiction Organizer to help students see how to collect all
of the important information about a novel.

E Connect

Review what students have learned about making connections to
their reading. Explain that the purpose for connecting to novels
helps readers better understand and enjoy what they are reading.

Ask the class to turn to page 291. Read aloud the Connect text at
the top of the page and the list of questions. Then read aloud the
excerpt from *Flat Stanley*. Discuss the connection one reader made
to the text. Ask students, "What connections can you make to this
excerpt?" Have volunteers share their ideas.

Wrap-up

Have students reflect on their understanding of the lesson by
asking them to respond to the following questions in their
Reading Notebooks.

■ Am I confused about anything I read so far about
   reading novels?

■ What questions do I still have about reading novels?

■ What parts of this lesson will I use next time I read a novel?

After students complete the activity, discuss their responses. Talk
about the similarities and differences among their answers.

Lesson 4 After Reading: Novel

For use with *Reader's Handbook* pages 292–293

Focus

In this lesson, students explore how to apply the After Reading stage of the reading process to a novel.

Getting Started

Give students a mini-writing assignment. Have them write a fictional story about a simple topic (a brother and sister at a park, on a boat, or at the beach). Guide them to have a problem and a solution in their story. Allow 10–15 minutes for this activity.

Teaching Approach

Explain to students that one of the most challenging aspects of applying the reading process to a novel is that often a week or more passes between the time readers first set their purposes and the time they finish reading the novel. Help students understand that taking the time to pause and reflect will help them pull together the entire reading process, from their initial preview to their final thoughts about the text.

F Pause and Reflect

Have students read the top of page 292. Then ask the class to answer the three purpose questions in their Reading Notebooks. When they've finished, have students talk about how well they were able to answer the questions. Ask those that answered the questions with ease to share what reading strategies or tools they relied on. Remind others who still have questions that rereading will help them find answers. Model for students how reading tools such as a Fiction Organizer and Character Map can help you answer these questions.

G Reread

Explain that when reading a novel strictly for fun, there is no need to reread unless readers want to clarify parts that are still confusing. When reading a novel for a class assignment, rereading plays a bigger role. First, students need to be aware of the parts of the novel that confuse them. If it involves a character, they might benefit from creating a Character Map. Most often, complicated plots give readers the most trouble. If that's the case, students might benefit from using a graphic organizer that focuses more on the novel's plot, such as a Story String or Storyboard.

H Remember

Ask students if they have ever read a great story, only to discover a few weeks later that they can barely remember what it was about. Explain that this happens when readers don't take the time after reading to think about ways to help them remember what they read.

Have students read page 293 on their own. Then talk about the purpose of a Storyboard. For some readers, drawing instead of writing the key plot events helps them better remember what they read.

Storyboard

FLAT STANLEY

Stanley becomes flat.	Stanley has fun.
Stanley becomes sad.	He stops being flat.

Wrap-up

Have students look over their story again from the beginning of Lesson 4. Ask them to trade papers with a student. Have students read each other's stories and then make a Storyboard.

Lesson 5 Review and Assess

Check Point

Use the Quick Assess checklist to informally evaluate students' understanding of how to read a novel. Based on their answers, divide them into two groups. Ask one group to complete the Independent Practice on the next page and the other group can do the Guided Practice in the *Applications Book and Word Work*.

Guided Practice

For students who need reinforcement in the reading a novel, use pages 147–155 in the *Applications Book and Word Work*.

Quick Assess

Can students

☑ apply the reading process to novels?

☑ name the basic parts of a novel?

☑ explain one tool to use to keep track of characters in a novel?

☑ explain two tools that help them remember what happened in the plot of a novel?

For students who need more word work, assign page 232 from the *Applications Book and Word Work* section on adding *ing*.

Independent Practice

Students with a strong understanding of the reading process and the strategy of using graphic organizers might apply their knowledge to another short novel.

After students choose a novel, have them do the following.

■ Write three or four reading purpose questions for the novel.

■ Make a Fiction Organizer about the reading, a Character Map about a main character, or a Storyboard that reflects their understanding of the main events of the novel.

Class Review

Divide the class into small groups. Have groups create brief quizzes (approximately three or four questions) to test others on their knowledge of the unit. Groups might include multiple-choice, short-answer, and matching questions in their quizzes. Remind groups to include questions from all parts of the unit. When they finish, ask groups to take the test themselves to work out any glitches and then trade with another group. Questions they might use include the following:

1. What are the purpose questions readers ask themselves before reading a novel?

2. What reading tool can readers use to help them keep track of the different story elements in a novel?

3. What is the definition of plot? Character? Setting?

Test Book

Use the short-answer and multiple-choice tests on pages 64–65 to assess students' understanding of the material presented in this week's lessons.

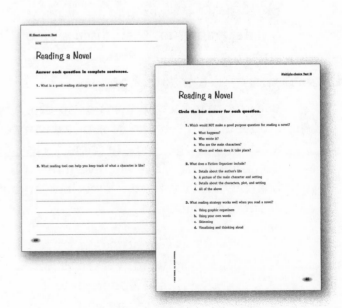

WEEK 30

Plot, Dialogue, and Theme

Goals

Here students will learn how to keep track of the events in a plot and consider the importance of dialogue and theme. This week's lessons will teach them to

- ☑ keep track of the events of a plot
- ☑ understand how the parts of a plot come together to create a cohesive whole
- ☑ recognize the importance of dialogue
- ☑ make inferences about theme

Background

Help students connect this week's lessons to their prior knowledge by asking them to

- ▪ recall stories and books they've found interesting and entertaining and then explain why
- ▪ define the term *plot*
- ▪ tell what they know about dialogue
- ▪ recall what they've learned about subject and main idea in preparation for their discussion of theme

Opening Activity

Use the first five minutes or so of every lesson this week to ask students to retell the plot of a favorite story. Because children ramble a bit at this age, require them to use only one sentence to retell a specific event. Write the events in a Story String as they tell them. Use the activity to reinforce how an author "strings together" the events in a plot.

Weekly Plan

Lessons	Summary
1. **Focus on Plot**	Work with students as they explore the characteristics of plot.
2. **Focus on Plot** (continued)	Introduce the terms *problem, climax,* and *solution* and help them to learn how to track key events in a plot.
3. **Understanding Dialogue**	Consider with students the importance of dialogue in a work of fiction.
4. **Understanding Theme**	Discuss theme and how it differs from the subject of a story.
5. **Review and Assess**	Informally assess students to decide if more guided practice is needed. Then give an assessment.

Lesson Materials

	Components	Pages
Plan	*Teacher's Guide and Lesson Plans*	374–385
Teach	*Reader's Handbook*	306–312, 329, 347
	Overhead Transparencies	3
Practice	*Applications Book and Word Work*	156–160, 233
Assess	*Test Book*	66–67

Lesson 1 · Focus on Plot

For use with *Reader's Handbook* pages 306–307

Focus

In this lesson, students explore the characteristics of plot and why it is important for readers to track the events of a plot when reading a story.

Getting Started

Plot is the backbone of a story. It is the series of events that connects the beginning of a story to its end. In most well-written stories, the plot builds steadily toward the climax, or turning point, and then moves with the same kind of assuredness toward the resolution, or ending.

In this lesson, you'll discuss characteristics of plot. Help students understand the movement of a plot by drawing a picture of a mountain on the board. Take a familiar story and show where the main events would be on the mountain sketch.

Teaching Approach

Start by putting plot in terms students will know. Use a well-known story, such as "Cinderella," and retell the plot. Ask students if they know any stories with plots they can retell. Be sure students understand the term *plot* before going on.

Before Reading

Begin the lesson by defining the term *plot*. Explain that plot is the action in a story. It is what keeps the reader reading from the beginning to the end.

Then have the class read page 306. Discuss the goals listed in the Goals box and invite students to share their own goals for the unit.

Goals

Goals

Here you'll learn how to:

✔ **keep track of the events of a plot**

✔ **understand how the parts of a plot work together**

Remind students that additional goals for the unit will be to learn how the reading process can help them understand what they read and how they respond to a plot. An additional goal is to learn tools that can help them track the action of a story.

Explain that most stories open with a little background information about the characters and setting. Sometimes the author provides that information in the first couple of paragraphs. Tell students to look for information about the plot in the first paragraphs of the story.

As an example, have students preview and then read the excerpt from *The Skirt* by Gary Soto (page 307). Ask them to make notes on character and action in a simple chart.

Story Opening

Characters	Action
Miata Ramirez	Miata yells for the bus driver to stop. Then she runs after the bus.
The bus driver	

Wrap-up

Have a student retell the definition of *plot* and explain how it is used. Then ask, "What is important to remember about plot? Why should readers pay attention to plot?"

Lesson 2   Focus on Plot (continued)

For use with *Reader's Handbook* pages 308–312

Focus

Here students consider *problem, climax,* and *solution* as literary terms and learn how to track key events in a plot.

Getting Started

Ask students to help make a list of stories they know well on the board. Add two columns to make a chart—one called "problem" and the other "solution." Ask them to name the problem and solution in each story. For example, ask, "What is the problem in *Charlotte's Web*? What is the solution?" Help them understand that the problem involves Wilbur and the possibility that he might be killed for food. The solution involves Charlotte, the spider, who makes Wilbur so famous that no one would ever dream of hurting him. Explain that a plot usually consists of a problem (conflict) and solution (resolution).

Teaching Approach

Ask students to read silently the explanatory text at the top of page 308 and the continuation of the excerpt from *The Skirt*. Then discuss the central problem in the story: that Miata has left her *folklórico* skirt on the bus. Point out that the title of the novel offers a clue about the story's major problem.

During Reading

Remind students that every plot has three general parts: beginning, middle, and end. Direct students to read the information in the handbook and follow along as you review the parts and discuss the function of each.

Then refer to the mountain sketch you drew on the board in Lesson 1. Explain that a plot's action is somewhat like the action of climbing a mountain. The plot builds as the climb gets steeper. Tell the class that the problem is usually introduced somewhere in the beginning section. In the middle, the problem is at its worst. This is called the *climax*. In the ending, the problem is often resolved.

Have students continue reading *The Skirt*. Ask them to keep an eye out for the climax. Where does it occur?

Story Organizer

TITLE The Skirt		
BEGINNING	**MIDDLE**	**END**
Miata forgets her skirt on the school bus.	Miata and her friend try to get the skirt.	Miata gets the skirt but gets a new one too.

Now ask students to recall what they know about the strategy of using graphic organizers. Have them discuss why this strategy might be helpful when focusing on the plot of a story. Then discuss the Story Organizer. Be sure to explain the importance of setting up the plot organizer *before* reading, so students can fill it in as they read along.

After Reading

Next, have students turn to page 312 in the handbook. Tell the class that a Plot Diagram like the one shown here can help readers figure out how the parts of a plot fit together. Students can be as brief or as detailed as they like when making notes in this organizer.

Plot Diagram

CLIMAX
Miata and her friend sneak onto a bus to get it.

PROBLEM
Miata has to get her skirt back.

SOLUTION
She wears two skirts to the dance.

Wrap-up

Ask students to create a graphic organizer that summarizes the plot of their favorite story. Then have them present their work to a partner and discuss the notes they made. After students have finished working, ask, "How did creating the graphic organizer help you better understand the events of the plot?"

Lesson 3 Understanding Dialogue

For use with *Reader's Handbook* page 329

Focus

In this lesson, students will explore dialogue as an element of
literature. In addition, they'll consider how a story's dialogue can
provide clues about character.

Getting Started

Have two students role play for the class a conversation in which
they tell a secret to each other. Encourage the students to be
dramatic and really get into the part. When they are finished, ask
the class to write what they heard. Check to see how they wrote it.
Some may do a paragraph and others may do a dialogue format.
Point out that the easiest way to write this is to use the dialogue
format. This is also the easiest way to follow as a reader.

Help students understand that dialogue is the conversation carried
on between characters in a piece of writing. Dialogue is important
because it can provide clues about the characters and explain and
advance the plot.

Teaching Approach

Ask students to tell what they know about dialogue. Ask, "What would
a story be like without dialogue?" Then write the words *characters*
and *plot* on the board. Explain the characterization clues a reader
might pick up from a piece of dialogue. Use the excerpt from *The Bee
Tree* on page 329 as an example. Tell students that they can use a
Double-entry Journal to help them think about key pieces of
dialogue.

Point out this model. Tell students that a Double-entry Journal is a
reading tool that helps them look at specific words and sentences.
Explain that it helps them make inferences and learn what the
author means but isn't saying.

Double-entry Journal

Quote	My Thoughts
"I'd rather be outdoors running and playing," said Mary Ellen.	Mary Ellen is a kid. She likes to have fun.

Using Speech Tags

Ask students to turn again to page 329. Define the term *speech tags* and ask students to identify the speech tags in the Polacco excerpt. Explain how these, too, can give clues about character.

Often the writer gives hints about a character in the speech tags. Ask students the difference between "he whispered softly," "he screamed," or "he said." Have student volunteers demonstrate how to say "I'm tired; I want to go home," using these different speech tags. Ask for other speech tags and have students model them. Help students see that speech tags can tell them something about the characters in a story.

Dialogue and Plot

Next, discuss how dialogue can explain or advance the plot of a story. Clarify that in a story, the characters might joke, make plans, and share information. This can give the reader clues about what will happen next and explanations of what happened before. Tell the class how important it is for a reader to "listen" to the conversations between characters. Point out an example of dialogue advancing a plot by reading aloud an excerpt.

Wrap-up

Ask students to look for clues about characters' personalities and motivations by focusing on the dialogue in their favorite short story or novel. Have students skim the text for examples of dialogue that offer clues about characters. Encourage students to use a Double-entry Journal to record their inferences. Then come together as a class to discuss the activity.

Lesson 4 Understanding Theme

For use with *Reader's Handbook* page 347

Focus

Here students learn what a theme is and how to find it in a work of literature.

Getting Started

Ask students to divide a piece of paper in half. On one side have them illustrate a time when they made a mistake. On the other half have them illustrate the same scene, but without the mistake. Have students share their drawings and explain what they learned from this situation. Tell them they just described the *theme* of a story.

Of all the literary concepts, theme troubles students the most. Even if they understand a story, poem, novel, or play completely, they are reluctant to take a chance and articulate the author's theme. You can demystify the subject by presenting a plan students can follow when thinking about the theme of a work.

Teaching Approach

Begin by explaining to students that most stories have a theme, which is the main idea, message, or lesson the author wants to get across in a story. In some cases, the theme will be articulated by a character or narrator. More often, readers will have to make inferences about theme. Show Overhead Transparency 3 and review the process of making inferences and connect it to theme.

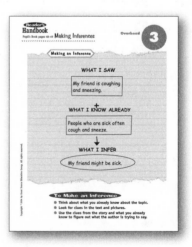

Introducing Theme

Tell students that authors do not always tell readers everything. That's why they have to make inferences as readers. Often they will have to infer the theme, or author's message about life.

Plan for Finding a Theme

Next, ask students to read the excerpt from *Spotlight on Cody* and consider the theme of the work. Walk them through the process by asking, "What is the topic of the passage? What is the author trying to tell you about the topic?"

Discuss how to find the theme of a story. Explain the following equation to students and how they use it:

Topic + What the author says about the topic = The author's theme

Make the point that theme is more than the topic of the work. It is the message the author has about the topic. Usually, the message will be universal—that is, it can apply to all people, instead of just a single character in a story.

Wrap-up

Finish the lesson with a review by asking students to make a picture dictionary page for each of the following literary terms:

■ plot

■ dialogue

■ theme

Ask students to explain the importance of understanding these elements when reading literature.

Lesson 5 Review and Assess

Check Point

Use the Quick Assess checklist to informally evaluate students' understanding of plot, dialogue, and theme. Based on their answers, divide them into two groups. Have one group do the Independent Practice on the next page, while the other group does the guided practice in the *Applications Book and Word Work.*

Guided Practice

For students who need reinforcement in recognizing the elements of plot, dialogue, and theme, use pages 156–160 in the *Applications Book and Word Work.*

Quick Assess

Can students

- ☑ tell what a plot is in their own words?
- ☑ identify the beginning, middle, and end of a plot?
- ☑ name and use a tool that helps them keep track of the events of a plot?
- ☑ read and understand a piece of dialogue?
- ☑ make inferences about an author's theme?

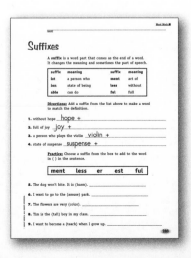

For students who need more word work, assign page 233 from the *Applications Book and Word Work* on suffixes.

Independent Practice

Students who have demonstrated a strong understanding of plot, dialogue, and theme can use their knowledge to help them read a folktale you've chosen beforehand. Good folktale collections include these:

■ *Wisdom Tales from Around the World* by Heather Forest

■ *Ashley Bryan's African Tales, Uh-Huh* by Ashley Bryan

■ *Latino Read-Aloud Stories* edited by Maite Suarez-Rivas

■ *The Storyteller's Start-Up Book: Finding, Learning, Performing, and Using Folktales* by Margaret Read MacDonald

■ *Favorite Folktales from Around the World* edited by Jane Yolen

■ *Norwegian Folk Tales Selected from the Collection of Peter Christen Asbjørnsen and Jørgen Moe* by Peter Christen Asbjørnsen and Jørgen Moe.

Class Review

Have students work together to plan the plot for a short story about an animal. Ask small groups to draw a Story Organizer on a piece of posterboard. Then have groups brainstorm the plot of their animal story, including the problem and solution. When all groups are finished, have them present their organizers to the class and explain the short story they're "planning" to write.

Test Book

Use the short-answer and multiple-choice tests on pages 66–67 to assess students' understanding of the material presented in this week's lessons.

Characters and Setting

Goals

Here students explore elements of character and setting in a work of fiction. This week's lessons will help them learn to

- ☑ find character clues
- ☑ tell the difference between major and minor characters
- ☑ see how a character develops over the course of a story
- ☑ explore the importance of setting
- ☑ see, or visualize, the setting of a story
- ☑ notice changes in the setting over the course of the narrative

Background

Help students connect this week's lessons to their prior knowledge by asking them to

- ■ define the terms *character* and *setting*
- ■ name their favorite literary characters and explain their choices
- ■ think of an example in which setting plays an important role in a book, movie, or television show

Opening Activity

Ask students to recall a favorite movie. Then ask them to list the most important characters, along with a brief description of what each character is like.

Next, ask them to describe the time and place of the movie and tell if and how it changes over the course of the story. Use the activity to introduce the idea that character and setting change in the same way as the plot changes and that both can provide valuable clues about the action and themes of a work.

Weekly Plan

Lessons	Summary
1. **Focus on Characters**	Work with students as they explore the element of character and distinguish between major and minor characters.
2. **Focus on Characters** (continued)	Help students read for character clues and understand the importance of tracking how a character changes over the course of a work.
3. **Focus on Setting**	Show students how to focus on time and place as they read a story.
4. **Focus on Setting** (continued)	Enhance students' understanding of setting and present tools that can help them understand it.
5. **Review and Assess**	Informally assess students to decide if more guided practice is needed. Then give an assessment.

Lesson Materials

	Components	Pages
Plan	*Teacher's Guide and Lesson Plans*	386–397
Teach	*Reader's Handbook*	313–325
Practice	*Applications Book and Word Work*	161–165, 234
Assess	*Test Book*	68–69

Lesson 1 Focus on Characters

For use with *Reader's Handbook* pages 313–316

Focus

In this lesson, students explore the element of character and distinguish between major and minor characters.

Getting Started

Ask students to choose a character from a book they think they are most like. Direct them to make a Web and list the character traits they share. Then have them draw a picture of the character and complete this sentence at the bottom.

"I'm most like _____ because _____."

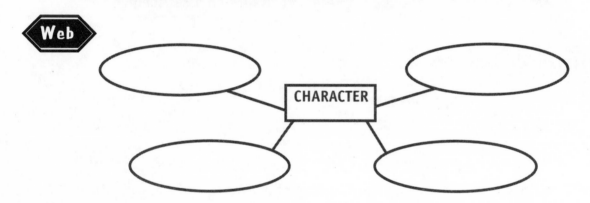

Web

CHARACTER

Teaching Approach

Define the term *character*. (Characters are the people, animals, or imaginary creatures that participate in the action of a story.)

Before Reading

Explain the difference between major and minor characters. Help students understand that the action of a story revolves around its major characters. Minor characters appear less often and are not as important to the plot.

Have students read the excerpt from *Jake Drake Know-It-All*. Ask, "Who is the major character in this story? How do you know?" Then read aloud the explanation of minor characters on page 314. Offer examples of minor characters students have read about in other works. Ask, "What is the difference between a major and a minor character?"

During Reading

Once students understand the concept of major and minor characters, begin your discussion of how to read for character clues. Direct students' attention to page 315. Ask another volunteer to read aloud the information under "Read for Clues," paying special attention to the three bulleted items. Tell the class that looking for these types of clues can help them better understand the characters. Ask

■ Why is it important to understand a character's thoughts and feelings?

■ Why do good readers pay attention to how the major characters interact with the other characters?

■ What are three ways an author can reveal information about a character?

Have students read the next excerpt. Then discuss the Character Map at the bottom of the page.

Character Map

WHAT HE SAYS AND DOES	WHAT OTHERS THINK
• loves computers • doesn't like "know-it-alls"	• Willie wants to work with him.

JAKE DRAKE

HOW HE LOOKS AND FEELS	HOW I FEEL
• thinks most kids he knows are pretty smart • likes being smart	• seems kind of funny • should be nicer to his best friend

Wrap-up

Draw a blank Character Map on the board and use it to analyze as a class a literary character students know well. Choose a character from a book you've read this year in class or a character students are likely to know from outside reading, such as Amelia Bedelia or Nate from the *Nate the Great* series.

⬭ Lesson 2 ⬭ Focus on Characters (continued)

For use with *Reader's Handbook* pages 317–319

Focus

In this lesson, students will continue their discussion of how to read for character clues and then explore the importance of understanding how a character changes over the course of a novel or story.

Getting Started

Ask students to think about themselves at the beginning of the school year. Encourage them to reflect on ways they have changed physically, academically, and emotionally. Tell them to jot down their thoughts in their Reading Notebooks.

Explain that most major characters undergo some kind of change over the course of a story. They become smarter or stronger or weaker or more foolish. These changes make it easier for the reader to relate to the character and connect the story to his or her own life.

Teaching Approach

Focus on change in a story and in a character. Give examples of characters students might know who have changed during the course of a story.

During Reading (continued)

Point out that understanding the changes a character undergoes can be a big help in understanding the plot of a story or novel. Very often a character's response to the action can provide clues about the character's personality, in addition to clues about what might happen next in the plot. In the best fiction, plot and character are so interwoven that it is difficult to tell which force is driving the other.

Have students turn to page 317 and read the next excerpt from *Jake Drake Know-It-All*. What brings about a change in Jake's feelings about himself and others? Point out the Character Change Chart on page 318 and discuss the handwritten notes.

Character Change Chart

BEGINNING	MIDDLE	END
• Jake wants to win the computer. • He doesn't want to work with Willie because he doesn't want to share the prize.	Jake tries to be a "know-it-all" just so he can win.	• Jake learns that it's better to work with someone than to win. • Jake and Willie stay great friends.

POSSIBLE THEME Working together is more important than winning a big prize.

Have students read the bottom two paragraphs on page 318. Discuss what Jake learns over the course of the story.

Discuss the theme shown at the bottom of the Character Change Chart. Remind the class that *theme* is the author's message about life. In this case, the theme involves the central character, Jake, but also has more universal applications. This is the mark of a good theme.

After Reading

Read aloud the top of page 319. Then have one volunteer at a time read and answer the four bulleted questions in the center of the page.

Explain to students that good readers plan on rereading bits and pieces of a novel or story in order to find out as much as they can about the central characters. If students are unsure of how a character changes over the course of the work, or they can't figure out what brings about a change in character, they should do some rereading. Model how to return to a text and skim for specific character clues.

Wrap-up

Bring students together to share what they learned about characters and character development. Review the difference between major and minor characters and the kinds of clues to look for when focusing on a character. Finish with a discussion of why it is important to understand how a character changes over the course of a story.

Lesson 3 Focus on Setting

For use with *Reader's Handbook* pages 320–322

Focus

Here students will learn characteristics of setting and discuss the ways in which time and place can be important to a story.

Getting Started

Read to students from a book of fiction. Focus on a passage with a description of the setting. Ask students to listen to the setting. Then discuss what they learned from it and draw a detailed picture of what they "see." Before students share their pictures, have them give their thoughts on the main words that should be included in the drawing. Have students revisit their drawings to make sure their pictures all show the key words.

Teaching Approach

In this lesson, you'll discuss setting. As you know, the setting provides context for the action of a story and helps readers visualize where and when the events of the story take place. It is a kind of lens through which the action occurs.

Before Reading

Discuss with students what they know about setting. List their thoughts on the board. Then explain that every story has a setting, a time and place in which the events unfold. Point out that some stories have very detailed settings, while other stories are set in such a way that time and place are not really important to the action of the story. Help students understand that their job as readers is to look for setting clues as they read.

Put the Setting Clues chart (see next page) on the board. Explain that these are the clues students need to look for to understand the setting. Ask if your students have anything to add.

Setting Clues

Time	Place
time of day day of the week month of the year season of the year historical period	specifics about rooms, homes, buildings, forests, and so on the city or town the state the country

Next, explain the types of setting clues students might look for and the places in which they might find them. Point out the importance of reading a story's first few paragraphs very carefully as they often give information on the setting. Then ask them to read and take notes on the opening for John Reynolds Gardiner's novel *Stone Fox* on page 321. When students have finished reading, discuss the setting clues they found. Ask, "What clues about time did you see?"

Have students turn to page 322 and read the second excerpt from the novel. Once again, ask students to tell the setting clues they found. Show the Setting Chart on page 322 and explain its uses.

Setting Chart

CLUES ABOUT TIME	CLUES ABOUT PLACE
early morning when grandfather stays in bed	small potato farm in Wyoming

Wrap-up

In anticipation of the lesson to come, have students visualize the setting of *Stone Fox*. Ask them to close their eyes and imagine the place where Little Willy and his grandfather live. Then have them draw a picture of what they imagined, referring to the excerpts for details as needed. Invite volunteers to share their art with the class.

Lesson 4 Focus on Setting (continued)

For use with *Reader's Handbook* pages 323–325

Focus

In this lesson, students will continue their exploration of setting and discuss tools they can use to help them understand and keep track of elements of time and place.

Getting Started

Begin by asking students to think about setting and character. Explain that paying attention to how a character reacts to a setting can help them better understand the character. For example, if a character screams and dives under the bed during a thunderstorm, the reader can infer that the character is a little jumpy, or nervous. Also, explain to students that a setting can sometimes reflect a character's likes and dislikes. Have students write a descriptive paragraph of their bedrooms—giving as much personal detail as possible. Then read all of them aloud. Have class members guess whose paragraph is read.

Teaching Approach

Explain that here you'll discuss things students can do and reading tools they can use to learn more about setting.

During Reading

An important part of understanding setting is being able to visualize the place and time the author describes. Help students learn to pay attention to the mental pictures they form as they read. Direct them to read the top of page 323 and then study the illustration of the setting of *Stone Fox*.

Look for Changes in Setting

Next, ask, "Why is it important to keep track of setting changes as you read?" Help students understand that a change in setting can mean a change in character and/or plot, too.

It may help students to use a Storyboard to track changes in setting. Have them draw a three-, four-, or six-celled Storyboard before they begin reading and then draw quick sketches of each new scene. They can add cells as needed. When they've finished, they'll have a visual that will help them "see" the setting of the story.

After Reading

Each time they finish reading a story or novel, ask students to take a moment or two to think about the importance of setting in the work and how it affects the action and characters of the story. Explain that writing Summary Notes will make it easier for them to remember key details of a setting.

► Summary Notes

WHERE AND WHEN
- on the farm in the fall
- in a store in the winter
- on a February night on Main Street

WHAT HAPPENS
- Grandfather gets sick.
- Willy needs money.
- Willy enters a dogsled race.

Wrap-up

Ask students to make a list in their Reading Notebooks of books they've read and the setting of each. Then ask them to define the term *setting*. When students have finished, ask them to share their lists.

Lesson 5 Review and Assess

Check Point

Use the Quick Assess checklist to informally evaluate students' understanding of character and setting. Based on their answers, divide them into two groups. Have one group do the Independent Practice on the next page, while the other group does the guided practice in the *Applications Book and Word Work.*

Guided Practice

For students who need reinforcement in understanding character and setting, use pages 161–165 in the *Applications Book and Word Work.*

Quick Assess

Can students

- ☑ tell what tools they can use to help them focus on character?

- ☑ explain why tracking changes in a character is important?

- ☑ define *setting* in their own words?

- ☑ describe tools they can use to help them visualize the setting and keep track of setting?

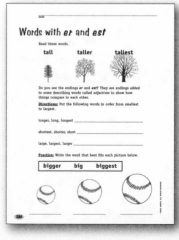

For students who need more word work, assign page 234 from the *Applications Book and Word Work* on suffixes *er* and *est.*

Independent Practice

Students who have demonstrated a strong understanding of characters and setting might apply their knowledge to a new short story or folktale. Provide a list of stories from which to choose. Then ask students to do one of the following.

▪ Create a Character Map for a major character.

▪ Complete a Character Change Chart for a major character.

▪ Write Summary Notes about the setting of the work.

Class Review

Ask students to gather in groups of three or four. Have them work together to develop a "Character Guidelines" or "Setting Guidelines" poster to display in the classroom. Each poster should give specific directions on how to focus on the characters or setting of a work. Encourage students to use terminology they've learned in class and to be as clear and succinct in their directions as possible.

Test Book

Use the short-answer and multiple-choice tests on pages 68–69 to assess students' understanding of the material presented in this week's lessons.

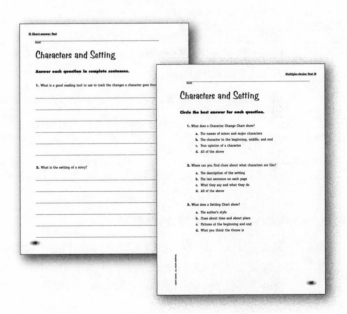

WEEK 32

Elements of Literature

Goals

Here students explore various elements of fiction, including mood, style, narrator, and imagery. During the week's lessons, you'll work with them to

- ☑ point out the use of mood in a passage
- ☑ understand author's style
- ☑ identify the narrator
- ☑ know what imagery is
- ☑ identify ways poets add interest to their work

Background

Help students connect this week's lessons to their prior knowledge by asking them to

- ▪ talk about what they know about mood
- ▪ discuss different types of narrators
- ▪ define *imagery*
- ▪ brainstorm elements of poetry that add interest and fun

Opening Activity

Tell students that in this unit they will explore elements of literature. Explain that an *element* is similar to a part; elements of literature are the features of fiction or poetry that make it special.

What elements do students predict will be part of this week's work? Ask pairs to list elements that they predict will be covered in this unit. Then create a master list of predictions. Next, direct students' attention to page 326 of the handbook. Compare the class list of predictions to the elements listed on this page. Discuss the similarities and differences between the lists.

Weekly Plan

Lessons	Summary
1. **Mood and Style**	Teach students the literary elements of mood and style and how to identify both in a piece of fiction.
2. **Narrator**	Help students learn how to determine the narrator of a piece of fiction.
3. **Imagery**	Enhance students' understanding of sensory language and how to find imagery in a poem.
4. **Alliteration, Onomatopoeia, and Personification**	Explore with students the literary elements of alliteration, onomatopoeia, and personification.
5. **Review and Assess**	Informally assess students to decide if more guided practice is needed. Then give an assessment.

Lesson Materials

	Components	Pages
Plan	*Teacher's Guide and Lesson Plans*	398–409
Teach	*Reader's Handbook*	327, 331, 333–337, 346
	Overhead Transparencies	31
Practice	*Applications Book and Word Work*	166–170, 235
Assess	*Test Book*	70–71

Lesson 1 Mood and Style

For use with *Reader's Handbook* pages 333 and 346

Focus

In this lesson, students will explore the literary elements of mood and style in a piece of fiction.

Getting Started

Ask student volunteers to explain how they can tell whether someone is in a good or bad mood. Explain that people give both verbal and nonverbal clues about their mood. Talk about various kinds of moods, such as happy, angry, and so on. Play a quick game of charades with different moods. Explain that just as people can have a variety of moods, so can stories and poems. Given what students know about how the term *mood* is used in everyday life, what do they think *mood* means in literature? Discuss their ideas.

Then ask student volunteers to define *style*. Ask them about the *style* of music they like or the *style* of their hair. What images come to mind when they hear the term? Discuss. Then ask students what they think *style* of writing means. List their ideas on the board.

Teaching Approach

Explain that in this lesson, students will explore these two elements of literature—*mood* and *style*.

Mood

Read aloud the top of page 333. Then read the excerpt from *Fantastic Mr. Fox*.

Help students see that mood is the feeling you get as you read. Do a Think Aloud, modeling your own "reading" of the mood in *Fantastic Mr. Fox*.

Help students understand that mood is how a story or poem makes them feel. Explain that sometimes the mood is very easy to detect. Other times, the mood is much more subtle and the reader has to dig hard for clues in the selection to determine its mood.

Style

Review students' ideas about the meaning of a writing *style*. Then read aloud the top of page 346. Make clear that authors have different ways of writing in the same way that people have different ways of dressing. These different ways add up to *style*.

Explain that an author's style is made up of at least three parts.

1. the author's choice of words
2. the kind and length of sentences an author uses
3. the author's use of special language, such as similes, metaphors, and imagery

Then read aloud the excerpt from *The Great Kapok Tree*. After reading, ask students to note the three highlighted parts. Point out how they correspond to the three components of style. Have students read the rest of page 346 on their own.

Wrap-up

To enhance students' understanding of mood, work as a class to list examples of common moods in literature, such as scary, funny, and sad. Draw a two-column chart on the board. Fill in the left-hand column with the types of moods. Then ask students to brainstorm examples of familiar stories or poems that match each type of mood.

401

Lesson 2 Narrator

For use with *Reader's Handbook* pages 334–335

Focus

Here students will learn how to determine the narrator of a piece of fiction.

Getting Started

Write the following excerpts on the board.

■ The children were freezing. Martha started to cry.

■ "I'm freezing," I said. I started to cry.

Talk about the similarities and differences between the two excerpts. To get students thinking about the importance of knowing who is telling the story, ask them such questions as

■ Who is telling the story in each excerpt?

■ In which excerpt is the person who is telling the story also a character in the story?

After discussing these questions, have students jot down their answers to the following.

■ Do you think it matters who tells a story? Why or why not?

Tell students that they will return to the last questions again at the end of the lesson.

Teaching Approach

Read aloud the excerpt on the top of page 334 of the *Reader's Handbook*. Ask a volunteer to read aloud the description of narrator at the bottom of the page. Review the excerpt with students. Point out the highlighted words that tell the reader who is telling the story.

First-person Narrators

Ask students, "What other words are clues that a story has a first-person narrator?" Work with students to develop a list of clue words, including *you, we,* and *us.*

Students may understand this concept more clearly if you focus on the point that the person telling the story is also *in* the story.

Third-person Narrators

Read aloud or have a volunteer read aloud the excerpt on page 335.

As students read the description of third-person narrator, point out the highlighted words in the excerpt. Again, ask students to think of other clue words that would signal a third-person narrator, such as *him, her,* and *it.* Ask students to compare these to those used in the first excerpt. Point out that the person telling this story is not *in* the story but stands outside of, or apart from, it.

Next, help students understand why readers need to pay attention to whom is telling the story. Explain that when a character in a story is also the narrator, the reader sees the action through that character's eyes only. Can students think of any disadvantages to this? Help them see that first-person narrators only tell their side of the story, while a third-person narrator generally tells a more objective account. Have students return to their responses to

■ Do you think it matters who tells a story? Why or why not?

Talk about how this lesson affected their answers to this question. Invite students to modify their responses as necessary.

Wrap-up

Have students work in pairs to practice identifying first-person and third-person narrators. Ask partners to choose three excerpts from the "Elements of Literature" section of the handbook (pages 326–347). Then have pairs create a chart similar to this one:

Title	First- or Third-person Narrator	Clue Words

⬭ Lesson 3 ⬭ Imagery

For use with *Reader's Handbook* page 331

Focus

Here students enhance their understanding of sensory language and sharpen their ability to find imagery in a poem.

Getting Started

Ask students to list the five senses: sight, hearing, feeling, smell, and taste. Then divide the class into five groups. Give each group an object and tell them they have to describe it by using the sense listed. They cannot say the name of the object.

- ■ lemon—taste
- ■ baking cookies—smell
- ■ ambulance siren—sound
- ■ sand paper—touch
- ■ rainbow—sight

Allow them to read their paragraphs and let the class guess what it is. Tell them they are using *imagery*.

Then offer the following definition: "Imagery is language that helps you see, hear, feel, smell, or taste something described." Discuss the definition. Explain that one reason that authors use imagery is to help readers feel more connected to the writing.

Teaching Approach

Begin by reminding students of what they've learned about reading poetry. Display Overhead Transparency 31 and have volunteers explain what a reader looks for when previewing a poem.

Looking for Imagery

Next, read aloud the excerpt from "Growing Old" on page 331. Read the excerpt straight through. Then have students do a second reading of the poem on their own.

Next, walk students through the description of imagery presented on page 331. Then think aloud your search for imagery in Henderson's poem. Focus your Think Aloud on how Henderson's language helps readers visualize Grandma Lee. Discuss how the imagery of the poem affects the mood (the atmosphere or feeling a work conveys).

Understanding Imagery

Ask students to extend their understanding about imagery by drawing what they see as you read aloud another poem to them. Then read aloud "Flea Fur All" (page 327) or "Pie Problem" (page 336). Have students spend five to ten minutes drawing what they see.

Then have students exchange their papers with a partner. Read the poem aloud again, and ask the partners to talk about the imagery they now see in the poem.

Reflect

Finish the lesson by asking students to write, in the form of a journal entry, the personal connections they made while reading "Growing Old." Who or what does the poem remind them of from their own lives? How does the poem make them feel? What would they like to say to the speaker of this poem? Invite two or three students to read aloud their entries.

Wrap-up

To extend your teaching—and strengthen students' ability to read and respond to imagery in a work—have students help you choose an excerpt from a familiar piece of fiction, such as *Charlotte's Web* or "Cinderella." Work as a class to find examples of imagery in the story.

Lesson 4 Alliteration, Onomatopoeia, and Personification

For use with *Reader's Handbook* pages 327, 336, and 337

Focus

In this lesson, students will explore the literary elements of alliteration, onomatopoeia, and personification.

Getting Started

Tell students that in this section of the handbook they will look at ways authors and poets have fun with words. Begin by asking students to recite the following.

■ She sells seashells down by the seashore.

See who can recite this the fastest without saying the words incorrectly. Talk about what makes these sayings fun, as well as tricky on the tongue. Then ask students to come up with an alternative sentence starting with the first letters of their first name.

Teaching Approach

Start by telling students you will talk about three different "fun" elements of literature in this lesson.

Alliteration

Begin the lesson by defining *alliteration*—the use of words with the same beginning consonant sound. Point out that the tongue twister includes an example of alliteration. Read aloud the poem on page 327. Do students see how alliteration adds fun and interest to the poem?

Onomatopoeia

Explain that poets and authors have other tools for adding fun to their work. Ask a volunteer to read aloud the "Pie Problem" by Shel Silverstein. Ask students if they see or hear any unusual words in the poem. Help them focus on *MMMM—OOOH-MY!* and *Chomp-Gulp.*

Talk about what makes this poem fun to read and hear. Do students note the poet's use of alliteration ("piece of pie")? Explain that words like *Gulp* and *Chomp* are examples of onomatopoeia. Then read aloud the description of onomatopoeia on page 336. Point out highlighted words in the poem. See if students can come up with other onomatopoeia words.

Personification

Have students reread the excerpt from "Flea Fur All" on page 327. Can fleas be filled with glee? Can they prance about and feel ecstasy? Explain that when poets and authors give nonhuman things human qualities, they are using *personification*. Have a volunteer read aloud "Labor Day" (page 337), which personifies summer. Point out the many ways in which the poet makes summer sound like a person. Then have students finish reading page 337.

Wrap-up

Ask students to look through "Reading a Poem" in the handbook as well as the poems used in "Elements of Literature" for examples of alliteration, onomatopoeia, and personification. Invite volunteers to read aloud their favorites.

Let students try writing some examples of these elements.

■ Have them all write a tongue twister with the letter *t*.

■ Describe the scene when a waiter drops a tray of food.

■ Write about a tree using personification.

Lesson 5 Review and Assess

Check Point

Use the Quick Assess checklist to informally evaluate students' understanding of various elements of literature. Based on their answers, divide them into two groups. One group can do the Independent Practice on the next page and the other group can do the guided practice in the *Applications Book and Word Work*.

Guided Practice

For students who need reinforcement in understanding these elements of literature, use pages 166–170 in the *Applications Book and Word Work*.

Quick Assess

Can students

- ☑ describe the mood and style of a passage?

- ☑ explain the difference between first-person and third-person narrator?

- ☑ tell the meaning of imagery in their own words?

- ☑ recognize alliteration, onomatopoeia, and personification in a poem?

For students who need more word work, assign page 235 from the *Applications Book and Word Work* on base words.

Independent Practice

Direct students who have demonstrated a strong understanding of the elements discussed to choose one or more additional elements of fiction to explore. Students should use their own words to define the element, explain how it is used, and provide an example that is different from the ones shown in the *Reader's Handbook*.

Class Review

To reinforce students' understanding of the various elements of fiction discussed in this section of the handbook, have the class play "20 Questions." Write the following elements on index cards.

- plot
- setting
- character
- theme
- mood
- style

- first-person narrator
- third-person narrator
- alliteration
- onomatopoeia
- personification

Fold the cards in half and place them in a bowl. Ask a student to pick a card from the bowl. Have the rest of the class ask the student "yes/no" questions about the element. If they cannot guess the element after 20 questions, put the card back in the bowl. Continue playing until the bowl is empty.

Test Book

Use the short-answer and multiple-choice tests on pages 70–71 to assess students' understanding of mood and style, narrator, imagery, alliteration, onomatopoeia, and personification.

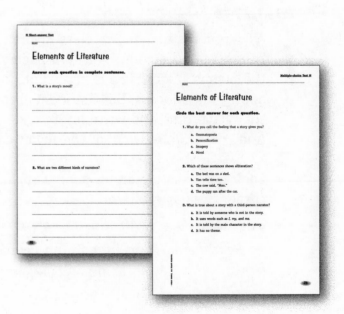

Reading a Poem

Goals

Here students read and respond to a poem called "Michael Is Afraid of the Storm." This week's lessons will teach them to

☑ understand what a poem means

☑ use the reading strategy of using your own words

Background

Help students connect this week's lessons to their prior knowledge by asking them to

■ reflect on any poems they've read or heard

■ talk about the easiest and the most challenging parts of reading poetry

■ read the title of the poem and make predictions about its content

Opening Activity

Ask students to bring to class favorite poems that they've found in books and magazines. Set up a poetry corner in your room and display the poems students have contributed as well as several children's poetry anthologies. Have students browse in the poetry corner when they have time and write brief "reviews" of the books and poems they find there. Share some of the reviewed poems with the class.

Look for these children's poetry anthologies and set up a reading corner in your classroom.

■ *Classic Poetry: An Illustrated Collection* edited by Michael Rosen

■ *Read-Aloud Poems for Young People* edited by Glorya Hale

■ *Over the Garden Wall* by Eleanor Farjeon

■ *Ants on the Melon: A Collection of Poems* by Virginia Hamilton Adair

Weekly Plan

Lessons	Summary
1. **Before Reading: Poem**	Work with students as they apply the Before Reading stage of the reading process to a poem.
2. **During Reading: Poem**	Teach students to apply the reading strategy of using your own words and to take notes in a Double-entry Journal as they read a poem.
3. **During Reading: Poem** (continued)	Continue to work with students as they apply a three-step plan that can help them read and connect to a poem.
4. **After Reading: Poem**	Enhance students' understanding of the After Reading stage of the reading process as they apply it to a poem.
5. **Review and Assess**	Informally assess students to decide if more guided practice is needed. Then give an assessment.

Lesson Materials

	Components	Pages
Plan	*Teacher's Guide and Lesson Plans*	410–421
Teach	*Reader's Handbook*	294–305
	Overhead Transparencies	1, 31
Practice	*Applications Book and Word Work*	171–179, 236
Assess	*Test Book*	72–73

Lesson 1 Before Reading: Poem

For use with *Reader's Handbook* pages 294–297

Focus

In this lesson, students learn to apply the Before Reading stage of the reading process to a poem.

Getting Started

Hand out lyrics to a current song your students may be familiar with. Let them read through it silently. Ask if they recognize any elements of literature. Then play the song for them. Explain that lyrics to a song are a form of poetry. Point out the way the song is organized, the rhyming and rhythm, and the style.

Teaching Approach

A Set a Purpose

Have students read silently page 294, paying particular attention to the Goals box.

Ask students, "What is your usual purpose for reading a poem?" Tell the class that there are two reading purpose questions that they can use for just about any poem.

■ What is the poem saying?

■ What makes this poem special?

Explain that the poem they're about to read is called "Michael Is Afraid of the Storm." Ask them to incorporate the title into two specific purpose questions and then jot down their reading purpose questions in their Reading Notebooks.

B Preview

Next, ask students to preview Gwendolyn Brooks's poem. Since previewing a poem is different from previewing other types of reading, you might want to walk them through the process. Point out the Preview Checklist at the bottom of page 295, and discuss the three elements listed there. Use Overhead Transparency 31 to help students preview the poem.

Preview Checklist

✔ title and author

✔ shape of the poem

✔ first and last lines

C Plan

After students preview "Michael Is Afraid of the Storm," explore how to make a plan for reading the poem. Direct students to turn to page 296 and read the text under Plan. Have them add to the bulleted list their own comments about the poem. Then remind the class that an important part of the reading process is choosing a strategy that can help them read, respond to, and remember the selection.

Ask the class to turn to page 297. Read aloud the information on using your own words. Help students understand that retelling a line or idea from a poem can make it easier for them to process— or think through—what the poet is saying.

Point out the Double-entry Journal on the page and discuss how to use this reading tool. Explain that this simple reading tool can help students understand what a poem means. Refer students to page 410 for more information on Double-entry Journals.

Wrap-up

Have a student summarize what the class has learned thus far about reading poetry. Ask, "What should you look for when previewing a poem? What strategy and reading tool can you use when you're reading a poem?"

Lesson 2 During Reading: Poem

For use with *Reader's Handbook* pages 298–300

Focus

Here students will learn to use their own words to help them understand a poem. In addition, they'll explore how a Double-entry Journal can help them read and respond to lines of a poem.

Getting Started

Divide the class into three groups. Give each group the same poem. Have one group read the poem once and then turn the paper over. The second will read through it twice and turn the paper over. The third group will read it three times. Prepare ten comprehension questions and have students complete them without looking at the poem. Discuss the answers. Most likely those that read the poem three times will get more correct answers than those who only read it once. Point this out to the class.

Teaching Approach

Remind students of their purpose for reading the poem. Before they begin, be sure students are reading with their Reading Notebooks and blank Double-entry Journals in hand.

Read with a Purpose

Explain to students that even the best readers make an effort to read a poem three times. Then show them a three-step plan they can use to get the most out of each reading.

> **Plan for Reading a Poem**

> **1.** first reading—read for meaning
> **2.** second reading—read for sound and shape
> **3.** third reading—read for language

1. First Reading—Meaning

Direct students to turn to page 298. Explain what it means to "read for meaning." Tell students to watch for words or lines that seem interesting or important. Ask them to write the quotations in the left-hand side of their Double-entry Journals and then use their own words to explain the quotes on the right-hand side.

◄ **Double-entry Journal** ►

QUOTES	MY WORDS
"Lightning is angry in the night."	Lightning is so scary. It's like someone gets mad all of a sudden.
"And crying's not for me."	Kids my age shouldn't cry.

Help students understand that because poets pack a lot of meaning in few words, each and every word in a poem will be significant. Students should think about what the words mean, how they sound, and what they look like.

Also remind students that no two readers will read—or interpret—a poem in exactly the same way. Explain that any idea they have about a poem is valid so long as they can point to the words or lines that support the idea.

2. Second Reading—Sound and Shape

After students finish reading page 299, have them turn to page 300 and read about the importance of paying attention to how a poem sounds and looks. Ask, "What repeated words did you notice in 'Michael Is Afraid of the Storm'? What do the words sound like and remind you of?"

Wrap-up

Have students work in small groups to take notes on the sound and structure of Brooks's poem. In particular, students should think about

■ repeated words and sounds

■ stanza patterns (number of lines per stanza and number of beats per line)

■ rhyme

Lesson 3 During Reading: Poem (continued)

For use with *Reader's Handbook* pages 301–302

Focus

In this lesson, students will continue their work with the three-step plan for reading a poem. In addition, they'll learn the value of making a personal connection to the poet's ideas.

Getting Started

Find a poem students have not heard before. Tell students to divide a blank piece of white paper into three sections. Read the poem out loud and then ask students to do a quick sketch of what they "see." Repeat this two more times. Discuss with students how their pictures changed each time.

Teaching Approach

Review on the board the three-step plan for reading a poem. Discuss why you might need multiple readings of a poem.

D Read with a Purpose (continued)

Explain that in this lesson students will learn about Step 3 of the reading plan for poems, as well as how to make a personal connection to the poet's words and message.

3. Third Reading—Language

Go over with students definitions for *simile, metaphor,* and *personification.* Be sure to explain the difference between similes and metaphors. Ask volunteers to give examples of each one to check that students understand.

Then have students read "Michael Is Afraid of the Storm" one final time. Encourage them to note any feelings, connections, and reactions the poem evoked in them. Have volunteers discuss Brooks's use of personification and how it can help the reader visualize the scene and understand Michael's fear.

 **Connect**

Review the three steps for reading poetry and have students discuss which step they found the hardest to complete and why.

◀ **Plan for Reading a Poem** ▶

1. First reading—read for meaning
2. Second reading—read for sound and shape
3. Third reading—read for language

Then explain the importance of making a personal connection to the poem. Have students turn to page 302. Read the three questions at the top of the page and ask students to write their answers to each one.

Explain to the class that reacting to a poem is an important part of understanding it. Sometimes a poet tries to provoke a certain reaction—anger, sadness, joy, fear—in order to create meaning.

Part of being an active reader is responding to what you read. As a reader, you have feelings, opinions, and reactions. Take note of them, because they can aid comprehension.

Point out the connections one reader made to "Michael Is Afraid of the Storm." Ask students to comment.

Wrap-up

Ask students to quickwrite about their connections to Brooks's poem. If you like, have students write in response to one of the following prompts.

■ I wonder why . . .
■ This made me think about . . .
■ My idea is . . .
■ I'd like to tell Gwendolyn Brooks . . .

Lesson 4 After Reading: Poem

For use with *Reader's Handbook* pages 303–305

Focus

Here students will strengthen their understanding of the After Reading stage of the reading process and consider how to use it with poetry.

Getting Started

Review with students the steps of the reading process. Display Overhead Transparency 1. Ask students to design a poster showing the eight steps in the process as they relate to reading a poem.

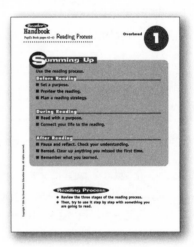

Teaching Approach

Remind students that "reading" does not end once their eyes have finished reading the last word. Reading is thinking. After a reader finishes with the words, it's time to think about and reflect on what they mean. Readers need to think back about their original purpose for reading. Did they find out what they wanted to learn? Help students see the importance of this last stage of the reading process, especially with poetry.

F Pause and Reflect

Remind students that the purpose of the Pause and Reflect step is to spend a moment considering what they've learned from a reading. Ask the class to turn to page 303. Write the three bulleted questions on the board and ask students to respond to each.

■ What is the poem saying?

■ What makes this poem special?

■ Can I explain the poem in my own words?

Reread

Keep in mind that the "Plan for Reading a Poem" presented in the handbook requires at least three readings of a poem. Model how to use the Reread step to clear up confusion with the language of a poem or to spot-check individual lines for comprehension problems.

Direct students to the Think Aloud. Explain to students that it is a model of the way they can go back after reading to clear up the meaning of a particular word or line.

Think Aloud

At first, I didn't get the part about the "busy dress." But now I think the "busy dress" is just a way of saying that the mother is moving around a lot.

I think Michael's eye is "wild" because he is scared. Maybe he's about to cry.

 Remember

Discuss the ways students can remember what they've read. Supplement the list with your own suggestions or have volunteers tell strategies they've used in the past that seem to work well.

Wrap-up

Ask students to write an entry in their Reading Notebooks in which they respond to Gwendolyn Brooks's language and message in "Michael Is Afraid of the Storm." Ask students to comment on whether or not they liked the poem. Point out that with understanding comes enjoyment. Careful analysis of a poem involves enjoying how the poem looks and sounds as well as what it has to say.

Lesson 5 Review and Assess

Check Point

Use the Quick Assess checklist to informally evaluate students' understanding of how to read a poem. Based on their answers, divide them into two groups. One group can do the Independent Practice on the next page, while the other group does the guided practice in the *Applications Book and Word Work.*

Guided Practice

For students who need reinforcement in the process of reading a poem, use pages 171–179 in the *Applications Book and Word Work.*

Quick Assess

Can students

- ☑ apply the reading process to a poem?

- ☑ explain and use the reading strategy of using your own words?

- ☑ explain the three-step plan for reading a poem?

- ☑ describe one reading tool that help with understanding a poem?

For students who need more word work, assign page 236 from the *Applications Book and Word Work* on root words.

Independent Practice

Students who have demonstrated a strong understanding of how to read poetry and the strategy of using your own words might apply their knowledge of reading to another poem by Gwendolyn Brooks. Show students anthologies of her work, and have them choose a poem they'd most like to read.

Then ask students to do the following:

■ Set a purpose and make a plan for reading the poem.

■ Use a Double-entry Journal to record their thoughts and feelings about the poem.

Class Review

Ask students to return to page 296 and read the poem one last time. Ask them to picture (visualize) the scene Brooks describes. Then have them use crayons and markers to create an illustration that reflects "Michael Is Afraid of the Storm." When they finish, have them use a line from the poem as a caption for their work and then share their art with the class. Review the strategy of using your own words, and explain to students that, in this case, they used art to retell what the poem was about.

Test Book

Use the short-answer and multiple-choice tests on pages 72–73 to assess students' understanding of the material presented in this week's lessons.

WEEK 34

Reading a Test and Test Questions

Goals

Here students explore strategies for taking tests. This week's lessons will help them learn to

☑ prepare for different tests and test questions

☑ use the strategy of skimming to find answers

Background

Help students connect this week's lessons to their prior knowledge by asking them to

■ talk about what they know about skimming

■ explore the more challenging aspects of taking tests

■ discuss the different kinds of test questions

Opening Activity

Explain to students that in the next few lessons they will learn how to apply the reading process to test-taking. Ask students to get ready for this section by reflecting on tests in their Reading Notebooks. Questions they might consider

■ How do I feel about taking tests?

■ What would I like to learn about taking tests?

■ What do I already do well when I'm taking tests?

Students will return to their reflections later in the lesson.

Weekly Plan

Lessons	Summary
1. **Before Reading: Tests**	Work with students to review the steps of this stage of the reading process. Discuss how to apply each step to a test and test questions.
2. **During Reading: Tests**	Teach students about fact and critical thinking questions and how to use the strategy of skimming.
3. **During Reading: Tests** (continued)	Explore with students how to answer inference questions on tests, as well as ways to connect to passages on a test.
4. **After Reading: Tests**	Help students explore how to apply the After Reading stage of the reading process to a test.
5. **Review and Assess**	Informally assess students to decide if more guided practice is needed. Then give an assessment.

Lesson Materials

	Components	Pages
Plan	*Teacher's Guide and Lesson Plans*	422–433
Teach	*Reader's Handbook*	350–361
	Overhead Transparencies	32, 33, 34, 36
Practice	*Applications Book and Word Work*	180–189, 237
Assess	*Test Book*	74–75

Lesson 1 Before Reading: Tests

For use with *Reader's Handbook* pages 350–354

Focus

Here students discuss how to apply the steps of the Before Reading stage to a test and test questions.

Getting Started

Invite volunteers to share how they study for a test. Talk about the importance of studying for a test as soon as the date is announced, rather than waiting until the night before. Then ask how students think the reading process can help them prepare for a test.

Teaching Approach

Read aloud the goals for the unit. Tell students they can do better on tests once they apply reading strategies to test-taking.

A Set a Purpose

Review with students the point of setting a purpose for reading. Explain that setting a purpose is just as important before taking a test as it is before reading a novel or a biography. Read aloud the two purpose-setting questions on the top of page 351. Explain that one of the biggest mistakes test-takers make is not understanding what is being asked of them.

B Preview

Read aloud the Preview text on page 351 and show students the checklist. Discuss the importance of each item. Ask one volunteer to model a preview using Overhead Transparency 32. When they've finished, ask, "What kind of reading is this, fiction or nonfiction?" Then point out the sample preview notes one reader made. Explain that looking over the questions before reading the passage will provide a focus for reading.

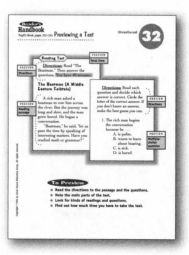

Plan

As a group, read the Plan section on page 354. Ask, "Which of the items listed did you notice in your previews?" Encourage volunteers to share other items they noted.

Next, talk with students about the importance of planning their time when taking a test. Previewing will give students an opportunity to get a feel for the test as a whole—planning their time will help students avoid getting stuck on one question or section of the test.

Next, explain that the reading strategy of skimming can help students through all stages of the reading process. Before reading, skimming is an excellent tool for looking over the reading passage and questions that follow. Read through the description of skimming on the bottom of page 354. Explain that skimming is only helpful if done correctly. Make sure students understand that skimming is not reading every word on the page; it is moving your eyes quickly across the page, looking for key words or phrases that catch your eye or fit your purpose.

Be clear with students that first they will need to read the passage and questions carefully. Then, to apply the strategy of skimming, they will look for key words. Students need to be clear that skimming does not replace reading but supplements it.

Wrap-up

 At the end of the lesson, have students skim the reading passage on page 352 to identify its characters. Ask them to run their fingers down the middle of the page as they skim and stop whenever they come across a new character. After students finish, come together as a class and discuss the activity. What did students find most challenging about skimming the passage? What might they do differently the next time they use the strategy?

Lesson 2 During Reading: Tests

For use with *Reader's Handbook* pages 355–356

Focus

In this lesson, students will learn about fact and critical thinking questions and how to use the strategy of skimming to help them answer questions.

Getting Started

Ask students to discuss what they know about multiple-choice tests. Do they know that there are "tricks" for answering questions correctly, even those they may not be sure of? Point out that one of these "tricks" is using the steps in the During Reading stage of the reading process, and the strategy of skimming.

Teaching Approach

Ask a volunteer to remind the class of their purpose for reading a test. Then post on the board the following two purpose questions and leave them up for the duration of the unit.

■ What is the test question asking?

■ What information do I need to answer it?

D Read with a Purpose

Make clear to students that, in order to answer questions about a reading passage correctly, they have to understand what they are reading. Have a volunteer read aloud the three tips for reading a passage on page 335.

Kinds of Test Questions

Read aloud the first purpose question: What is the test question asking? Remind students that understanding the question is the key to answering it correctly. Explain that there are two main types of multiple-choice test questions: fact questions and critical thinking questions. Use Overhead Transparencies 33 and 34 to help make your point.

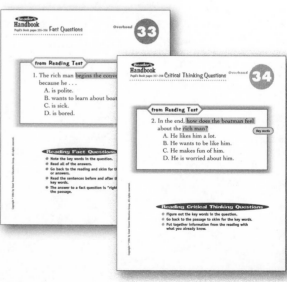

Fact Questions

Explain to students that fact questions are those in which the answer is "right there" in the passage. The trick is to find the fact in the reading. Point out that this is where the strategy of skimming comes in handy. Ask students to look over the sample test question on the top of page 356. Have them note the highlighted key words in the question. Tell students that these key words are what they skim for in the reading passage.

from Reading Test
Key words

> **1.** The rich man begins the conversation because he . . .
>
> **A.** is polite.
> **B.** wants to learn about boating.
> **C.** is sick.
> **D.** is bored.

Model for students how to skim for the key words in the question. Be sure students understand that they need to highlight key words in each question and then go back to the passage and skim for them.

Read with students the process of answering the question by reading aloud the rest of page 356. Stop as needed to discuss and clarify. Talk about the role skimming played in answering the question successfully. Remind students that they only have a certain amount of time (40 minutes) to complete the whole test. If they had to read every word of the passage again for every question, they most likely would run out of time before finishing the test.

Wrap-up

Have students work in pairs to write another fact question for "The Boatman." Remind them that the correct answer to a fact question should be "right there" in the passage. Point out that because this is a multiple-choice question, they will need to come up with three incorrect answers as well. When students complete the activity, have them exchange with another pair and answer each other's questions.

Lesson 3 During Reading: Tests (continued)

For use with *Reader's Handbook* pages 357–359

Focus

In this lesson, students learn how to answer inference questions on tests. They also explore ways to connect to passages on a test.

Getting Started

Review what students learned about answering fact questions in the previous lesson. Clear up any confusion students have about this type of question. Then ask students to look over the two last test questions on page 353. Do students think they will be able to find the answers in the passage? Point out that many test questions cannot be answered simply by skimming the passage. Explain that in this lesson students will learn how to answer the second type of test questions, critical thinking questions that require inferences.

Teaching Approach

Clarify for students what *inference* means. It requires that they, as readers, put together what they read with what they already know.

D Read with a Purpose (continued)

Review what students learned about making inferences. Remind them that making inferences involves "reading between the lines." The answers to this type of critical thinking question, unlike those for fact questions, are not right there in the passage. Then go over the inference equation.

> **Inference Equation**

| information from the reading | **+** | what I already know | **=** |

| my inferences |

◀ from Reading Test ▶

2. In the end, how does the boatman feel about the rich man?

    A. He likes him a lot.
    B. He wants to be like him.
    C. He makes fun of him.
    D. He is worried about him.

Walk students through the steps to take in order to answer the question correctly. Again, talk about the importance of skimming the passage in order to find the correct answer. Use Overhead Transparency 36 to support your instruction. Explain to students how they need to put together their own experience with what they learn from the reading.

E Connect

Ask a student volunteer to describe the last step in the During Reading stage of the reading process. Can students think of ways they can connect to "The Boatman"? Then have students look at how one reader made connections on page 359 of the handbook.

Wrap-up

Give each student two index cards. Tell students that they will use these cards to create fast fact cards for the two types of test questions. Information students might list on their cards include:

■ type of question

■ what it is asking

■ tips for answering it

Encourage students to include any additional information that will help them remember how to answer the questions. When students finish, have them keep the fast fact cards on hand for review before tests.

⬭ Lesson 4 ⬭ After Reading: Tests

For use with *Reader's Handbook* pages 359–361

Focus

In this lesson, students explore how to apply the After Reading stage of the reading process to a test.

Getting Started

Review what students have learned so far about using the reading process when taking tests. Clarify any questions students still have about answering fact questions and inference questions and the strategy of skimming.

Then explain that in this lesson the class will explore how to apply the steps in the After Reading stage of the reading process to a test. Invite a student volunteer to describe the three steps in the stage.

Teaching Approach

Have volunteers tell what they do when they finish taking a test. Do they go back over the questions? Do they make sure they've answered every question? Taking the time to use the steps in the After Reading stage of the reading process will help them improve their grade on the test.

F Pause and Reflect

Direct students' attention to the bottom of page 359. Have a volunteer read aloud the explanation of how to pause and reflect after taking a test. Make clear how these After Reading questions connect to students' original purpose for reading. Invite the class to list additional questions they might ask themselves now.

 Reread

Explain to students that the Reread step gives test-takers a chance to go back to questions that gave them trouble. Because most tests are timed, it makes sense for students to answer all the questions they know first and then spend the remaining time working on the more challenging ones.

Discuss with the class strategies they use currently when they come to test questions that they cannot answer. Then go through the sample question on page 360.

Point out the steps one reader took to find the answer, including identifying the key word and making inferences. Explain that if students still cannot find the correct answer, they can at least narrow down their choices by getting rid of any obvious wrong answers. For example, do students think that any story's main lesson would be answer choice A, "Always learn to swim"? Eliminating wrong answers will give students a better chance of selecting the right one.

H Remember

Have students turn to page 361 and read the top of the page. Then discuss the suggestions for how to remember information in a test. Point out that it is best for students to discuss tests in small groups after the test is over. Explain that because the purpose of most tests is to find out how much students learned about a subject, it is important to know the right answers, even if students learn them after completing the test.

Wrap-up

Have students reread the questions and their responses to them from the unit's opening activity (page 422 of this *Teacher's Guide*). Ask students if working through this section of the handbook changed how they would answer the questions. Have students modify their responses in their Reading Notebooks based on their new understanding of taking tests.

Lesson 5 Review and Assess

Check Point

Use the Quick Assess checklist to informally evaluate students' understanding of how to read tests and test questions. Based on their answers, divide them into two groups. Ask one group to complete the Independent Practice on the next page and the other group can do the guided practice in the *Applications Book and Word Work.*

Guided Practice

For students who need reinforcement in the reading process and the strategy of skimming, use pages 180–189 in the *Applications Book and Word Work.*

Quick Assess

Can students

☑ describe the process of how to prepare for a test?

☑ preview a test?

☑ explain how to use the strategy of skimming?

☑ tell the difference between fact and critical thinking questions?

For students who need more word work, assign page 237 from the *Applications Book and Word Work* on more root words.

Independent Practice

Students with a strong understanding of the reading process and the strategy of skimming might apply their knowledge to another set of test questions. (Standardized tests often include practice tests.) Have students apply the three stages of the reading process to the test questions. Ask them to label each question "fact" or "inference." When students complete the questions, ask them to reflect on the following question in their Reading Notebooks:

■ Did using the reading process help you answer the questions? If so, tell how. If not, tell why.

Class Review

Divide the class into three groups. Assign each group a different stage of the reading process: Before Reading a Test, During Reading a Test, After Reading a Test. (If you have too many students in a group, further divide the groups into subgroups and assign them one or two steps from their stage.) Have students work together to come up with two or three multiple-choice questions that explore their stage in the process. (Examples: What are two purpose questions for taking a test? Why is skimming a helpful strategy to use with tests?) After groups finish their questions, combine the questions into one master test. Have groups work through the questions, using what they learned in this lesson as a guide.

Test Book

Use the short-answer and multiple-choice tests on pages 74–75 to assess students' understanding of the material presented in this week's lessons.

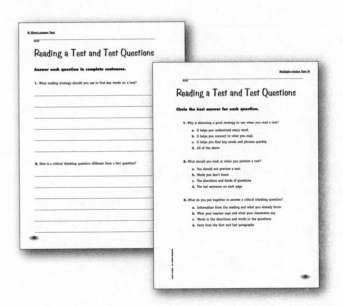

Reading Tests and Language Tests

Goals

Here students will explore techniques that can help them improve their performance on reading and language tests. In this week's lessons, they will learn to

- ☑ read and understand the directions on a reading test and a language test
- ☑ use the reading process to help them answer test questions
- ☑ read and answer different types of questions
- ☑ check their answers after they've finished a test

Background

Help students connect this week's lessons to their prior knowledge by asking them to

- ■ reflect on their strengths and weaknesses as test-takers
- ■ talk about their goals for taking reading tests and language tests
- ■ predict how they might use the reading process with a reading test
- ■ discuss the types of language test questions they find most difficult

Opening Activity

Ask students to talk about tests. Why do you have them? What purpose do they serve? What's it like to take them? What tests have they taken up to this time? Help students start to recall what they know already about tests.

Weekly Plan

Lessons	Summary
1. **Focus on Reading Tests**	Explore the components of a reading test and learn how to read a passage and answer the factual questions.
2. **Focus on Reading Tests** (continued)	Continue your discussion of reading tests. Discuss how to answer fact and critical thinking questions.
3. **Focus on Language Tests**	Support students as they learn to prepare for and read a language test.
4. **Focus on Language Tests** (continued)	Explore strategies for reading, understanding, and answering, the questions on a language test.
5. **Review and Assess**	Informally assess students to decide if more guided practice is needed. Then give an assessment.

Lesson Materials

	Components	Pages
Plan	*Teacher's Guide and Lesson Plans*	434–445
Teach	*Reader's Handbook*	362–375
	Overhead Transparencies	4, 9, 32, 34
Practice	*Applications Book and Word Work*	190–195, 238
Assess	*Test Book*	76–77

Lesson 1 Focus on Reading Tests

For use with *Reader's Handbook* pages 362–364

Focus

In this lesson, you'll work with students as they learn the elements of a reading test and consider reading test questions.

Getting Started

Tests are a fact of life, both inside and outside the classroom. New laws require elementary, middle school, and high school students to take state-mandated standardized tests in most subject areas, especially reading and math. In this lesson and the three that follow, you'll work with students to develop strategies and learn tips they can use with various types of reading and language tests.

Teaching Approach

Begin by explaining that the purpose of a reading test is to assess students' ability to read, comprehend, and respond to fiction and nonfiction reading passages. The handbook lesson features a test on a nonfiction passage. Review with students key test-taking terms. Display Overhead Transparency 32 as a way of reminding students what they have learned about using the reading process with in-school tests.

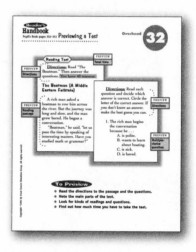

Talk with students about test-taking basics. The first and most important tip for doing well on tests is to read carefully. Remind students to relax, take a deep breath, and read the passage slowly and carefully. Then have students start with the question. Read it carefully, and then read all the answer choices. This single tip can do a lot to improve students' performance on tests.

Prepare

Explain to students that two test-taking tips helpful *before* the test are preparing and previewing. Students should understand by now that preparation is key to succeeding on all types of tests. Discuss how students can prepare for a reading test. Direct their attention to page 363 and read aloud the Listen, Practice, and Get Ready items at the top of the page. Explain to students that sharpening their ability to use the reading process with fiction and nonfiction is another excellent way to prepare for a reading test. Finish by discussing the importance of listening to what the test will be about and asking questions to clear up any confusion.

Preview

Stress the importance of taking a minute or two to preview the test to come. Tell students to mark the questions they feel will be the easiest to answer. If possible, they'll answer these questions first when it comes time to take the exam.

Point out the Preview items at the bottom of page 363. Then have students preview the sample test on page 364. Ask, "What did you notice about the reading passage? What did you notice about the test questions?" Post on the board a chart like the one below. Ask students to help you complete the chart by adding their own preview comments.

Preview Chart

	My Notes
What did you see in the directions?	
What is the title of the reading passage?	
What do the first and last sentences tell you?	
How many questions are there?	
What kinds of questions are they?	

Wrap-up

Reserve the final 10 or 15 minutes of the class period for students to read and take notes on the sample reading passage (page 364). Ask them to write their During Reading notes in their Reading Notebooks. Students will use these notes in the lesson to come.

Lesson 2 Focus on Reading Tests (continued)

For use with *Reader's Handbook* pages 365–368

Focus

Here students learn how to read and respond to fact and critical thinking questions on a reading test.

Getting Started

Begin the lesson by asking a student to summarize "Killer Whales" (page 364). Explain to the class that on a reading test the answers to factual questions can be found "right there" in the passage. Even so, students will still need to activate their prior knowledge of a topic whenever they can.

Teaching Approach

Start by helping students understand what it means to "read" a question carefully.

During Reading

Ask students to turn to page 365. Ask a volunteer to read Question #1. Then read it again, emphasizing the key words. Explain the key words in the question and in the answer choices.

> **Sample Question**
>
> 1. Which of these sentences is <u>not</u> true of killer whales?
>   - **A.** They are fast swimmers.
>   - **B.** Sometimes they eat birds.
>   - **C.** They have no teeth.
>   - **D.** Humans are their enemy.

Find the Answers

Next, discuss how to find answers to a fact question. Explain the process of returning to the reading, skimming, and finding key words that are in the question. Stress the importance of reading one sentence before and one sentence after finding the key words in the passage.

Thinking Aloud

Explain how the strategy of thinking aloud can help students puzzle out the answer to a question. Have a volunteer read aloud the Think Aloud on page 366. Discuss as a group.

◀ **Think Aloud** ▶

The correct answer has to be C. I see a sentence right there that tells about the whale's sharp teeth. So sentence C is <u>not</u> true.

Tell students that the purpose of a Think Aloud is to help them go step-by-step. Many test questions require two or even three steps to answer, and a Think Aloud will help students follow the steps in order.

Draw Conclusions

Once students understand how to find the answer to fact questions, review the process of answering inference and other critical thinking questions. Have the class turn to page 367. Then ask them to read sample question 2 and decide how they'd answer it. Tell students that critical thinking, or inference, questions require them to think about what they read and make an inference. The writer doesn't always tell them everything. Display Overhead Transparency 4 if students need help drawing conclusions.

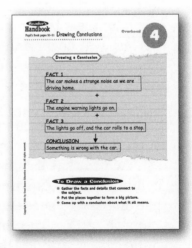

Wrap-up

Direct students to the text on page 368. Read aloud "Summing Up." Stop to discuss individual items as needed. Remind students that many of the techniques they've learned in "Focus on Reading Tests" they have seen before in "Reading a Test and Test Questions" (pages 350–361).

Lesson 3 Focus on Language Tests

For use with *Reader's Handbook* pages 369–372

Focus

In this lesson, students will learn how to prepare for and read a language test.

Getting Started

Begin by asking students the purpose of a language test. Then ask, "What subjects are covered on a language test?" Depending on your curriculum, students might suggest spelling, grammar, punctuation, editing, and research skills. Display a sample test and ask students to recall their experiences with that particular test.

Teaching Approach

Begin with a review of general techniques for preparing for tests, such as studying a little each night, working with a study group, and using note cards.

Before Reading

Have students read the three preparation tips listed on page 370. Ask volunteers to summarize the importance of listening to what the test will cover and studying old quizzes and worksheets. Also emphasize the importance of rereading key parts of the class text and completing any practice tests you distribute.

Show students the three items to watch for when previewing a language test. Add to that list the item "context clues." Explain to the class that one key to succeeding on language tests is knowing how to use context clues to find the meaning of an unknown word. Display Overhead Transparency 9 and review with students how to find and then use context clues.

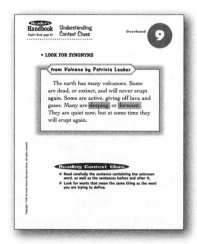

During Reading

Very often, language tests will be divided into parts. The first will contain grammar questions, the second research skills questions, and so on. Each new section will contain a new set of directions for students to follow. Stress that students must read every set of directions they come to on a language test.

Have students turn to page 372. Ask them to follow along as you read aloud sample Question #1. Discuss the highlighted key words.

◄ **from Language Test**

1. Seela, a truck driver, has to drive from Indiana to Texas. What would help her find the best road to take?

2. How should the underlined part of the sentence below be written?

3. Which word is spelled incorrectly?

As these examples show, students need to follow different directions throughout a test. Emphasize to students that much of what makes a test challenging is the demands it places on readers. They must first read the directions, then the test question or stem, and last the answer choices. Prepare students for this challenge and encourage them.

Wrap-up

Ask students to return to sample Question #2 (page 371). Have them copy the question into their Reading Notebooks and then highlight key words in the question and answer choices. Discuss students' highlighting.

Lesson 4 Focus on Language Tests (continued)

For use with *Reader's Handbook* pages 372–375

Focus

In this lesson, students continue their exploration of language tests and learn how to read the questions and answers.

Getting Started

Review with students what they learned thus far about language tests and how to prepare for them. Then display Overhead Transparency 34. Discuss once more the process involved in answering critical thinking questions. Stress the value of eliminating incorrect answer choices as you go.

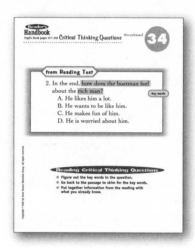

Teaching Approach

Start by reviewing critical thinking questions. Tell students that they will learn part of the answer from what they read, and they will have to supply part of the answer from what they think about what they learned.

During Reading (continued)

After students read the question and highlight the key words, their next step is to figure out the answer. Explain that a good strategy is to try to answer the question on their own first, without looking at the answer choices. Ask, "What do you think is the answer to sample question number 1?" Once students have their provisional answer, they should read through all four choices to see which matches the answer they've come up with. Write the Plan for Answering a Multiple-choice Question on the board.

Plan for Answering a Multiple-choice Question

1. Read the question.
2. Think of the answer.
3. Read the four choices.
4. Choose the best answer.

Being Test Smart

Then have students turn to page 374. Discuss what it means to be "test smart." Explain the difference between making a wild guess and making an *educated* guess. Help students understand that being "test smart" means choosing the answer that is most likely correct. Have them read the Think Aloud at the bottom of the page.

Think Aloud

> This question is hard. I feel like probably and recieves are both spelled incorrectly. But I'm going to guess recieves is wrong. It looks stranger to me than probably. I think receives might be the correct spelling.

After Reading

Read aloud the four tips listed at the top of page 375. Discuss ways for checking your work on a language test. Remind students that very often their first answer will be the correct answer and that going back and rethinking every single question can lead to trouble. Encourage students to develop their own method. One good way is to return to the easiest questions to double-check that you've marked the correct answer. Another is to look again at the very hardest questions and ask yourself, "Which answer makes the most sense?" Encourage students to give their answers a "common sense" check, not to second guess all of their answers.

Wrap-up

Have students read to themselves the bulleted items under Summing Up. Finish with a discussion of which tip discussed in the lesson seems the most useful. Have volunteers explain why.

Lesson 5 — Review and Assess

Check Point

Use the Quick Assess checklist to informally evaluate students' understanding of how to prepare for and take reading and language tests. Based on their answers, divide them into two groups. Have one group do the Independent Practice on the next page and the other group do the guided practice in the *Applications Book and Word Work*.

Guided Practice

For students who need reinforcement in taking reading and language tests, use pages 190–195 in the *Applications Book and Word Work*.

Quick Assess

Can students

☑ explain how to answer fact questions?

☑ describe what is needed to answer critical thinking questions?

☑ identify what the question on a language test is asking for?

☑ explain the importance and crossing out wrong answers and making smart guesses?

For students who need more word work, assign page 238 from the *Applications Book and Word Work* on contractions.

Independent Practice

Students who have demonstrated a strong understanding of how to apply the reading process and strategy can use their knowledge to help them complete practice reading and language tests. If possible, download sample tests from your state's Department of Education website. Have students work together to complete the reading and language components. Then have them discuss the following:

■ the type of reading passage they were asked to read

■ what the reading questions were like

■ what the language questions were like

■ the tools and strategies they used to help them answer the questions

Class Review

Ask students to write one factual question and one critical thinking question. Then ask students to exchange papers with a partner. See if they can decide which question is factual and which is a critical thinking question.

Test Book

Use the short-answer and multiple-choice tests on pages 76–77 to assess students' understanding of the material presented in this week's lessons.

Writing Tests and Math Tests

Goals

Here students will explore techniques that can help them improve their performance on writing and math tests. In this week's lessons, they will learn to

- ☑ read and understand the directions on a writing test
- ☑ plan and write their answer
- ☑ prepare for and preview a math test
- ☑ read and understand math questions

Background

Help students connect this week's lessons to their prior knowledge by asking them to

- ■ talk about their goals for taking writing tests and math tests

- ■ recall strategies that work well with most types of tests.

Opening Activity

Ask students to work in groups of three or four and discuss what helps them do well on tests. Have each group create "Five Tips for Success." Then share the tips from all of the groups. Focus students on succeeding on tests and on the idea that test-taking tips *can* help them succeed.

Weekly Plan

Lessons	Summary
1. **Focus on Writing Tests**	Work with students as they explore the components of a writing test and learn how to plan a response to a writing prompt.
2. **Focus on Writing Tests** (continued)	Discuss planning, writing, and checking their answers to a writing test question.
3. **Focus on Math Tests**	Support students as they learn to prepare for and preview a math test.
4. **Focus on Math Tests** (continued)	Explore how to use visualizing and thinking aloud to understand and answer the questions on a math test.
5. **Review and Assess**	Informally assess students to decide if more guided practice is needed. Then give an assessment.

Lesson Materials

	Components	Pages
Plan	*Teacher's Guide and Lesson Plans*	446–457
Teach	*Reader's Handbook* *Overhead Transparencies*	376–391 25, 26, 33, 35
Practice	*Applications Book and Word Work*	196–202, 239
Assess	*Test Book*	78–79

Lesson 1 Focus on Writing Tests

For use with *Reader's Handbook* pages 376–379

Focus

Explore with students the components of a writing test and learn how to plan their response to a writing prompt.

Getting Started

Successful test-takers know techniques they can use to help them read and perform well on tests. Following the steps in the reading process is one. Use this lesson to emphasize the benefits of using the Before Reading, During Reading, and After Reading stages of the process even when taking a writing test.

Teaching Approach

Begin by explaining that the purpose of a writing test is to assess students' ability to read and then respond to a writing prompt. Clarify the test-taking vocabulary students need to know for this lesson: *directions, prompt, purpose, topic sentence, supporting details,* and *signal words.* Provide examples of each.

Before Reading

Point out to students that preparation is one key to succeeding on a writing test. They can do some of the preparation in the days leading up to the test. Direct students' attention to the three tips listed on page 377.

Provide sample writing tests that students can read and respond to. Download practice tests from your state's Department of Education website. Set aside five minutes at the beginning of class to discuss a sample question. Highlight the key words. Help students get into the habit of reading for the topic and type of writing they're being asked to do.

Walk students through the Preview items shown at the bottom of page 377. Explain the purpose of each item and why it is important.

Writing Test

> <u>**Directions:**</u> Everybody loves a party! Write <u>how to</u> ❶ ❷ plan a really great birthday party. Write at least ❸ one paragraph. When you finish, ❹ proofread your work.

Taking apart a sample essay question or prompt will help students know what to look for.

During Reading

Reiterate the importance of finding key words in the prompt. These will provide valuable information about the topic of the writing and the kind of essay or paragraph students are being asked to write. Then discuss reading tools students can use to plan their responses. Begin by explaining the Process Notes organizer on page 379.

Process Notes

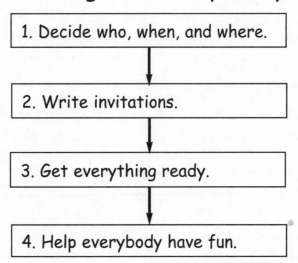

Planning a Birthday Party

| 1. Decide who, when, and where. |

↓

| 2. Write invitations. |

↓

| 3. Get everything ready. |

↓

| 4. Help everybody have fun. |

Wrap-up

Discuss why Process Notes work well with the prompt shown on page 378. Then ask students to thumb through the Reading Tools section of the handbook and suggest reading tools that would work for other types of writing, including descriptive and persuasive.

Lesson 2 · Focus on Writing Tests (continued)

For use with *Reader's Handbook* pages 380–382

Focus

Here students continue their exploration of how to plan, write, and check their answer to a writing test question.

Getting Started

Begin by displaying Overhead Transparency 35. Discuss writing test questions and the language students might expect to see in the writing prompt. Talk about any vocabulary terms that might be difficult.

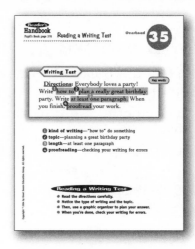

Teaching Approach

Explain that first students looked at how to read a writing prompt. Here the focus will be on how to plan and write the answer.

During Reading (continued)

Show students how to budget their time on a writing test, using ten minutes to plan, five minutes to check their work, and the remainder of the time to do the writing and revising. Help students understand how important it is that they stay within their time constraints so that they don't end up running out of time.

Next, walk students through the sample answer. Point out the topic sentence and discuss the relationship between it and the four steps that follow.

Sample Answer

PLANNING A BIRTHDAY PARTY

There are four steps you need to follow
to plan a good party. First, decide who
to invite and when and where to have
the party. Second, write and send out the
invitations. The third step is to get everything
you need and then to set it all up. That means
food, balloons, and games. Make everything
look nice! Last, help everybody have fun.

> **Topic sentence**

> **Signal words**

Remind students that, with writing tests, it is not how much they
write but how organized, correct, and interesting the writing is.

After Reading

Explain to students that on a writing test they'll be judged on their
ability to stay focused and follow the conventions of standard
English. This means that if they wander away from the topic at
hand, they'll have points subtracted. The same is true if they make
capitalization, punctuation, or spelling errors.

For this reason, it's vital that students take the time to edit and
proofread their writing. Remind them of the writing process and the
importance of steps 3 and 4.

Ask students to follow along as you read the checklist on page 381.
Discuss which of the items has caused them trouble in the past and
then write a sentence or two telling how they might avoid making
the same mistakes on future writing.

Wrap-up

Ask students to write a sample paragraph about how to do or make
something. Have students use the writing prompt in the book as a
model. Then have them create Process Notes that give three to four
steps to follow.

Lesson 3 ▸ Focus on Math Tests

For use with *Reader's Handbook* pages 383–386

Focus

Here students will learn how to prepare for and preview a math test and find keywords.

Getting Started

Open the lesson by asking students to discuss the easiest and most challenging aspects of taking a math test. Then have student volunteers share what they do to prepare for a math test. Do they make use of practice tests at the end of a chapter? Do they review key terms and work sample problems? List their responses on the board. Work with students to compare the ways they study for math tests with how they study for other types of tests.

Next, have volunteers share techniques they use *during* a math test. Once again, discuss the similarities and differences between math tests and other content area exams. Point out that even though math tests follow a different format than social studies or reading tests, there are some general tips that work well for all types of tests.

Teaching Approach

Have students read page 383 of the *Reader's Handbook*. Review general techniques for preparing for tests, such as memorizing key terms, taking practice tests, and getting a good night's sleep the evening before the exam.

Before Reading

Walk students through the three preparation tips listed on page 384. Discuss the importance of listening to what the test will cover, working sample problems, and studying their textbook. Another good way of preparing for a math test is to form a study group.

Preview

Display Overhead Transparencies 25 and 26 and discuss the similarities between previewing a math *text* and previewing a math *test*. Help students modify techniques shown on Overhead Transparencies 25 and 26 so that they work as before-reading strategies to use with a math test. Have students preview on their own the sample math test shown on page 385. Point out that there are two multiple-choice questions and a word problem. Students can expect to see more than one type of question on almost any type of math test they take.

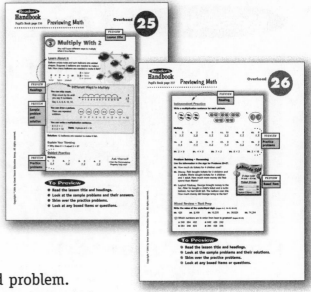

During Reading

Next, have students turn to page 386. Explain that one of the biggest problems students have when taking a math test is that they don't read carefully. Help them get into the habit of highlighting key words in the directions and key words and numbers in the problems. Show students the highlighted version of sample problem 1.

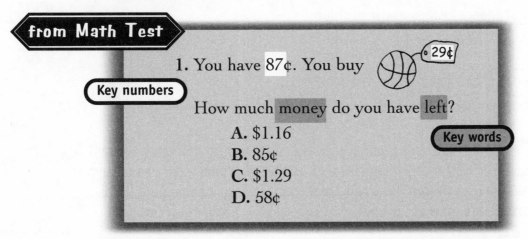

Focus students on the key words in the questions. Tell them that they will have to find the key words on their own on their next test.

Wrap-up

Ask students to return to sample Question #2 (page 385). Have them read the question and highlight the key words and numbers. Then discuss if these were the key words they identified.

Lesson 4 Focus on Math Tests (continued)

For use with *Reader's Handbook* pages 386–391

Focus

In this lesson, students learn how to use visualizing and thinking aloud to understand and answer math questions.

Getting Started

Review with students what they have learned about test-taking throughout this unit. What techniques do they find most helpful? Then have a volunteer remind the class of the process involved in answering a multiple-choice question. If needed, display Overhead Transparency 33 and ask students to follow along as your volunteer discusses the steps.

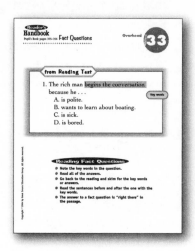

Teaching Approach

After students read a math problem, their next step is to figure out how to solve it. Two important questions to ask are the following:

■ What do I know? (This is the *given*.)

■ What do I need to find out? (This is the *unknown*.)

Have students return to sample problems 1 and 2. Ask them to tell the given and the unknown in each problem. Then have them turn to page 387 and read the explanation at the top of the page and the Think Aloud that follows.

Think Aloud

The first question is how much money is left. That means I need to subtract. I know I started with 87¢. I bought a ball that cost 29¢. To solve the problem, I have to subtract 29 from 87. I need to line up the numbers.

Students' next step is to solve the problem. Once again, the strategy of thinking aloud can help here. Have students read the Think Aloud on page 388. Discuss the solution to the problem.

Next, ask students to turn to pages 389 and 390. Review the strategy of visualizing and talk about how to use it with math. Have students look at the illustration at the top of the page and read silently the Think Aloud for question 3 that follows.

Visualizing

Be sure students understand the value of using Visualizing and Thinking Aloud with math tests.

Wrap-up

Use the After Reading page of the lesson to help you bring closure to the "Focus on Math Tests" lessons. Read aloud the three tips listed at the top of page 391. Then have students read to themselves the bulleted items under the head Summing Up. Finish with a discussion of the techniques discussed in the lesson. Which seem the most useful? Ask volunteers to explain why.

Lesson 5 Review and Assess

Check Point

Use the Quick Assess checklist to informally evaluate students' understanding of how to read a writing or math test. Based on their answers, divide them into two groups. One group can do the Independent Practice on the next page and the other group can do the guided practice in the *Applications Book and Word Work.*

Guided Practice

For students who need reinforcement in taking writing and math tests, use pages 196–202 in the *Applications Book and Word Work.*

Quick Assess

Can students

- ☑ explain how to preview and prepare for writing anf math tests?

- ☑ describe a way to plan their writing?

- ☑ tell what to do when checking their writing?

- ☑ identify different types of math questions?

- ☑ explain how visualizing and thinking aloud can help them answer math questions?

For students who need more word work, assign page 239 from the *Applications Book and Word Work* on homophones.

Independent Practice

Students who have demonstrated a strong understanding of how to answer writing and math test questions should use their knowledge to help them complete practice writing and math tests. If possible, download a sample test from your state Department of Education website. Have students work together to complete the writing and math components. Then have them report on the following:

■ the type of essay or paragraph they need to write

■ the organizer they would use to plan their writing

■ the type of math problems they'd need to solve

■ the strategies and tools they'd use to solve those problems

Class Review

Put the students in three groups. Ask groups to make a test-taking guide for writing and math. Have them divide their guides into three parts: Before, During, and After. Encourage them to refer to the handbook as needed as they create their guides.

Test Book

Use the short-answer and multiple-choice tests on pages 78–79 to assess students' understanding of the material presented in this week's lessons.

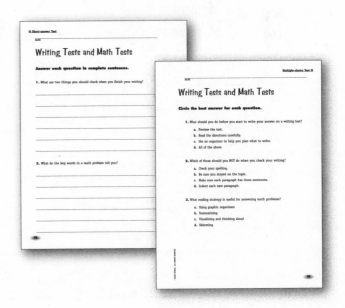

Reading Tools

Blackline Masters

Twenty of the reading tools in the Reader's Almanac of the *Reader's Handbook* are included in this *Teacher's Guide and Lesson Plans* book in a format suitable for copying. Use the blackline masters that follow to reinforce and supplement the lessons in the handbook.

Cause-Effect Organizer	Process Notes
Character Change Chart	Setting Chart
Character Map	Storyboard
Double-entry Journal	Story Organizer
Fiction Organizer	Story String
5 W's and H Organizer	Summary Notes
Key Word Notes	Timeline
K-W-L Chart	Venn Diagram
Main Idea Organizer	Web
Plot Diagram	Website Card

CAUSE-EFFECT ORGANIZER

A Cause-Effect Organizer helps you sort out causes and the effects coming from them. It shows the relationship between them.

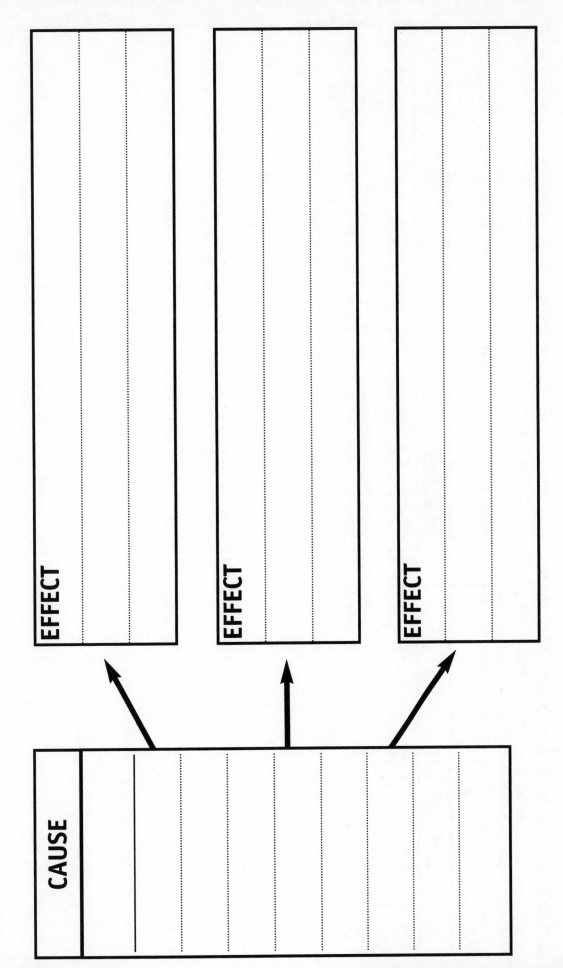

CAUSE

EFFECT

EFFECT

EFFECT

Character Change Chart

Use a Character Change Chart to show how a character grows and changes from the beginning to the end of a story, folktale, or novel. Knowing how a character changes can help you understand a lesson or theme.

BEGINNING	MIDDLE	END

THEME:

CHARACTER MAP

Use a Character Map to help you remember details about a character from a story or novel.

NAME _____

WHAT OTHERS THINK ABOUT CHARACTER

HOW I FEEL ABOUT CHARACTER

CHARACTER'S NAME

WHAT CHARACTER SAYS AND DOES

HOW CHARACTER LOOKS AND FEELS

DOUBLE-ENTRY JOURNAL

A Double-entry Journal helps you take a closer look at a small part of a reading. Use it to restate a couple of lines in your own words or to react to the writer's ideas.

QUOTES	MY WORDS

FICTION ORGANIZER

Use a Fiction Organizer to help you remember the details of a story or novel.

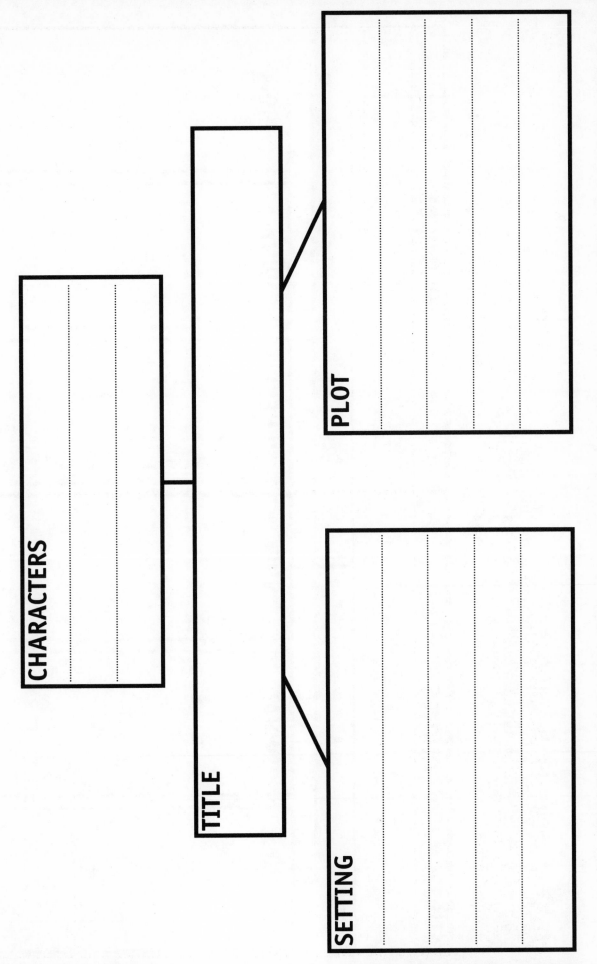

CHARACTERS

TITLE

PLOT

SETTING

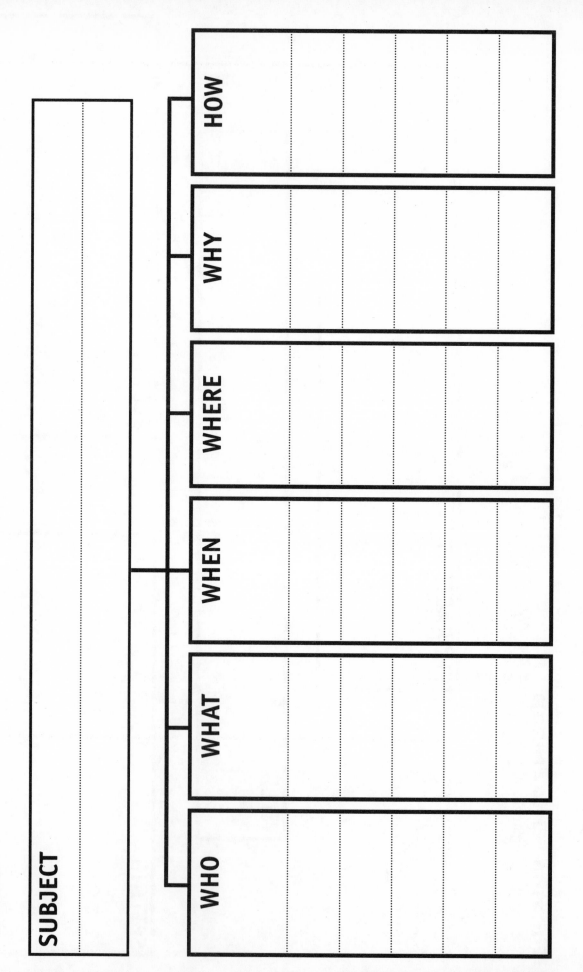

5 W's and H Organizer

You can use a 5 W's and H Organizer to keep track of key information about a subject. It helps you organize details about *who, what, when, where, why,* and *how.*

NAME

SUBJECT

WHO

WHAT

WHEN

WHERE

WHY

HOW

KEY WORD NOTES

Key Words Notes help you pick out the important words or topics from a reading. They work well for many kinds of reading—from articles and information books to textbooks and biographies.

KEY WORDS	NOTES

K-W-L Chart

A K-W-L Chart helps your organize what you already know about a subject and decide what you want to find out. It also gives you a place to list the main things you have learned.

WHAT I KNOW	WHAT I WANT TO KNOW	WHAT I LEARNED

Main Idea Organizer

A Main Idea Organizer help you find the most important idea and keep track of the smaller details.

SUBJECT

MAIN IDEA

DETAIL

DETAIL

DETAIL

PLOT DIAGRAM

A Plot Diagram helps you understand the action of a story or novel.
It helps you see what the main problem is, how the action builds to
a climax, and how the problem is solved at the end.

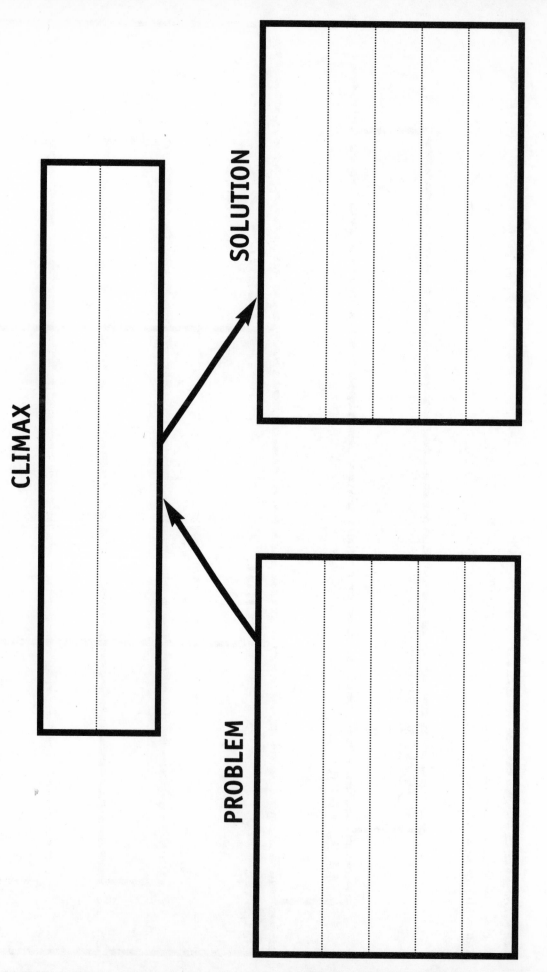

CLIMAX

SOLUTION

PROBLEM

PROCESS NOTES

Process Notes help you keep track of a series of steps or events. They are especially useful when you need to understand how things grow or change, how something works, or how to do something.

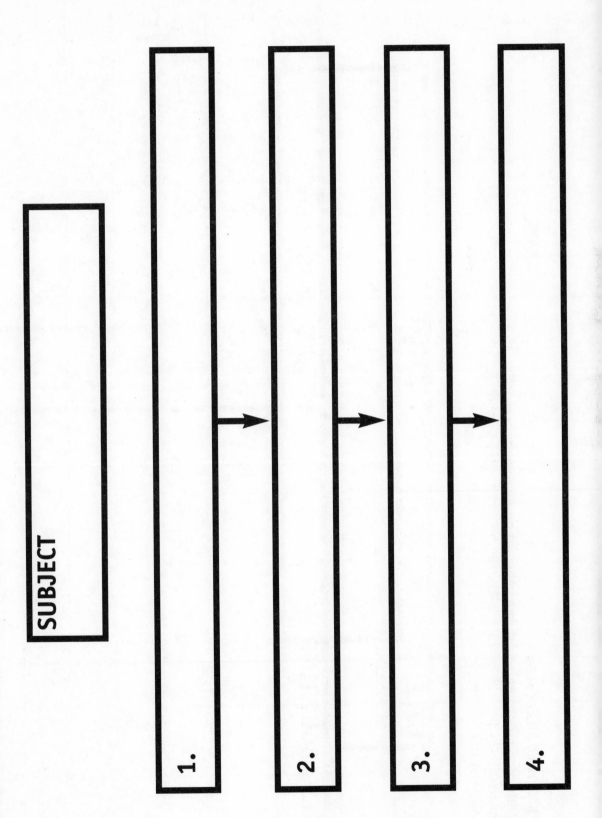

SUBJECT

1.

2.

3.

4.

SETTING CHART

Use a Setting Chart to help you remember when and where a story takes place.

TITLE

CLUES ABOUT TIME

CLUES ABOUT PLACE

STORYBOARD

A Storyboard uses words and pictures to help you remember what happens in a story or novel.

TITLE

1.

2.

3.

Story Organizer

Use a Story Organizer when you want to tell what happens in a story.

TITLE	

BEGINNING	MIDDLE	END

STORY STRING

A Story String helps you keep track of the different events that happen in a story or novel. Use a Story String to help you remember the order of events.

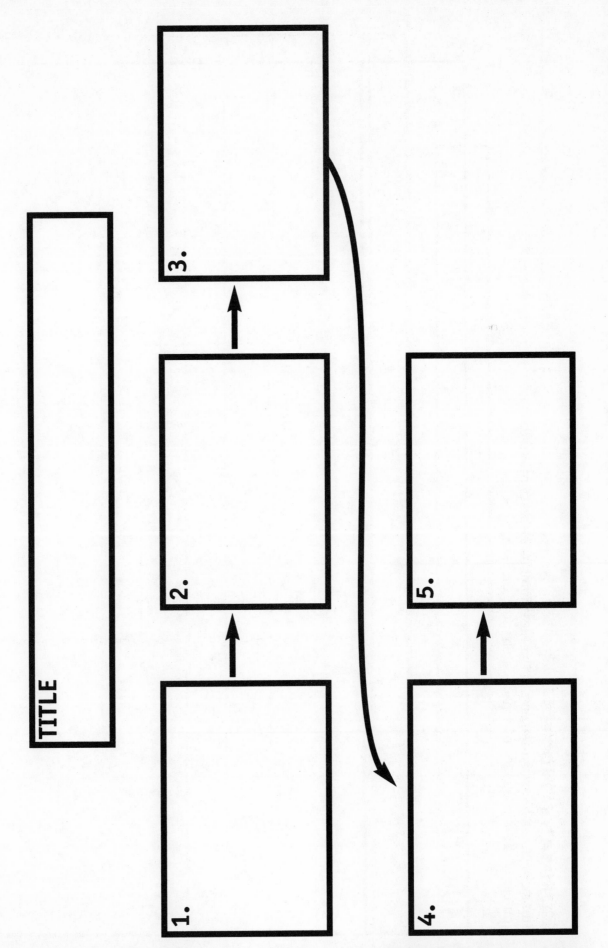

TITLE

1.

2.

3.

4.

5.

SUMMARY NOTES

Summary Notes help you remember the most important parts of a reading.
You can write a summary of a page, a chapter, or even a book.

SUBJECT	
1.	
2.	
3.	
4.	
5.	

TIMELINE

A Timeline lists events in the order they happened. Use a Timeline when you want to remember *what* happened and *when* it happened.

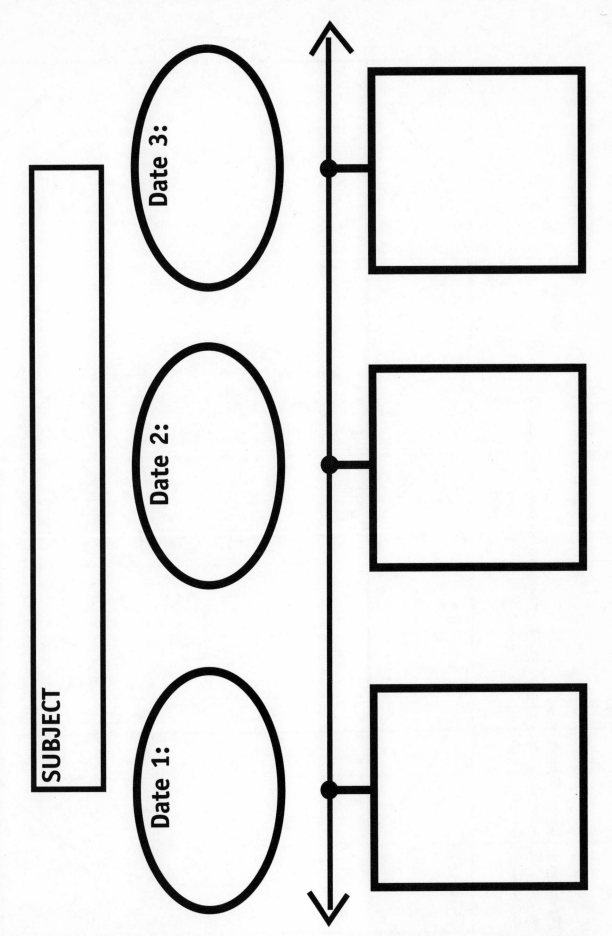

SUBJECT

Date 1:

Date 2:

Date 3:

VENN DIAGRAM

A Venn Diagram helps you compare and contrast two things. Use it to understand how two things are the same or different.

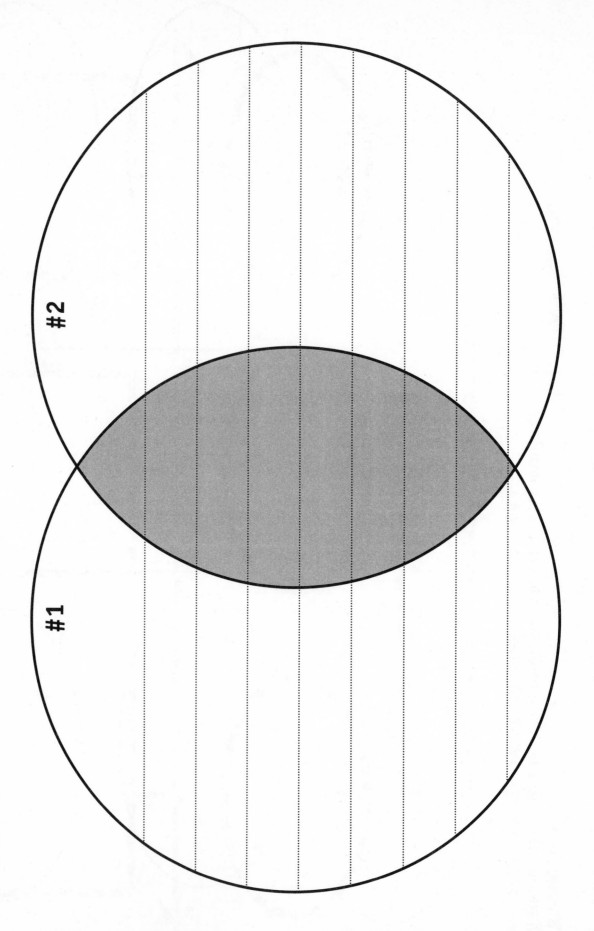

#1

#2

WEB

A Web is a simple tool for taking notes. Use it to organize information, brainstorm ideas, and remember details.

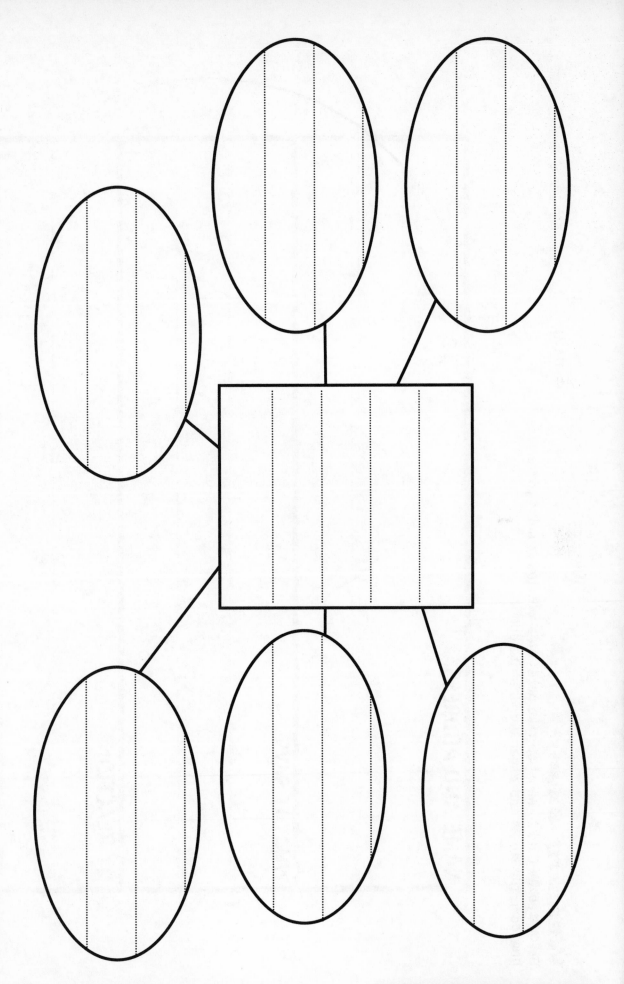

Website Card

Use a Website Card to help you take notes on a website. It helps you decide
how good the site is and remember what it's about.

NAME AND ADDRESS	

WHAT IT SAYS

MY REACTION

Acknowledgments

165, 166 From THE AMERICAN HERITAGE CHILDREN'S DICTIONARY, 1998.

188, 190 From TROMBONES by Bob Temple. Copyright © 2003 by The Child's World, Inc. Reprinted with permission of The Child's World, publisher and copyright holder.

197, 212 From KOALAS, by Emilie U. Lepthien. Copyright © 1990 by Children's Press, Inc. Reprinted by permission.

244 "Bubble, Bubble, Spittlebug" by Beverly J. Letchworth from HIGHLIGHTS FOR CHILDREN April, 2003, Vol. 58, No 4, Issue 618. Copyright © 2003 by Highlights for Children, Inc., Columbus, Ohio. Reprinted by permission.

256 Reprinted with permission from BENJAMIN FRANKLIN: PAINTER, INVENTOR, STATESMAN by David A. Adler, © 1992.

256 From BENJAMIN FRANKLIN by David A. Adler, illustrated by Lyle Miller, 1992. Reprinted by permission of Holiday House.

270 From GIANT PANDAS by Patricia A. Fink Martin. © 2002 by Children's Press. Reprinted by permission.

281 Screen captures from www.sandiegozoo.org. All rights reserved. Reprinted by permission.

293 http://www.sportlines.com

293 KID'S ALMANAC FOR THE 21ST CENTURY.

304 From COMMUNITIES: ADVENTURES IN TIME AND PLACE by J. Banks, et al. Copyright © 2001, 2000, 1999 McGraw-Hill School Division, a Division of the Educational and Professional Publishing Group of The McGraw-Hill Companies, Inc. Reproduced by permission of The McGraw-Hill Companies.

316 From *Harcourt Science*, Pupil's Edition, Grade 3, copyright © 2002 by Harcourt, Inc., reprinted by permission of the publisher.

329, 331, 332 From *Houghton Mifflin Mathematics*, Level 3 by Vogeli, et al. Copyright © 2002 by Houghton Mifflin Company. Reprinted by permission of Houghton Mifflin Company. All rights reserved.

346 From DISCOVERY WORKS, Level 3 by Badders, et al. Copyright © 2003 by Houghton Mifflin Company. Reprinted by permission of Houghton Mifflin Company. All rights reserved.

352, 357 "The Lion and the Mouse" from AESOP'S FABLES © 2000 by Jerry Pinkney. Used with permission of Chronicle Books LLC, San Francisco. Visit ChronicleBooks.com.

365 From FLAT STANLEY by Jeff Brown, illustrated by Steve Bjorkman. Text copyright © 1964 by Jeff Brown. Illustrations copyright © Steve Bjorkman. Used by permission of HarperCollins Publishers.

404 "Michael Is Afraid of the Storm" from BLACKS by Gwendolyn Brooks. Reprinted by consent of Brooks Permissions.

Lesson Index